Resilience, Emergencies and the Internet

This book traces how resilience is conceptually grounded in an understanding of the world as interconnected, complex and emergent.

In an interconnected world, we are exposed to radical uncertainties, which require new modes of handling them. Security no longer means the promise of protection, but it is redefined as resilience – as security in-formation. Information and the Internet not only play a key role for our understanding of security in highly connected societies, but also for resilience as a new program of tackling emergencies. Social media, cyber-exercises, the collection of digital data and new developments in Internet policy shape resilience as a new form of security governance. Through case studies in these four areas this book documents and critically discusses the relationship between resilience, the Internet and security governance. It takes the reader on a journey from the rise of complexity narratives in the context of security policy to a discussion of the Internet's influence on resilience practices, and ends with a theory of resilience and the relational. The book shows how the Internet nourishes narratives of connectivity, complexity and emergency in political discourses, and how it brings about new resilience practices.

This book will be of much interest to students of resilience studies, Critical Security Studies, Internet Politics, and International Relations in general.

Mareile Kaufmann is senior researcher at the Peace Research Institute Oslo (PRIO), has a post-doc in the Department of Criminology and Sociology of Law, Oslo University, and holds a PhD from Hamburg University.

Routledge Studies in Resilience
Series Editor: David Chandler
University of Westminster

The *Routledge Studies in Resilience* series is interested in publishing a broad range of high-quality contemporary research into the processes, spaces, policies, practices and subjectivities through which resilience is seen to operate.

Securitizing Global Warming
A Climate of Complexity
Delf Rothe

Resilience, Emergencies and the Internet
Security In-Formation
Mareile Kaufmann

Resilience, Emergencies and the Internet

Security In-Formation

Mareile Kaufmann

LONDON AND NEW YORK

First published 2017
by Routledge
2 Park Square, Milton Park, Abingdon, Oxon OX14 4RN

and by Routledge
711 Third Avenue, New York, NY 10017

Routledge is an imprint of the Taylor & Francis Group, an informa business

© 2017 Mareile Kaufmann

The right of Mareile Kaufmann to be identified as author of this work has been asserted by her in accordance with sections 77 and 78 of the Copyright, Designs and Patents Act 1988.

All rights reserved. No part of this book may be reprinted or reproduced or utilized in any form or by any electronic, mechanical, or other means, now known or hereafter invented, including photocopying and recording, or in any information storage or retrieval system, without permission in writing from the publishers.

Trademark notice: Product or corporate names may be trademarks or registered trademarks, and are used only for identification and explanation without intent to infringe.

British Library Cataloguing-in-Publication Data
A catalogue record for this book is available from the British Library

Library of Congress Cataloging-in-Publication Data
A catalog record for this book has been requested

ISBN: 978-1-138-29098-3 (hbk)
ISBN: 978-1-315-26574-2 (ebk)

Typeset in Times New Roman
by Wearset Ltd, Boldon, Tyne and Wear

Contents

List of figures vii
Acknowledgments viii
Preface xii

PART I
Interconnectedness, emergencies and resilience 1

1 The emergency paradigm 3
2 Resilience is the answer!? 16
3 Thinking for and from relationality 44
4 From program to programming 64

PART II
Resilience as a way of governing the Internet 77

5 Resilience and spatiality 79
6 Resilience and affect 101

PART III
Resilience as a way of governing through the Internet 127

7 Resilience and the digital 129
8 Resilience and the network 154

PART IV
Conclusions 183

9 A theory of resilience and the relational 185

  Index 213

Figures

0.1a	STAAT/Random IV	x
0.1b	STAAT/Random V	x
3.1	3 × interconnectedness: the three vertices of this book	45
8.1	NRK Twitter-timeline of 22 July Attacks in Norway	156
8.2	Coding nodes: theme cluster "Facebook"	158

Acknowledgments

The support I have experienced while writing this book means a lot to me. I am grateful to everyone who offered appreciation, criticism, advice, insight, interviews, ideas or other delightfulness along the way. I am particularly indebted to some of you that need naming.

With profound gratitude I would like to mention:

Michael Dillon and Julian Reid, for coining the analytic term *in-formation* (cf. Dillon 2000; Dillon and Lobo-Guerrero 2009; Dillon and Reid 2009); the concept has influenced this book's theoretical argument, which is why they have generously allowed me to employ it in the subtitle.

David Chandler, for creating various platforms for critical resilience research and for inviting me to be part of them.

Jorinde Voigt, for allowing me to reproduce her evocative artworks.

Peter Burgess, for his strategic investment into my development as a researcher.

Susanne Krasmann, for her clever, factual and supportive guidance during my dissertation project that influenced this book.

Urs Stäheli and Ulrich Bröckling, for their constructive feedback on my PhD thesis which has shaped the writing of this manuscript.

My peer-reviewers, for pointing me toward the parts that needed development;

Lynn P. Nygaard, for positioning and empowering women in research and her extensive knowledge on publishing.

My dear colleagues from the "Negotiating Values" (NECORE) project, our work contributed directly to this book.

My friends and colleagues in the Security Research Group at the Peace Research Institute Oslo, for inspiration, necessary confusion and discussion.

My husband and my family, for being an indispensable support in mind and spirit.

The research for this book was conducted at the Peace Research Institute Oslo (PRIO), in particular within the framework of the Norwegian Research Council (NRC)-funded project: "Negotiating Values: Collective Identities and Resilience after 22/7" (NECORE), the NRC/PRIO-funded "Positioning Women for Research Professorship" (POWER), as well as the NordForsk-funded project "Nordic Centre of Excellence for Security Technologies and Societal Values" (NordSTEVA).

Copyrights and permissions

Permission was acquired from both the artist Jorinde Voigt and BONO Billedkunst Opphavsrett i Norge to reprint her artworks "STAAT/Random IV" and "STAAT/Random V" in the preface. © Jorinde Voigt/BONO 2016.

Permission was acquired from the Staatliche Museen zu Berlin, specifically Andreas Schalhorn, to quote the Exhibition Flyer "System und Sinnlichkeit. Zeitgenössische Zeichenkunst von Tom Chamberlain bis Jorinde Voigt" in the preface.

Parts of Chapter 2 appeared previously in German in "Das Unbekannte regieren: Risiko trifft Resilienz." *Kriminologisches Journal* 47(4): 264–278 (2015). Permission was acquired from Julius Beltz GmbH & Co. KG.

Sections of Chapter 5 appeared previously in "Resilience governance and ecosystemic space: a critical perspective on the EU approach to Internet security," *Environment and Planning D: Society and Space* 33(3): 512–527 (2015).

Sections of Chapter 6 appeared previously in "Exercising emergencies: Resilience, affect and acting out security," *Security Dialogue* 47(2): 99–116 (2016).

A version of Chapter 7 appeared previously as Mareile Kaufmann (2016) "The Digitization of Resilience." In: Chandler, David and Jon Coaffee (eds) *The Routledge Handbook of International Resilience*. London: Routledge. 106–118.

Sections of Chapter 8 appeared previously in "Resilience 2.0: social media use and (self-)care during the 2011 Norway attacks," *Media, Culture & Society* 37(7): 972–987 (2015).

Permission was acquired from the Norwegian public service broadcaster NRK to reprint the figure *"Terrordøgnene på Twitter"* © nrk.no that appears in Chapter 8.

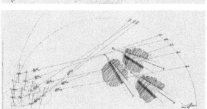

Figure 0.1a
STAAT / Random IV
© Jorinde Voigt/BONO 2016
full reference on next page

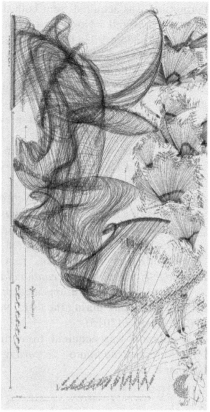
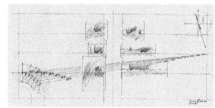

Figure 0.1b
STAAT / Random V
© Jorinde Voigt/BONO 2016
full reference on next page

STAAT / Random IV
(Matrix 4: Algorithmus Adlerflug; Strom; Top 100 Popsongs (Takt - weise); elektrische Impulse / doppelte Fraktalsequenz; Puls/min.; Standpunkt; Akustisches Feld: Doppelte Akustische Impulse (Volume in %; Dauer in Sek.; Loop); Rotation; Himmelsrichtung; Windrichtung; Windstärke; 2 küssen sich – Aktionsablauf / Generationen 1-11; C4-Detonation; Temperaturverlauf; Richtungsansammlungen/ Wirbel / Loop; Schussfeld)

Jorinde Voigt
Berlin 2008
Aus einer Serie von 11 Diptychen
Ohne Rahmen 1 Diptychon jeweils oberer Teil (STAAT): 230 × 115 cm + unterer Teil (Random): 67 × 115 cm
Mit Rahmen 1 Diptychon insgesamt jeweils: 306,02 × 124,05

(Oberer Teil (STAAT): 238,35 cm × 124,05, Unterer Teil (Random): 67,67 × 124,05 cm)
Framed each diptych: 10.04 × 4.07 ft
(upper part (STAAT): 7.82 × 4.07 ft + lower part (Random): 2.22 × 4.07 ft)
Installation insgesamt: Höhe 306,02 cm × Breite: 1375 cm

Bleistift, Tinte auf Papier
Unikat

STAAT / Random V
(Matrix 5: Algorithmus Adlerflug; Strom; Top 100 Popsongs (Takt - weise); elektrische Impulse / doppelte Fraktalsequenz; Puls/min.; Standpunkt; Akustisches Feld: Doppelte Akustische Impulse (Volume in %; Dauer in Sek.; Loop); Rotation; Himmelsrichtung; Windrichtung; Windstärke; 2 küssen sich – Aktionsablauf / Generationen 1-11; C4-Detonation; Temperaturverlauf; Richtungsansammlungen/ Wirbel / Loop; Schussfeld)

Jorinde Voigt
Berlin 2008
Aus einer Serie von 11 Diptychen
Ohne Rahmen 1 Diptychon jeweils oberer Teil (STAAT): 230 × 115 cm + unterer Teil (Random): 67 × 115 cm
Mit Rahmen 1 Diptychon insgesamt jeweils: 306,02 × 124,05

(Oberer Teil (STAAT): 238,35 cm × 124,05, Unterer Teil (Random): 67,67 × 124,05 cm)
Framed each diptych: 10.04 × 4.07 ft
(upper part (STAAT): 7.82 × 4.07 ft + lower part (Random): 2.22 × 4.07 ft)
Installation insgesamt: Höhe 306,02 cm × Breite: 1375 cm

Bleistift, Tinte auf Papier
Unikat

Preface

The 2013 exhibition *System and Sensuality* by the Ernst Schering foundation in Berlin displayed a collection of non-figurative, minimalist drawings, some of which resembled scientific notes, others looked like abstract landscapes or dancing geometrical shapes. All of these elements are combined in Jorinde Voigt's works "Staat/Random IV and V" displayed above. According to a journalist's observation some of these graphical elements generated the philosophical effect that everything in this world is interconnected (Ruthe 2013). The exhibition's flyer described the complexity of the drawings through the seemingly incidental, yet

> systematic, conceptual use of the line – the draughtsman's essential means of expression. Inherent in this systematic character, however, are also a distinct sensuality and vitality. This especially applies to the many works that consist in grid-like or cell-like linear compactions, which can, at times, appear to mutate into random or seemingly chaotic forms.
>
> (Schalhorn 2013)

I quote this text here, because it formulates well why the aesthetics of the drawings invoked associations to my own work. Not only is the line a visualization of relatedness and interconnectedness – a central theme of this book, but the description of the way in which the line is put to use summarizes well how complexity speaks to both the random and emergent, and also the systematic and orchestrated (in that context, it is noteworthy that the titles of the graphics displayed above translate as "State [pol.]/Random"). Together, orchestration and emergence effectuate what the author of the exhibition's introductory text characterized as "sensual" and "vital" (ibid.), which again speaks to the subject matter of this book. The concept of resilience builds on a sense of being interconnected with the complex *system world* to the extent that the question about life itself is at the heart of it. While the artworks at the exhibition offered a different form of speech (Ruthe 2013), thus a visual entry point to a complicated topic, this book seeks to trace and to word a critical inquiry into the themes of interconnectedness, complexity, governance and security, all of which converge in the concept of resilience. It provides a critical discussion of resilience as a way of governing in interconnected societies and as a new mode of administering and managing security that is based on insecurity.

Before introducing the inquiries and arguments of this book in the first chapter, I would like to reflect about what it means to formulate or to word such an argument and to share some insights that I gained along the way. First, I experienced that one shouldn't underestimate the performative effects of doing research. The moment an argument is formulated, thoughts are not merely expressed, but the chance exists that the argument creates effects, even bringing particular phenomena into being. Such a trajectory was traceable with regards to the resilience discourse, as for the past decade resilience was and still is a concept in the making, or as Dillon and Reid would put it: it is in-formation (2009). The rise of the term in different governmental contexts, the recent focus on (re-)conceptualizing resilience and filling it with meanings, the attempt to make it measurable by developing resilience metrics, the decisions taken to base political programs on it and make interventions in the name of resilience literally created a multiplicity of resilience phenomena. This does, by no means, exclude the critical assessments of the concept, since devoted critical attention to resilience also contributes to the recognition of its power and presence – which led Neocleous to the conclusion that the term should be avoided altogether (Neocleous 2013).

To take it further: being part of a scholarly discourse that discusses resilience critically not only contributes to a certain acknowledgment of the concept itself, but the performative effects of taking a critical stance, of bringing into being and contributing to a critical discourse, are also not to be underestimated. Critical assessments of resilience can easily be misunderstood as misanthropic, especially by institutions that are used to the positive, empowering framing of the term. Being aware of and grappling with this effect is particularly relevant in an environment such as the Peace Research Institute Oslo, which is in regular exchange with policy makers and, for example, the International Federation of the Red Cross, which has recently adopted resilience as one of its key conceptual approaches. The intention of this project and its critical stance is not to contribute to a negative view on life as such. Rather the opposite, the aim is to point to those instances and aspects of resilience that are tied to questions of power, agency and the political – and especially to those points where resilience as a way of governing denies them.

It should become obvious from this book that the critical resilience discourse did get to work and has, by now, produced manifold effects. Another important lesson to learn, however, was that critique as a method of analysis is not exempt from the performative effects of doing research. In the case of writing this book it means that the formulation of some arguments came to re-influence my thinking, sparking processes of reflexivity. For example, the work on resilience in interconnected societies also re-influenced my understanding of the world as radically relational, as is expressed in poststructuralist terminology and methodology. At some point, however, it struck me that some of the critical narratives and premises of poststructuralism seemed to overlap with the discourse I sought to criticize, which equally subscribes to an understanding of the world as relational and in flux. At that point I had to pause and re-investigate my own critical stances in order to take critique even more seriously. It was most helpful here to read Dillon's (2000; Dillon and Lobo-Guerrero 2009; Dillon and Reid 2009) works contrasting complexity and poststructuralism, which have influenced the argument of this book.

My project came to a second halt when I wanted to combine a critical argument about the use of digital technologies in resilience governance with the field research that I had conducted about the use of social media after the 2011 Norway attacks. From my empirical findings it became clear that I could not be as critical as I intended to be. Most of the individuals interviewed did not experience the use of social media after the attacks as depoliticizing, intrusive or as a medium that affectively forged their relationship to emergency governance. The fact that I had to provide for a more fine-grained argument about resilience vis-à-vis the digital and vis-à-vis the networked, taught me that a critical stance alone cannot guarantee a reasonable critique. In fact, sometimes it produces blind spots or obscures heterogeneity.

While any research project is probably furnished with hiccups, halts and moments of re-orientation, I experienced a particularly memorable pause when an acquaintance of mine challenged the ubiquity and the why of security studies altogether: security – why do we need so much of it? Potentially he posed this question for the same reason that Neocleous (2013) would argue to resist the investigation of specific buzzwords, such as resilience: through our explorations of in/security we may even (re-)create it. I am guessing that this question will follow me around in the future, but my preliminary answer to this is in line with the argument I presented above about studying resilience in the first place. In the resilience discourse in particular, the question about security is intimately tied to the question about being alive. An engagement with security then also engages with the quality of being alive and the extent to which life can actually be lived without the overwhelming experience of domination, standardization, depoliticization and limitation of agency. While explicit normative suggestions are not the aim of this book, any criticism forwarded within the realm of these pages is eventually intended to provide insights into that which limits and expands agency and the chances for being political. Resisting this form of investigation would constitute a silent agreement with whatever politics confronts us with – it would be passive and disregardful of meaning and life.

References

Dillon M (2000) Poststructuralism, Complexity and Poetics. *Theory, Culture & Society* 17(5): 1–26.
Dillon M, Lobo-Guerrero L (2009) The Biopolitical Imaginary of Species-being. Theory, Culture and Society 26(1): 1–23.
Dillon M, Reid J (2009) *The Liberal Way of War. Killing to Make Life Live*. London: Routledge.

Neocleous M (2013) Resisting Resilience. Radical Philosophy 178 (March/April). Available at: www.radicalphilosophy.com/commentary/resisting-resilience (accessed 27 February 2017).

Ruthe I (2013) Eine andere Art von Sprache. Berliner Zeitung. Available at: www.berliner-zeitung.de/kunst/kupferstichkabinett-eine-andere-art-von-sprache,10809186,22200192.html (accessed 26 July 2016).

Schalhorn A (2013) System und Sinnlichkeit. Zeitgenössische Zeichenkunst von Tom Chamberlain bis Jorinde Voigt. Kupferstichkabinett – Museum of Prints and Drawings, Staatliche Museen zu Berlin. Die Sammlung Schering Stiftung. Flyer zur Ausstellung.

Part I
Interconnectedness, emergencies and resilience

Part 1

1 The emergency paradigm

I remember the year resilience became big news. Operating the symbolism of clashing ideologies in an interconnected world the front page of *Newsweek*'s September 2011 issue featured one of two planes flying into the Twin Towers, subtitled with colossal lettering: "RESILIENCE" (Newsweek 2011). Strikingly, the subtitle of *Time* magazine's online feature about the tenth anniversary of 9/11 read: "Portraits of resilience" (Time 2011). Only a few months later the *Guardian* speculated whether 2012 would in fact be the "year of the R word" (Juniper 2011). The way in which the *Guardian*'s contextualization of the buzzword speaks to the narratives, conceptual foundations and rationalities that this book investigates is utterly indicative:

> New concepts of course reflect the times in which they are born. In the 1960s and 70s, conservation was the buzzword. It implied the need to reduce our impact and to set aside areas where nature could be left unmolested. In the 1980s sustainability became prevalent. It arose from the need to reach an accommodation between efforts to reduce poverty while also meeting pressing environmental goals. Resilience is different. It signals a need to deal with inevitable major shocks, including those which are impossible to predict.
>
> (Juniper 2011)

Indeed, uncertainty and inevitable disaster play a central role in resilience discourses. If one were to think of resilience as a protagonist, it would feature exclusively in discourses, tales and stories of survival in a complex, unpredictable world. It describes an ongoing activity of rebounding or recoiling and springing forward in response to strain – a process that was first formulated for ecosystems (Holling 1973) and in the context of childhood adversities (Garmezy 1973). The concept then moved from ecology and psychology into other disciplines, such as socio-ecology (Adger 2000) and engineering (Roylance 2001), and has finally been adopted into security policy (UNISDR 2005). The term itself, as the peak in resilience articles on Google Trends indicate, is not only tied to narratives of terror attacks, but also to economic crashes or unexpected collapses in schools, sports and human spirit. The domains in which resilience operates are numerous. Since the early 2000s, the referencing index for resilience continued to rise with no stagnation in sight (Google trends 2015, search: "resilience"), and academic publications about resilience have doubled between 2010 and 2015 (cf. Dunn Cavelty *et al*. 2015). Resilience is no longer big news. It has arrived. The fact that resilience describes character attributes in the online game *World of Warcraft* or in facelift cosmetics, shows how mundane and everyday the term has become – at least in the Anglophone world. One of the major success stories of resilience is, however, in the field of emergency management and security governance, which is not surprising given the conceptual linkage of resilience to shocks and uncertainty.

Resilience has become a guiding theme for the United Nations and European Union as well as for many national policies that address different kinds of emergencies such as developmental, cyber or climate issues. Within such discourses resilience is framed as the panacea for treating emergencies. The recurrent diction of uncertainty and inevitable disaster indicates that resilience builds upon a broader epistemological fundament of complexity thinking. It implies an understanding of the world as radically interconnected and relational; it describes a world in which the constant interaction of different parts gives rise to emergencies that have to be met with the adaptation and evolution (cf. Hayles 1999; Dillon 2000; Urry 2005a). Insecurity, then, is internal to complex systems. And one such system, proclaimed by security policies, is society itself. Following the rule of complexity, insecurity is a part of society's functioning and resilience becomes the necessary ability to learn from and adapt to it (Duffield 2012). Resilience thus expresses a specific understanding of the world. And as this understanding becomes settled in political thinking, resilience develops into a way of governing insecurity. The extent to which current discourses and practices in security policy embrace the idea of an interconnected and complex world, how they frame the emergence of emergency as a problem of increased complexity and present resilience as the solution is one of this book's endeavors. To study resilience as a way of governing means to look at those discourses and practices that share the objective of creating resilience. This does not only refer to governance exercised by governmental bodies, but it also includes Foucault's notion of "self-governing" – processes by which the individual acts upon the self (Bröckling *et al*. 2011; cf. Foucault 1988). While at first glance resilience seems to represent the optimal form of security governance in a complex, emergency-ridden world, this book points to the peculiarities and ambiguities of this form of governing, which both targets and thrives upon society's inherent insecurities. It traces the many ways in which resilience asks us to live *through* emergencies, to live a life in constant trans-formation, and it reflects on the way in which interconnectedness reflects the governmental program of resilience.

This book illuminates the interconnected relational society as well as its inherent insecurities and resilience from a particular angle – the Internet. It is no coincidence that the epistemological awareness of complexity and the limits of certainty, the rise of digital technology and the concept of resilience became prominent aspects of security governance at a similar point in time. This book documents and critically investigates the overlap of these emerging trends in security governance that have not yet been considered together (with exception of Duffield 2016). Chapters 2, 3 and 4 outline theories for consideration and explain how resilience is different from risk and how – with the rise of digital technologies – resilience is both a specific program and a subject of programming within security governance. The growing presence of the Internet in societal interactions nourishes not only narratives of interconnectedness and complexity in political discourses, but it also sets a new stage for resilience policies. The European Union's Agency for Network and Information Security, for example, reframes the Internet as an "interconnection ecosystem" (ENISA 2011) that is in need of resilience. This, as argued in Chapter 5, affects the very understanding of the Internet as a space. A tool to instill resilience is, for example, a cyber-exercise used in order to safeguard the space that seems to be so crucial to contemporary societies. Cyber-exercises, this book argues in Chapter 6, reveal how resilience works as a way of acting-out security.

Studying resilience as a way of governing the Internet not only provides deeper insights into the ontological, epistemological, temporal and spatial workings of resilience, but it also adds a new dimension to resilience. Through informationalization and digitization of social activities, resilience becomes more than a program of security governance, it becomes subject to programming. *Digital humanitarians*, *Effective altruism*, and *Disaster resilience through big data* are a few of the approaches that harness digital tools and information to instill different forms of resilience governance. Chapter 7 explores how the properties of digital code come to re-determine practices of resilience and self-governing, while Chapter 8 analyzes how social media are being used to deal with emergencies in a self-organized manner. All of these findings are reflected on in the concluding chapter (9), which formulates a theory of resilience and the relational.

As such, this book not only sets out to critically discuss the links between interconnectedness, resilience, emergencies and insecurity, but it does so by investigating resilience as a way of *governing the Internet* and a way of *governing through the Internet*. The Internet offers vast opportunities to explore a world and specifically a security that is in-formation (Dillon 2000); it provides a milieu to study interconnectedness and how it relates to resilience as a way of living through emergence and emergencies. The book utilizes these opportunities by combining case studies and theoretical reflections. Its empirical observations are based on a selection of four cases: two of which deepen our understanding of resilience as a way of governing the Internet itself and two that provide insights into resilience as a way of governing through the Internet. All of them are chosen for their explanatory power and their symbolic meaning vis-à-vis resilience as a governmental program. They signify overarching trends in government and have become important milestones in governmental practices with an outspoken reference to resilience and the Internet. They offer insights on the workings of resilience and the way in which rationales, practices, and technologies of resilience and interconnectedness relate to, reinforce and reflect each other.

6 *Part I: Interconnectedness and emergencies*

The first of four cases is an analysis of the European Internet security policies that the European Union Agency for Network and Information Security (ENISA) implements. Not only do these policies build on a re-imagination of the Internet as a complex ecosystemic space, but the shift in understanding the Internet as an ecosystem also legitimizes and enforces resilience as a way of governing this space. This case combines an analysis of policies and discursive strategies – their inherent understanding of connectedness, hardware, software and insecurity – with an analysis of information technological concepts, such as protocol and the so-called *self x*. The focus on resilience that operates in specific, interconnected topologies produces insights about the governance of complex and connected spaces at large – a theme that will, in all likelihood, become more important in future security governance.

The second case study focuses on the idea of *self x*. It illustrates the way in which security exercises are key to instigating self-organization – one of the central aspects of resilience programs. Significantly, self-organization is equally important in the context of technological emergencies, such as cyber-attacks, as it would be in other kinds of disasters. The cyber-exercise not only signifies the role of connectivity for imaginaries of insecurity and resilience, but it also serves as an entry point to understand how *affect* and *being affected* becomes an important empirical and theoretical tool to conceptualize resilience as a way of acting-out security. Exercises are a classic tool in security governance and as such, they remain an important source of insight into the workings and rationalities of governmental programs.

The third case study moves from the perspective of exploring resilience as a way of organizing the security of the Internet or connected topologies to the way in which the Internet itself is used to instill resilience practices and form resilient subjects. Chapter 7 investigates different European emergency management practices, documents, and policies that include digital information in their resilience programs. The use of digital information for governmental practices is a growing trend that has been discussed before (cf. Dillon and Reid 2009; Boyd and Crawford 2012; Amoore 2013; Andrejevic and Gates 2014). However, in this case digital information also signifies the rationales and principles of being in-formation and of constantly adapting oneself to given circumstances: a key element of the resilience program. Digital information here foregrounds the logics of patterns and prioritizes a focus on effects over causes, which is also a central feature of resilience itself. Resilience is mainly interested in the reaction to disruption – not in keeping spaces or subjects safe from disruption. As a governmental program it addresses effects. This study shows how various digital resilience practices can be grouped into three aspects of managing the effects of emergencies: (i) mapping the status quo of emergencies; (ii) directing the trajectory of emergencies; and (iii) learning from past emergencies for the future.

The final case study then draws our attention from the significance of the digital for resilience to the networked aspect of the Internet and information. It examines the use of social media during the Norway terror attacks in 2011 to understand how spontaneous, networked resilience practices came about. The case moves the perspective from the resilience program as planned by governmental institutions to the way in which the emergency population itself enacted resilience, what social media users did with their access to information and how/what they thought about deploying social media during emergencies. This is one of the first studies to involve interviews and look at this trend systematically. While this case can be discussed as a successful installation of governmental practices of freedom and instigation – as a technology of the self – it also illuminates the not-planned and spontaneous aspects of resilience that may question resilience as a top-down program.

The four cases then, not only feed into the systematic study of resilience as a way of governing the Internet, but also as a way of governing through the Internet. The first case of each part focuses rather on the role of governmental institutions in the instigation of resilience, while the second cases of each part provides the perspective of the role of the population and that which potentially challenges governmental rationalities. As the cases indicate, this book focuses mainly on the relationship between the Internet and resilience programs that concern emergency management in Europe and beyond. However, it does not address the connections between humanitarian discourses of resilience and the Internet, as Duffield (2016). The case studies and their respective reflections, however, do feed into a theory of resilience and the relational that has the ability to speak to many different contexts of complexity and in/security. Complexity and insecurity are major themes in various contemporary discourses.

A world in-formation: insecurity revisited

All is movement. We have entered the Information Age. Everything is connected to everything else. These are at least the narratives that the complexity discourse of the past decades has successfully instilled in our everyday lives (cf. Castells 1996; Hardt and Negri 2000; Barabási 2003). In fact, the idea that our world is marked by radical interconnectedness stretches from physics, biology, mathematics, ecology, chemistry and economics to architecture, consultancy, consumer design, fiction, management, New Age, organizational studies, town planning and much more (Urry 2005a: 2). Thrift argues that the number of outspoken references to interconnectedness and complexity burgeoned throughout the 1990s:

> Metaphors of complexity may be a sign of something of wider cultural interest and most especially a greater sense of openness and possibility concerning the future, based upon new cultural senses of time that acknowledge that things are complex and cannot be easily apprehended, models of time that are not foundational but still allow grip. In other words, I want to suggest that a new structure of feeling is emerging.
>
> (Thrift 1999: 53)

Complexity theories paint a picture of a postmodern world that "tends toward a smooth space defined by uncoded flows, flexibility, continual modulation, and tendential equalization" (Hardt and Negri 2000: 327). Hardt and Negri see a world evolving that is understood to be a de-territorialized apparatus without a center of power; it is spatially mobile and marked by exchange (ibid.).

By today, such perceptions of complexity are not only present (Urry 2005a: 2), but their epistemological premises have been "seamlessly absorbed across the socio-economic and environmental policy spectrum" (Duffield 2012: 479). The fact that complexity thinking and related discourses have become commonplace provides a breeding ground for the concept of resilience. In order to comprehend the politics and workings of resilience it is gainful to retrace the basic assumptions of complexity thinking and how knowledge about complexity became "conventional wisdom" (ibid.). It adds to understanding why the concept of resilience appears to be so compelling at this particular point in time and why resilience narratives speak to the current "structure of feeling" (Thrift 1999: 53).

A starting point for the reiteration of the complexity discourse is the feedback loop and the way in which information is considered a mode of relating. Eventually, the complexity discourse takes us to the point where *everything* is understood to be interrelated and in-formation whereby emergence becomes the driving force that determines the evolution of any interconnected system. This centrality of emergence in interconnected societies is also what challenges the idea of the ability to control situations of insecurity *ex ante*. Emergence abandons the concept of external insecurities and the idea that their entrance into society can be apprehended. Emergence internalizes insecurity. It draws the governmental focus from that which causes situations of insecurity toward the necessity of dealing with effects of disasters and shocks. The paragraphs that follow describe this development in more depth with a focus on central events.

An important entry point to complexity thinking has been the conceptualization of the feedback loop in the 1940s. Norbert Wiener and his colleagues originally designed it as a control mechanism in the field of systems engineering. The feedback loop simply describes a flow of information that travels from systems to observers and back into systems in order to foster stability (Wiener 1948; von Foerster 1974; Bateson *et al.* 1976). This systemic information exchange was enabled by the codification of information on the one hand and the condition of interconnectedness on the other. Thus, information exchange was not only conceptualized as the ability to send information, but also as the capacity to receive information (Dillon and Reid 2009: 67ff.). Information exchange was not an isolated process, it was a mode of relating and a vantage point for self-reflexivity, which became a prominent concept in cybernetics (von Foerster 1974), or in the discipline of biology and sociology as autopoiesis (Maturana and Varela 1980 [1973]; Luhmann 1984). Through the feedback loop and the processing of information observers became part of the system they observe.

However, information transmission did not only occur in singular, closed feedback loops. Information was understood to mobilize and assemble audiences as well as multiple feedback loops, which gave rise to the concept of the network (Dillon and Reid 2009: 68). Ever since, networked ontologies have heavily influenced theories of science, but also the understanding of society and politics.

A number of scholars have tied complexity thinking to the idea of network-based social structures. Castells, for example, suggested that networks are "highly dynamic, open systems, susceptible to innovating" (Castells 1996: 470) and a key mode of social organization:

> [T]he core activities that shape and control human life in every corner of the planet are organized in global networks: financial markets; transnational production, management, and the distribution of goods and services; [...] the Internet networks of interactive, multipurpose communication; culture; art; entertainment; sports; [...] religion; the criminal economy; and the transnational NGOs and social movements.
> (Castells 2009: 25).

This led Castells to conclude that networks are no less than a ubiquitous mode of existence in the global network society (ibid.). This relational mode of existence is not exclusively dependent upon but as the engineering concept of the feedback loop illustrates, it is heavily influenced by the idea of technology.

One of the latest determinants here is the rise of digital technology and the way in which it reinforces interconnectedness. However, as much as the effect of digital technologies is that they, too, seem ubiquitous, framing "contemporary notions of everything from cultural identity to war" (Galloway and Thacker 2007: 10). Galloway and Thacker remind us that the ubiquity of digital technology is far from being a global one "or from being the bedrock of society" (ibid.: 10). Similarly, Graham argues that the Internet especially is a network with highly selective connections (Graham 2013: 10). The singularity proclaimed by the Information Age and the Global Network Society can surely be questioned vis-à-vis the various kinds of effects that rising digital connectedness brings about. Acknowledging that digital connectivity is unevenly distributed, the everydayness of digital technologies, so some scholars argue, still accelerates information exchange, it forms and multiplies new interrelations (Barabási 2003; Urry 2005a, 2005b; Galloway and Thacker 2007). The increasing digitization of information is thus understood to reinforce and illustrate the effects of interconnectedness and information exchange. Such narratives about digital connectivity add a new facet to discourses of complexity.

While the digital dimension of interconnectedness and its relationship to resilience will be explored in more depth at a later stage in this book it is worth noting at this point that the digital also expedites an epistemology, which is typical for interconnected societies. The traceability, storability and computability of digital information enable specific forms of reflexivity, such as automated analytics and sense-making from large numbers (cf. Boyd and Crawford 2012; Gitelman and Jackson 2013). As a result, patterns become a central mode of creating knowledge (cf. Dillon and Reid 2009: 55ff.; Amoore 2013: 129ff.; Andrejevic and Gates 2014) and information begins to inter-act with its environments through form. Information does not only *per*form, because it constitutes the basis for reflexivity and learning (Hayles 1999), but information exchange and analysis *create form and patterns* that institute changes within their recipients.

This formative capacity is one of the key features of complex information exchange: it is said to drive adaptation and change as it creates form. This is why digital information exchange also becomes increasingly relevant to different ways of instilling resilience. Another commonality of resilience and digital information exchange is that they both focus on effects rather than on causes. While resilience expresses a response to disasters ex post facto and works with the effects of shocks, the patterns of digital analytics – the myriad correlative calculations digital information enable – equally focus on the computation of effects rather than causes. This epistemological analogy may explain why resilience and digital analytics speak well to each other in the governance of interconnected societies and the emergencies they accommodate.

The emergency as a paradigmatic form of insecurity

Complexity thinking adheres to the idea that everything is "in-formation," meaning that everything is in a process of becoming, developing and evolving (Dillon 2000: 9). In complex societies, multiple, parallel and highly recursive feedback loops of traveling information lead to emerging formations and reformations (Dillon and Reid 2009: 69ff.). As a result, the possibilities for mastery become increasingly limited as endless interconnections renounce any conscious design and lead to "unpredictable evolutions" (Hayles 1999: 225). Emergence challenges the idea of controlled feedback and introduces a shift in the ontology and ethos of the interconnected society. The ultimate aim of a system is no longer to remain stable, but to learn from and adapt to failure in order to survive (Maturana 1987). The goal of any system is now to follow the "laws of becoming" (Dillon and Reid 2009: 60) and to "evolve the capacity to evolve" (Hayles 1999: 243). The only way of managing or governing the capacity of becoming is, it seems, through resilience.

The feedback loop thus initiated a paradigm shift from essentialist and reductive epistemologies toward complexity, emergence and resilience. As the legacy of the feedback loop resilience relinquishes the previously dominant episteme of a world that can be controlled, a world that is geared toward stability and equilibrium. The now obsolete paradigm of stability implied an understanding of security that would seek to keep disruptions outside the system. Here, phenomena would be studied and understood in isolation and large changes would produce large effects (Urry 2005a: 4), which allows for the idea of control. With the rise of the emergency paradigm, however, the world would no longer be characterized by pre-formation, but by being in-formation:

> In prioritizing the mode of relating, accepting that temporality is an operator rather than a mere parameter, and conceiving of "bodies" in terms of the contingent assemblages and ensembles (systems) that are a function of their diverse modes of relating, it [complexity science] simultaneously subverted the epistemic structures upon which both Newtonian physics and great scientific taxonomic enterprises of the last 200 years were said to be based.
> (Dillon and Reid 2009: 73)

Complexity thinking thus recasts the world as an assemblage of continuous information exchange: dynamic, emergent, contingent and always at the edge of chaos, far from a stable state. Emergency could no longer be kept outside the system, but had become an integral part of it.

Complexity leads to a growth of disorder, to plurality, diversity and creativity. In such an interconnected world, phenomena are studied as contextual and are not reducible to elementary laws or simple processes (Urry 2005a: 6f.). Small changes can produce large impacts and systematic effects that are different from their parts, as well as large changes that can produce small effects only, as becomes visible with, for example, the concept of the tragedy of the commons where the acting of individual parties does not necessarily feed into a common good or a needed change at an overarching level. Time is neither understood as fixed nor as absolute; it is contextual, flexible, variable and dependent on the system it relates to (Urry 2005a). This dynamic of becoming however, implicates nonlinearity and "a sense of contingent openness and multiple futures, of the unpredictability of outcomes in time-space" (ibid.: 3). Complexity and interconnectedness not only induce the "end of certainty" as Prigogine proclaims (1997: 189), but are considered "the worst enemy of security" (Schneier 2001). Complexity narratives of radical interconnectedness and radical uncertainty have been tied into the security discourse as a fundamental threat. Within global politics infinite interconnectedness has led to the emergency as the ultimate insecurity, unexpected and dangerous. Here, feedback loops and emergence are framed as the perpetual possibility of "synchronous failure" (Pelosky 2002). In fact, since the 1960s policy reports warned about the vulnerabilities of a world that is "knitted together by transportation, power and communication systems designed for efficiency not security" (Brown 2006: 51; cf. Dunn Cavelty and Giroux 2015). Undeniably, the rise of cyber- or critical infrastructure- vulnerabilities, climate change and global economic instabilities reinvigorated and further fine-tuned this focus on the interconnected and the uncontrollable.

In 2011, the European Parliament, for example, called for a collective brainstorming-exercise to "identify structural changes to be initiated in order to prepare the European Parliament for a more complex and challenging environment" (European Parliament 2013: 2). The core narrative of their resulting reports is pervasive: since multiple levels and actors interrelate with diverse technologies on an everyday basis, change is accelerated in an unprecedented way. This change may lead to forms of networked and technology-driven democracy on the one hand, but emergent threats and risks on the other (European Parliament 2013). Concepts such as the snowballing of disasters and transboundary emergencies feature prominently in European Security policies (cf. Council of the European Union 2010; European Commission 2010a,b): "Europe's interconnected arteries move people, goods, capital and services, but can also propel once-minor threats to new heights" (Rhinard 2007: 11). Uncertainties with regards to time, place and magnitude of disruption culminate in imaginaries of cascade and domino effects, of immanent and imminent insecurity that should inform security decision-making:

Experts predict the number of [...] emergencies to rise in the near future. They point to modern society's ever-increasing complexity and the close links between the various life-sustaining systems, all of which provide minor glitches with plenty of potential to develop into full-blown emergencies. They also point to the rise of catastrophic transboundary threats to societal security such as fundamentalist terrorism, climate change and bioengineering, with governing authorities in a race against time to deal with them.

(Boin and Sundelius 2007: 35)

Within this insecurity discourse the threats emerging from interconnectedness take a variety of forms. The interconnectedness of infrastructures creates new vulnerabilities as the flow of goods, data and people can be interrupted by strikes, network failure and congestions (cf. Lewis 2006). Increased interconnectedness also allows for the circulation of harm, whether this refers to viruses (cf. Gaouette 2014 on Ebola's tolls in the interconnected world; cf. Parikka 2007 on digital contagions) or threatening ideas (cf. von Behr *et al.* 2013 on radicalization in the digital era). It can also generate new, mediated forms of violence (Grusin 2004). Duffield summarizes that the international security apparatus imagines its domain "as a potentially borderless social-ecological terrain shaped by the emergent properties of radically interconnected contingent events" (2012: 479) and security now "occupies a magical space of flows where butterflies can flap their wings in Australia and cause hurricanes in America" (ibid.). It is a terrain of emergencies, which may only be mastered by resilience – the strategic engagement with and of insecurity.

References

Adger WN (2000) Social and Ecological Resilience: Are They Related? *Progress in Human Geography* 24 (3): 347–364.

Amoore L (2013) *The Politics of Possibility. Risk and Security Beyond Probability.* Durham, NC: Duke University Press.

Andrejevic M, Gates K (2014) Big Data Surveillance: Introduction. *Surveillance and Society* 12(2): 185–196.

Barabási AL (2003) *Linked: How Everything is Connected to Everything Else and what it Means for Business, Science, and Everyday Life.* New York: Plume.

Bateson G, Mead M, Brand S (1976) "For God's Sake, Margaret!," *CoEvolutionary Quarterly*, 10 June: 32–44.

Boin A, Sundelius B (2007) Managing European Emergencies: Considering the Pros and Cons of an EU Agency. *EPC Working Paper No. 27: Building Societal Security in Europe: The EU's Role in Managing Emergencies.*

Boyd D, Crawford K (2012) Critical Questions for Big Data. Provocations for a Cultural, Technological, and Scholarly Phenomenon. *Information, Communication and Society* 15(5): 662–679.

Bröckling U, Krasmann S, Lemke T (2011) From Foucault's Lectures at the Collège de France to Studies of Governmentality. An Introduction. In: Bröckling U, Krasmann S,

Lemke T (eds) *Governmentality. Current Issues and Future Challenges.* New York/Abingdon, Oxon: Routledge. 1–33.
Brown KA (2006) *Critical Path: A Brief History of Critical Infrastructure Protection in the United States.* Washington, DC: George Mason University Press.
Castells M (1996) *The Rise of the Network Society.* Cambridge, MA: Blackwell Publishers.
Castells M (2009) *Communication Power.* Oxford: Oxford University Press.
Council of the European Union (2010) *Draft Internal Security Strategy for the European Union: "Towards a European Security Model."* 5842/2/10.REV2. Available at: http://register.consilium.europa.eu/pdf/en/10/st05/st05842-re02.en10.pdf (accessed 11 August 2016).
Dillon M (2000) Poststructuralism, Complexity and Poetics. *Theory, Culture and Society* 17(5): 1–26.
Dillon M, Reid J (2009) *The Liberal Way of War. Killing to Make Life Live.* London: Routledge.
Duffield M (2012) Challenging Environments: Danger, Resilience and the Aid Industry. *Security Dialogue* 43(5): 475–492.
Duffield M (2016) The Resilience of the Ruins: Toward a Critique of Digital Humanitarianism. *Resilience – International Policies, Practices and Discourses.* 15 March: 1–19. Available at: http://dx.doi.org/10.1080/21693293.2016.1153772 (accessed 27 February 2017).
Dunn Cavelty M, Giroux J (2015) The Good, the Bad, and the Sometimes Ugly: Complexity as Both Threat and Opportunity in National Security. In: Kavalski E (ed.) *World Politics at the Edge of Chaos: Reflections on Complexity and Global Life.* Albany, NY: SUNY Press. 209–227.
Dunn Cavelty M, Kaufmann M, Søby Kristensen K (2015) Resilience and (In)security: Practices, Subjects, Temporalities. *Security Dialogue* 46(1): 3–14.
ENISA (2011) *Inter-X: Resilience of the Internet Interconnection Ecosystem.* Full report. Available at: www.enisa.europa.eu/publications/interx-report/at_download/fullReport (accessed 11 August 2016).
European Commission (2010a) *Communication from the Commission to the European Parliament, the Council, the European Economic and Social Committee and the Committee of the Regions. Delivering an Area of Freedom, Security and Justice for Europe's Citizens, Action Plan Implementing the Stockholm Programme. COM(2010) 171 Final.* Available at: http://eur-lex.europa.eu/LexUriServ/LexUriServ.do?uri=COM:2010:0171:FIN:EN:PDF (accessed 11 August 2016).
European Commission (2010b) *Communication from the Commission to the European Parliament and the Council. The EU Internal Security Strategy in Action: Five Steps Towards a More Secure Europe. COM(2010) 673 Final.* Available at: http://eur-lex.europa.eu/LexUriServ/LexUriServ.do?uri=COM:2010:0673:FIN:EN:PDF#page=2 (accessed 11 August 2016).
European Parliament (2013) *Preparing for Complexity. The European Parliament in 2025. The Answers.* Available at: www.europarl.europa.eu/the-secretary-general/resource/static/files/preparing-for-complexity--the-european-parliament-in-2025--the-answers-en--2nddraft-.pdf (accessed 11 August 2016).
Foucault M (1988a) *The History of Sexuality. Volume 3: The Care of the Self.* New York: Vintage Books.
Galloway AR, Thacker E (2007) *Exploit: A Theory of Networks.* Minneapolis, MN: University of Minnesota Press.

Gaouette N (2014) Ebola's Toll Threatens Security in Interconnected World. *Bloomberg News*. Available at: www.bloomberg.com/news/2014-10-14/ebola-s-toll-threatens-security-in-interconnected-world.html (accessed 11 August 2016).

Garmezy N (1973) Competence and adaptation in adult schizophrenic patients and children at risk. In: Dean SR (ed.) *Schizophrenia: The first ten Dean Award Lectures*. New York: MSS Information Corp. 163–204.

Gitelman L, Jackson V (2013) Introduction. In: Gitelman L (ed.) *"Raw Data" is an Oxymoron*. Cambridge, MA: The MIT Press. 1–14.

Google Trends (2015) Google trends search "Resilience." Available at: www.google.com/trends/explore#q=Resilience (accessed 11 August 2016).

Graham M (2013) Geography/Internet: Ethereal Alternate Dimensions of Cyberspace or Grounded Augmented Realities? *The Geographical Journal* 179(2): 177–182.

Grusin R (2004) Premediation. *Criticism* 46(1): 17–39.

Hardt M, Negri A (2000) *Empire*. Cambridge, MA: Harvard University Press.

Hayles K (1999) *How We Became Posthuman. Virtual Bodies in Cybernetics, Literature and Informatics*. Chicago: University of Chicago Press.

Holling CS (1973) Resilience and Stability of Ecological Systems. *Annual Review of Ecology and Systematics* 4: 1–23.

Juniper T (2011) Will 2012 Be the Year of the R Word? *Guardian*, 14 December. Available at: www.theguardian.com/sustainable-business/resilience-sustainable-development (accessed 11 August 2016).

Lewis TG (2006) *Critical Infrastructure Protection in Homeland Security. Defending a Networked Nation*. Hoboken, NJ: Wiley & Sons.

Luhmann N (1984) *Soziale Systeme: Grundriß einer allgemeinen Theorie*. Frankfurt: Suhrkamp.

Maturana H (1987) Everything is Said by an Observer. In: Thompson W (ed.) *Gaia, a Way of Knowing*. Great Barrington, MA: Lindisfarne Press. 65–82.

Maturana H, Varela F (1980 [1973]) Autopoiesis and Cognition: The Realization of the Living. In: Cohen RS, Wartofsky MW (eds) *Boston Studies in the Philosophy of Science 42*. Dordrecht, Netherlands: D. Reidel Publishing Co.

Newsweek (2011) *9/11 – Ten Years of Fear, Grief, Revenge, Resilience*. Cover available at: www.spd.org/2011/09/9-covers-part-3.php (accessed 11 August 2016).

Parikka J (2007) *Digital Contagions. A Media Archaeology of Computer Viruses*. New York: Peter Lang Publishing.

Pelosky RJ (2002) *Synchronous Failure: The Real Danger of the 21st Century*. Washington, DC: The Elliot School of International Affairs, George Washington University.

Prigogine I (1997) *The End of Certainty*. New York: Free Press.

Rhinard M (2007) Societal Security. An Emerging Role for the European Union. *EPC Working Paper* No. 27: Building Societal Security in Europe: The EU's Role in Managing Emergencies.

Roylance D (2001) *Stress-Strain Curves*. Available at: http://ocw.mit.edu/courses/materials-science-and-engineering/3-11-mechanics-of-materials-fall-1999/modules/MIT3_11F99_ss.pdf (accessed 11 August 2016).

Schneier B (2001) *A Plea for Simplicity You Can't Secure What You Don't Understand. Information Security*. Available at: www.schneier.com/essay-018.html (accessed 11 August 2016).

Thrift N (1999) The Place of Complexity. *Theory, Culture and Society* 16(3): 31–69.

Time (2011) *Time [Beyond 9/11] Portraits of Resilience*. Available at: http://content.time.com/time/beyond911/ (accessed 4 March 2015).

UNISDR (2005) *Hyogo Framework for Action (2005–2015) "Building the Resilience of Nations and Communities to Disasters."* Available at: www.unisdr.org/2005/wcdr/intergover/official-doc/L-docs/Hyogo-framework-for-action-english.pdf (accessed 11 August 2016).

Urry J (2005a) The Complexity Turn. *Theory, Culture and Society* 22(1): 1–14.

Urry J (2005b) The Complexities of the Global. *Theory, Culture and Society* 22(1): 235–254.

von Behr I, Reding A, Edwards C, Gribbon L (2013) Radicalization in the Digital Era. The Use of the Internet in 15 Cases of Terrorism and Extremism. *RAND Europe*. Available at: www.rand.org/content/dam/rand/pubs/research_reports/RR400/RR453/RAND_RR453.pdf (accessed 11 August 2016).

von Foerster H (1974) *Cybernetics of Cybernetics*. Urbana, IL: University of Illinois.

Wiener N (1948) *Cybernetics: Or Control and Communication in the Animal and the Machine*. Paris and Cambridge, MA: MIT Press.

2 Resilience is the answer!?

Governing uncertainty

The academic complexity narratives of the 1980s and 1990s, such as Habermas's *Die Neue Unübersichtlichkeit* [*New Obscurity*] (1985), Beck's *Risikogesellschaft* [*Risk Society*] (1986) or Luhmann's argument about *security as social fiction* (1991) are by today an inherent part of public security discourse. The vulnerabilities of the interconnected society (Nato 2002), the unpredictability of global terrorism (*The Economist* 2005) or the uncontrollable effects of global warming (*National Geographic* 2010) are at the heart of political discussions about the uncertain future of society. The more complex a society with its different cultural groups, its entanglement with technologies, its market- and climate-dependencies, its circulating bacteria and viruses – in short: with its manifold exchange processes and feedback loops, the more that interruptions, disturbances and emergencies move from the realm of the possible into the realm of the necessary. Prigogine describes the consequence of complexity as the "end of certainty" (1997: 189). Thus, security policies that do not engage with the unknown future seem to miss their mandate.

Uncertainty, the unknown, and the uncontrollable indeed characterize the modern understanding of security and insecurity. This is highlighted not only in policy narratives but also in concrete political models, practices and techniques, which aim to tame and govern the unknown future (Hacking 1990; Aradau and van Munster 2011). One such security practice is risk. In the 19th century Liberalism formulated risk as a way of governing insecurity that appeared in the form of the unknown future (Donzelot 1984). Ever since then, the interest in governing the unknown has increased (Aradau and van Munster 2011) – especially in relation to the complexity discourse that has burgeoned throughout the past decades.

Information is a key component of risk calculation, which is why risk practices are on the one hand a direct consequence of increased information flow. They are, on the other hand, deployed as a strategic approach to organizing the uncertainties caused by increased interconnectedness and complexity. The intent of risk calculation is to make future crises calculable in order to prevent, control, manage or manipulate their realization. Risk thus gives form to the regulation of uncertainties to come and it does so through calculation (Aradau and van Munster 2011: 17ff.; cf. Ewald 1991, 2002; Dillon 2007; de Goede 2012). As a mode of governing, it assumes that a pattern of future insecurity exists, which can be identified before it materializes. Because the existence of such a pattern is the basis of risk calculation, risk practices often reinforce categorization and normalization.

However, the capacity to calculate such patterns of future insecurity is challenged in the face of ever-rising uncertainty. As a result, risk's efforts to foresee the crises to come were reinvented over time. Risk practices began to transcend the calculation of probabilities: calculus gave way to intuition and probability was transformed into possibility. The precautionary principle here symbolizes the very tipping point from risk as the prevention of a future-made-known into strategies that seek to avert future insecurities that are radically uncertain. The latest critical assessments of risk-oriented practices thus describe the response to the incalculable and erratic as characterized by anticipation (Ewald 2002; Amoore 2007), imagination (Aradau and van Munster 2008, 2011), premediation (Grusin 2004; de Goede 2008), and speculation (de Goede 2012). Amoore describes how scientific data itself would

> begin to incorporate the emotional affective and speculative domains, while, on the other hand, knowledges considered to be "non-scientific" are authorized as science. Data-led algorithms that model and track the movement of bodies or objects through space now coalesce with intuitive, speculative and inferential knowledges that imagine future scenarios.
>
> (2009: 55)

These political practices of *pre-* and *anticipatus*, Latin for "taken before or to take care ahead of time" (Dictionary.com 2014: *anticipate*), are practices of forestalling and averting failure to take place. Their goal is to keep insecurity outside the system, or manage it in a way that the least possible impact occurs. Such models of governing the uncertain future acknowledge the existence of emergencies, but consider them to be external to society. They use information and patterns to project emergent futures in order to keep them outside of society. Such a politic of protection, prediction, planning and intervention, so Duffield argues, is symptomatic of modernity (2012). The emergency is here considered a random, isolated or an unplanned side effect. The response that anticipatory and preventative practices provide to radical uncertainty is thus an increase in techno-scientific security politics of speculation, novel models of pattern recognition and algorithms – a trend that has risen to new levels with the digitization of information. However, the overall ambition of such models is to control uncertainty and to keep the materialization of danger outside society. They assess the uncertain future in order to minimize or control damage (Aradau and van Munster 2008: 25).

Politics of prevention, preparedness, pre-emption and precaution have, particularly in the past three decades, inspired an extensive critical discourse on the idea of governing through insecurity. They have been criticized to increasingly employ epistemic uncertainty and dystopian futures in order to legitimize specific security practices. Even though such practices eventually seek to avert the materialization of insecurity, they do, at the same time, reinforce insecurity through the production of fear of the unknown (cf. Beck 1986; Massumi 1993; Furedi 1997, 2006; Altheide 2002; Ewald 2002; Robin 2004; Aradau and van Munster 2008, 2011; de Goede 2008; O'Malley 2009).

While the notion of risk shaped the security policy of a whole era, the notion of insecurity that it responds to and reinforces has recently begun to change, and the political practice of risk is encountering an ontological challenge. As described above, anticipation and prevention work on the assumption that an active subject can effectively act on its environment in order to avert insecurity. Risk is thus fundamentally based on subject-object binaries. The objective of risk practices to keep insecurity outside the system is fundamentally different from an understanding of insecurity that has emerged in the past few years which considers threat as "quasiuniversal" (Dunn Cavelty and Giroux 2015: 215) and most importantly system-inherent. The idea that the "protective capacity of space is obliterated" and that "there is no place that is safe from attack" (ibid.) features strongly in the insecurity discourse of the past five years and describes the gist of complexity thinking. It is present in many narratives ranging from international terrorism (Heath-Kelly 2015) to climate catastrophes (Oels and Methmann 2015). Such insecurities, so the discourse goes, can only be met by "complete system response" which re-shuffles subject-object positions. This logic lies at the heart of resilience, which the remainder of this book is dedicated to. Now that risk and resilience coexist as two models of governing uncertainty, important questions emerge. To what extent are the basic understandings of "being" and "knowing" that inform the concept of resilience different from those that inform risk? What kind of security practices does resilience generate and which temporal dimensions do they speak to? Which role does resilience foresee for the citizen?

Resilience does not replace risk, both practices occur simultaneously and this does not have to be contradictory. In fact, risk and resilience can both be situated in a security discourse of preparedness, which complicates a clear-cut distinction between them. In practice, both programs focus largely on the governance of future emergencies and crises, which is why the terms are often used synonymously and are discursively blurred. Both of them subscribe to a form of insecurity that is relevant to the politics of circulation (Dillon and Reid 2009): risk and resilience are both practices which aim to secure or steer smooth exchange processes and information flow. They seek to promote "good" and avoid "bad" circulation (Boy 2015). In order to do so, risk policies involve the citizen as a cautious, calculating and self-insuring subject. Furthermore, resilience foregrounds the responsible and active subject. However, by placing subject and object in dynamic assemblages the origins of disruption can, at least in part, not be known, calculated or insured against. Threats can no longer be prevented by a prudent, preventive subject alone. Political strategies that emphasize the necessity of resilience argue that within a complex world, the "promise of linear modes of governing and understanding" (Chandler 2014a: 13) has come to an end. Rather than through means of insurance and probability that prevent insecurity, strategies of resilience embrace insecurity and engage with it through system-wide complex adaptive processes. Insecurity is thus no longer considered external, but internal to the system that the citizen is embedded in. Consequently, the general population will have to face threats through reflection and self-govern its contingent position within such complex assemblages.

In order to better understand this unique ontology, epistemology and temporality, the next section introduces the resilience discourse in detail. It starts out by tracing the rise of resilience from the 1970s across different fields and introduces a general mapping of that which characterizes resilience. The understanding of this world as interconnected and uncertain features here as the common vantage point for all the different writings on resilience. This chapter moves then from a more general mapping of the concept toward the way in which the discourse can be subdivided and organized according to the different critiques of resilience. While the larger part of resilience literature understand it as positive empowerment, others see it as the advent of fundamental insecurity, as a new form of self-governance or as a way of exercising critique.

The rise of resilience

A brief look at the etymology of resilience indicates the extent to which the concept is already embedded in a processual logic of disruption and response. Resilience derives from the Latin word *resiliens*, which describes an ongoing activity of rebounding or recoiling. It is a composite of *Re-* meaning *back* and *salire*, which is often translated as *to jump, to leap*. The grammatical modus that expresses repeated and habitual actions is related to the verb *to result*, which also means *to spring forward* (Online Etymology Dictionary 2012). The term itself thus describes an ongoing, result-oriented process of reacting and rebounding, which may also produce "a leap forward." As such, it points to the emergent aspects of resilience that lead to evolution.

Despite its increasing circulation across disciplines, such as ecology (e.g., Folke *et al*. 2003), psychology (e.g., Luthar *et al*. 2000) or political science (e.g., Brassett *et al*. 2013), and political domains, for example development and aid (e.g., UNDP 2014a), climate change (e.g., UNISDR 2005) and cyber-security (ENISA 2011), the concept of resilience remains ambiguous. A consistent definition or conceptualization does not exist (Kirk and Theobald 2010). This may be traced back to the fact that resilience was coined in two disciplines simultaneously: ecology and psychology. Even though Schoon claims that almost all literature refers "in one manner or another to various works by C. S. Holling" (2005: 2) citing his 1973 article "Resilience and Stability of Ecological Systems" (Holling 1973), this mainly relates to works in the field of ecology, sociology or political sciences.

Holling's notion of resilience originally criticized the pathology of command-and-control natural resource management (Holling and Meffe 1996). He and a broad scholarship following his legacy define resilience as "the amount of change a system can undergo [...] and still retain the same controls on function and structure," which is linked to "the degree to which the system is capable of selforganization, [...] learning and adaptation" (Walker et al. 2002: 5–6). Soon after Holling's conceptualization of resilience for the ecological context gained prominence, interrelations between ecological and societal systems were explored (cf. Adger 2000). This resulted in an integration of ecological thinking into sociology and vice versa. In the spirit of Holling's original definition, socio-ecological resilience requires

> communities and societies to have the ability to self-organise and to manage resources and make decisions in a manner that promotes stability. Most important of all, resilience requires societies to have the capacity to adapt to unforeseen circumstances and risks.
>
> (Adger 2003: 3)

This parallels the conceptualization of resilience in engineering science, which defines it as "the ability of a material to absorb energy when it is deformed elastically and return to its original shape on release of load" (Davis 2004: 270; cf. Pimm 1984, 1991; Lovins and Lovins 2001; Roylance 2001). Similar conceptualizations of resilience can be found in information technology (cf. Woods 2006).

At the same time as Holling, Norman Garmezy explored the relevance of adaptation within the development of children at risk (1973). In 1974 he coined the term resilience in the psychological context (Garmezy and Streitman 1974). Ever since, psychology has further developed theorizations of resilience whereby most incorporate the idea of adaptation as Luthar et al. find:

> Resilience refers to a dynamic process encompassing positive adaptation within the context of significant adversity. Implicit within this notion are two critical conditions: (1) exposure to significant threat or severe adversity; and (2) the achievement of positive adaptation despite major assaults on the developmental process.
>
> (2000: 543)

Since the early 2000s, resilience has been adopted into various disciplines and fields as a concept of dealing with disruption. By now, resilience refers to a variety of objects and individuals that are embedded in relational contexts: it is explored as a property of materials (Roylance 2001: 9; Davis 2004; Schoon 2005) or complex networks, such as the Internet (ENISA 2011). Resilience is supposed to work across multiple scales, referring to individuals (Rutter 1990; Masten et al. 1990; Kaplan 1999; Luthar et al. 2000), communities (Pimm 1991; Longstaff et al. 2010), societies or socio-ecological systems (Gentry and Kobasa 1984; Walker et al. 2002; Folke et al. 2003), organizations (Home and Orr 1997), markets (Peron et al. 2012) or infrastructures (Amin 2002). Processes

(Jontunen and Hyvönen 2014), social systems (Cudworth 2013) and movements (Newlands 2013) are also studied with regards to their resilience.

Irrespective of the field it is deployed in, resilience always speaks to a situation of insecurity, which can occur in the past, present or future. It emerges as a response to stress (Lösel et al. 1989; Kaplan 1999; Rolf and Glantz 1999; Luthar et al. 2000; Adger 2003; Bohle 2007), disturbance (Walker et al. 1981; Holling 1995; Gunderson 2000; Lovins and Lovins 2001; Rieger et al. 2009; Longstaff et al. 2010), adversity (Masten et al. 1990; Luthar and Zigler 1991; Werner and Smith 1992; Kaplan 1999), risk (Rutter 1990; Masten and Powell 2003; Titus 2006) or simply change (Holling 1973; Adger 2000; Carpenter et al. 2001; Walker et al. 2004; Woods 2006). All of these insecurities are framed as the result of increased global interconnectedness and complexity, which has also been recognized by the political institutions that seek to instigate resilience (UNISDR 2005; IFRC 2012; European Commission 2012).

In many definitions resilience is understood as a mechanism to maintain or re-establish the original state of a given system after disruption. Resilient systems are here understood to be tolerant (Woods 2006), flexible (Hale and Heijer 2006), elastic (Davis 2004), redundant (Rosenzweig 2010) or robust (Perelman 2007) as they mainly seek to "retain essentially the same function, structure, identity, and feedbacks" (Walker et al. 2004: 6f.; cf. Pimm 1991; Quinlan 2003; Folke 2006; Longstaff et al. 2010). The goal is then to "remain in a particular configuration" (Walker et al. 2002: 19; cf. Holling 1973; Carpenter et al. 2001). Material would, for example, be considered resilient if it was "unaffected by the applied stress" (Roylance 2001: 9) or would not suffer damage (Davis 2004), which is why this understanding of resilience is prominent in engineering. What this also implies is that there are limits to resilience: systems may collapse, disappear, move, deform or break when reaching their resilient limits (Handmer and Dovers 1996; Smithers and Smit 1997; Walker et al. 2002; Roylance 2001).

Other conceptualizations of resilience consider disruption to be a driver for change and resilience as the adaptive capacity that changes a system. In a society that considers itself as a product of constant circulation (Dillon 2000; Lash 2006), the emergency is not only an inevitable accompaniment of exchange processes, but an opportunity for new formation and development. Disruption and resilience, then, contribute to a system's evolution. Following this understanding, resilient systems and individuals are dynamic (Garmezy 1990; Luthar and Zigler 1991; Werner and Smith 1992; Luthar et al. 2000). They don't only bounce back, but leap forward, which is tied to the concept of adaptation, the idea of learning from disruption and exploiting instabilities (Walker et al. 2002). Longstaff et al. associate, for example, a community's adaptive capacity with the ability to remember experiences in order to "use that memory [...] to learn, innovate, and reorganize resources in order to adapt to changing environmental demands" (2010: 7). Similar thinking occurs in psychology, where a positive outcome despite major adversity is tied to adaptation (cf. Kobasa 1979; Garmezy 1990; Luthar et al. 2000). Resilience would then allow for "renewal [...] and emergence of new trajectories" (Folke 2006: 259), for "disturbance-driven change" (Walker *et al*. 2002: 19) and "developmental progression" (Luthar *et al*. 2000: 3). Many authors consider both understandings of resilience – sustaining and developing with change – to coexist (cf. Holling 1973; Walker *et al*. 2002; Folke 2006). Handmer and Dover's typology, for example, suggests that resilience reaches from systems aimed at stability via those that change at the margins to a form of resilience marked by openness, flexibility and adaptation (1996; newly picked up by Bourbeau 2013, 2015). Resilience, here, means to create conditions for entrepreneurial commitment and evolution (Zebrowski 2013).

What follows from these recurrent aspects of the resilience concept is that insecurity is not only understood as an inherent part of our world, but this insecurity needs to be dealt with in a self-organized manner. This implies that any form of recovery is organized by drawing on internal resources (Rauh 1989; Kaplan 1999; Carpenter *et al*. 2001; Folke *et al*. 2003; Longstaff *et al*. 2010). Systems then "reorganize in the absence of direction, or to obtain resources from outside sources" (Longstaff *et al*. 2010: 7). Self-organization is thus understood as the contrary of two states: "lack of organization," or "organization forced by external factors" (Carpenter *et al*. 2001: 766), which also applies to non-human systems. In the context of critical infrastructure security, for example, Gustavsson and Ståhl refer to resilience as self-healability, because it is the "property that enables a system to perceive that it is not operating correctly and […] make the necessary adjustments to restore itself" (2008: 86).

The insecurity of the unknown future is here the engine for competition, adaptation, self-organization and progression. While risk governance techniques respond to this uncertainty with the means of what can be described as new prudentialism (O'Malley 2009), having the citizen embrace risk by calculating, minimizing and insuring against eventualities in a self-responsible fashion (Baker and Simon 2002), resilience responds to increasing complexity by asking the citizen to embrace emergencies. The citizens now assume the responsibility to organize themselves, to create local forms of security and to provide their local knowledge for overarching emergency management activities (Kaufmann 2013). This includes, for example, the sharing of important crisis information (Kaufmann 2015), the storage of nutrition in case of supply chain disruption (Bundesamt für Bevölkerungsschutz und Katastrophenhilfe n.d.), psychological training for dealing with trauma (Neocleous 2012; Howell 2012), or an imaginative spirit for identifying individual solutions to climate catastrophes (Duffield 2012; Oels and Methmann 2015). With resilience, the responsibility to establish security is decentralized to render emergency management more effective. Where risk techniques calculate the unknown in order to prevent it, resilience would, for example, calculate the best possibilities for reaction in case of emergency. One of such practices is, for example, enabled through social media and apps, through which citizens can report incidents, which are then translated into frequencies and marked as "zones" that need help most urgently (Meier 2011).

The design of resilience to embrace complexity and answer insecurity via processes of self-organization is at the core of the promise and the criticism that it inspires. Bourbeau, for example, notices a general positive bias in resilience literature. He observes that most contributions imply a position that "resilience is good and must be promoted" (2013: 9), as it provides the answer to insecurity. In response, he calls for analyses that investigate the promises and the pitfalls of resilience in International Relations contexts (Bourbeau 2015). Seen from a promising angle, resilience could even be framed as a criticism of the linearity, reductionism, artificiality and closure-orientation of modern governance, which seeks to create certainty and stability by means of control, since it originated as a response to command and control regimes (Holling and Meffe 1996):

> In a non-linear world of interactive or emergent causality any top-down attempts to direct and control the social world fly in the face of the "real" processes of social causation, leading to counterproductive or unintended outcomes. Resilience-thinking is thereby constantly drawing lessons from the real and complex appearances of the world to learn that liberal artifice – the constructed world of linear cause and effect and reductionist binaries – is a barrier to be overcome through new ways of conceiving the world that is to be governed.
>
> (Chandler 2014a: 12)

Assessments of the promises of resilience, however, have lately been confronted with rising criticism. What follows is an overview of current resilience discourses that tend to either adopt or criticize resilience as a strategy of dealing with disruption. The process of mapping clarifies which discourses of resilience this book is aware of and speaks to. Moreover, the gaps in research or literature it addresses and the conceptual discourses it identifies with will be expanded on toward the end of this chapter.

Resilience as empowerment

While it is contested that resilience actively lowers the exposure to threat (Prior and Eriksen 2013), the larger part of socio-ecology and psychology discourses suggest that resilience reduces sensitivities to disruption for individuals, communities or systems (cf. Garmezy 1973; Holling 1973; Handmer and Dovers 1996; Rolf and Glantz 1999; Amin 2002; Adger 2003; Folke *et al.* 2003; Gustavsson and Ståhl 2008; Mark *et al.* 2009, to name but a few). The conclusion drawn from this is that resilience can and should be enhanced. Advocates of resilience identify self-organization as not just the only available means of dealing with contingency, but also as a chance for change (Holling 1973) and a form of empowerment, emphasizing that the process of confronting adversities can be energizing (Shih 2004).

This stance is heavily reflected in policy discourses that seek to "build back better" (UNISDR 2010) or enhance resilient capacities altogether (cf. European Commission 2012, 2013a,b, 2014b; IFRC 2012, 2013; UN 2012a,b; UNDP 2011, 2014a,b; UNESCAP 2013; UNISDR 2012a,b). During the past decade such discourses have become particularly prominent in the disaster policies of the Anglophone world, such as the UK (e.g., Challen *et al.* 2010), the US (e.g., US Department of Homeland Security 2013) and Australia (e.g., Australian Government 2011), but the concept has also been adopted by intergovernmental bodies, such as the United Nations (UN 2012a) and the European Union (European Commission 2010). Making systems, individuals, communities or complete societies resilient is by now an explicit political agenda, which targets especially those that are thought to be vulnerable or particularly exposed to danger. The United Nations Office for Disaster Risk Reduction's (UNISDR) "Hyogo Framework for Action" (HFA) from 2005 was one of the first major political resolutions to include resilience in disaster management strategies. As a response to complex emergencies (UNISDR 2005: 22), the plan foresees to strengthen resilience as

> [t]he capacity of a system, community or society potentially exposed to hazards to adapt, by resisting or changing in order to reach and maintain an acceptable level of functioning and structure[.] This is determined by the degree to which the social system is capable of organising itself to increase this capacity for learning from past disasters for better future protection and to improve risk reduction measures.
>
> (UNISDR 2005: 4)

The framework was followed by a range of UN policies on resilience with a definite upsurge from 2011 onwards. The vast range of these policies are forwarded by the UNISDR and the United Nations Development Program (UNDP), which situate resilience in the context of humanitarian and development issues in the global South. Resilience is here the strategic answer to phenomena that are difficult to control, such as the effects of climate change and other natural hazards (cf. UN 2012a, 2014; UNISDR 2014), but also economic crises (UNESCAP 2013). The central aim is to weave resilience into the fabric of societies (UNDP 2014a), targeting communities (UNDP 2014b), the people (UN 2012b "Resilient people resilient planet"; UNDP 2011 "Towards Human Resilience"), or cities as a whole (UNISDR 2012a,b "Making Cities Resilient" campaign). The European Commission's disaster risk reduction strategy from 2011 reflects the UN's priorities and emphasizes the importance of the role that crisis populations can play for disaster resilience in particular (European Commission 2011).

Similar to the UNDP's and UNISDR's programs, the EU issued several strategies to foster resilience in the global South in order to deal with natural hazards (European Commission 2013b "Increasing Resilience by Reducing Disaster Risk in Humanitarian Action") and food crises (European Commission 2012 "The EU approach to resilience," 2013a "Action Plan for Resilience in Crisis Prone Countries," 2014a "Building Resilience to food and nutrition crisis in the Sahel and West-Africa"), but also more broadly with violence and conflict (European Commission 2014b "Building Resilience: The EU's Approach"). All of these policies refer to resilience as the ability of individuals, households and communities to withstand, absorb, recover and bounce back from, cope with or adapt to shocks timely and efficiently. This also parallels the International Federation of the Red Cross's (IFRC) approach to resilience, which is captured in the IFRC's *Contribution to the Preparation of the European Commission Communication on Resilience* (European Union Red Cross Office 2012) and the extensive discussion paper, *The Road to Resilience* (IFRC 2012), as well as the Options for Including Community Resilience in the Post-2015 Development Goals (IFRC 2013), all of which present resilience as an important strategic concept for the IFRC's overall commitment. The IFRC's documents emphasize in particular the importance of local ownership and people-centered approaches for resilience, as well as the fact that it refers to adaptive processes before, during and after crises (European Union Red Cross Office 2012).

Even though the concept is most widely used in humanitarian policies, resilience has also been adopted into the EU's Internal Security Strategy, which foresees to build resilience to natural and man-made disasters (European Commission 2010). Beyond general disaster and emergency management, resilience is more concretely integrated into EU Internet security policies, where it is linked to critical information infrastructures that adapt to and recover from failure and survive in the face of threats (European Commission 2009; ENISA 2011).

Resilience is not only present in policy discourses, but it has also been linked to cultural traditions, to mentalities of

> always being on a journey, both external and internal [...]. A tradition of constant striving, of constantly recreating one's self, of living in uncertainty, of being an outsider in an established system.
> (Siapno 2011: 58)

Resilience is here instantiated in ceremonies and rituals that help to come to terms with one's life and to deal with loss, displacement and violence (ibid.).

Such positive framings of resilience are also symptomatic of the large body of popular resilience literature and courses (e.g., "Developing Personal Resilience," "Becoming a Resilient Person," "Resilience and Stress Management Training Course"), which mainly address the fields of management and self-help. In his book *From Crisis to Recovery*, Doherty, for example, defines resilient people as those who "are more likely to notice positive meanings within the problem they face" (2010: 105). The process of embracing disruptions as opportunity for development, then, is considered a positive asset or trait, which greatly reflects the law of emergence. In fact, resilience has become the "lingua franca of survival" (Duffield 2016). This law is also what governs the evolutionary development of living systems, "which requires that they engage in a continual process of exposure to danger [...]. We may even pre-emptively create the conditions for the catastrophic so that we can control its emergence on our terms" (Evans and Reid 2014: 61).

Resilience as insecurity

This very understanding of resilience as adaptive capacity also constitutes the entry point for critical assessments of resilience by different research traditions. Some authors question whether resilience at all qualifies "as an organizing concept with sufficient logical and emotional resonance to yield systematic theoretical and research inquiry that will make it a lasting contribution" (Liddle 1994: 167). In particular, the notion of adaptation is criticized as conceptually boundless and unspecific (Fujita 2006). Other authors subscribe to the idea of adaptation, but mention that the outcome of a resilience process is not necessarily positive: "[i]t may prove very difficult to transform a resilient system into a more desirable one" (Folke 2006: 259; cf. Carpenter *et al.* 2001). Resilience can thus also be a negative characteristic, because some systems, situations, norms, or regimes can be resilient to a needed transformation (Bourbeau 2013). Resilience processes may furthermore happen "at the expense of changes in the capacity of ecosystems to sustain the adaptation" (Folke 2006: 260), which can again generate traps and breakpoints (ibid.).

These critical assessments, however, do not address the fundamental challenges that arise when resilience is understood as a way of governing. Together with other scholars, Lentzos and Rose started conducting Foucaultian assessments of resilience and exposed resilience to be a systematic technique of strengthening "subjective and material arrangements so as to be better able to anticipate and tolerate disturbances in complex worlds without collapse" (Lentzos and Rose 2009: 243). As that, they find, resilience is merely another risk-oriented and liberal practice of governing, which utilizes subjective states of insecurity, alertness, suspicion and surveillance as a means to legitimate an extension of security practices into everyday existences (ibid.).

Indeed, epistemological claims about uncertainty play an important role in the critical discourse about resilience, even though other authors find that they are in fact quite different from those claims that regimes of risk make. Aradau, for example, distinguishes between different epistemic regimes. Risk would be an episteme that allows for the taming of uncertainty. The interconnected world, however, is characterized by the episteme of surprise – the unexpected, disruptive, emergent challenge. Only in an environment infused with uncertainty and surprise does resilience get to work. Here, security remains desirable, however, "the problematisation of surprising events renders its promise impossible, to be replaced by resilience" (Aradau 2014: 87). Resilience is then a stand-in for security. Grove goes one step further in arguing that resilience has become the official policy response for fabricated uncertainties (Grove 2014). Within an interconnected world, so the governmental narrative goes, there is no protection from danger, but we embrace the reality of its immanence (Peters 1987). Danger and disruption are framed as an integral part of the complex, disordered world (Schipper and Pelling 2006; O'Malley 2009; Bahadur *et al.* 2010; Duffield 2012). Instead of surrendering to danger, practices and strategies of resilience seek to embrace and utilize it. As molecular biology and complex systems theory teach us, complex emergencies require system-wide responses – a response of dynamism, evolution and renewal. In the spirit of the battle-call "bounce back better!" emergence and emergency are exploited as opportunities for development and resilience is understood as that which generates development with change (cf. Folke 2006). As such,

> [r]esilience embodies the neo-Darwinian promise that if organizations and individuals can rise to the challenge of permanent threat, if they are not fazed with external dystopia, they can reinvent themselves anew as more flexible and adaptive, becoming altogether better and more agile models of their old selves.
>
> (Duffield 2012: 486)

Duffield formulates here a biopolitical critique of resilience practices. Foucault's notion of biopolitics describes the various forms of governing that target man as a living being; they manage life itself and characteristics specific to life, such as "birth, death, production, illness" (Foucault 2003: 242). Resilience then constitutes a biopolitical form of governing, in which exposure to danger is recast as a constitutive process, which Evans and Reid criticize as "insecure by design" (2014: 38ff.). The resilient subject is not a victim (ibid.). Danger is not a phenomenon it seeks freedom from. Quite the contrary: the resilient subject needs danger to prosper and extend life. The ontological conditions formulated by discourses of complexity, however, will also leave the resilient individual with no choice. In a world in which danger is understood as endemic and has been recast as a condition for being alive, the subject has no other opportunity but being resilient.

This "self-reductionism to a purely biological state of being" (Evans and Reid 2014: 63) undermines freedom, since we have to "live through the source of our endangerment" (ibid.: 169). Resilience is thus criticized as inherently depoliticizing, since resilient subjects are expected to accept danger as a state of being instead of challenging it politically (Neocleous 2012; cf. Howell and Voronka 2012; Howell 2012). Understood through resilience, insecurity is not the result of uneven political distributions that can be changed, but the "unavoidable consequences of living in an emergent and interconnected world" (Grove 2014: 244). Because resilience forecloses the tackling of any underlying issues that lead to danger in the first place, resilience has been criticized as "self-imposed powerlessness" (Jontunen and Hyvönen 2014: 208). It "disavows the transformative capacity of collective political action and remains hostage to the limits of knowledge" (Aradau 2014: 87). Oels and Methmann illustrate this depoliticizing and non-transformative trend using an example from the field of climate politics:

> By accepting that dangerous levels of climate change are inevitable, resilience deprives us of our capacity to foster a more secure world in which climate change is tackled through the transformation of lifestyles and energy

systems. Politics, to put it bluntly, is reduced to the decision between staying or going.

(Oels and Methmann 2015: 53)

However, the fact that resilience deprives the subject of its transformative capacities, so Evans and Reid argue (2013), has even more drastic consequences. If the ultimate aim of resilience is to harness the constant exposure of threat in order to make life live and thrive, life itself would equally become continuous and never-ending. Life without death, however, cannot imagine what it means to turn the world upside down: "[i]t is impossible to live meaningful without knowing how to die. Abandoning death forces us to give up the prospect of self-renewal" (Evans and Reid 2013: 83). Resilience is thus found to be inherently nihilistic: its pursuit for infinite survival eventually nurtures the political will to nothingness (Evans and Reid 2013).

Grove reminds us of the fact that the ontology of complexity, which justifies this form of depoliticization, is not a given. He argues that it is part of a political program, an immunitary style of governing that encodes an artificial adaptive capacity within society the main aim of which is not to threaten existing order (Grove 2014). Despite the fact that these are powerful critical arguments, a thorough conceptualization of transformation vis-à-vis adaptation needs more critical attention, which we will return to in the course of this book. The book will also further develop the argument that resilience is not replacing the promise of security – the state of being *sed cura*, which is Latin for *without worry*, but resilience recasts security as an activity. With resilience, security becomes a constant interplay of insecurity and security, which can entail depoliticizing effects, but also harbor new forms of agency. The question as to whether resilience actually instills agency, or merely a laissez-faire kind of governance, as well as a redistribution of responsibilities, is also relevant in the critical discourse we will now turn to.

Resilience as self-governance

As we have seen, the concept of adaptation is often coupled with another key aspect of resilience theory: the role of self-organization. If resilience is about survival in the face of threats, only oneself can know where and how to adapt. Conceptually, resilience emphasizes the role of self-reflection and engagement, whether that concerns the individual, an organization, a community or society at large. This presupposes a sense of being interconnected with the rest of the contingent world: the resilient subject can only be self-reflective if it internalizes the dangers of the world that it needs to adapt to.

This form of reflection and self-organization, so Malcolm argues, is not an organic development, but a governmental strategy (2013). He describes this development as a bargain struck between the citizen who acquires extra knowledge and learns to use local resources, and the state that can count on the citizens' engagement (2013: 319). Rogers, whose entry point to understanding resilience is the community, finds that governmental engagement tactics can be both empowering in a positive way and responsibilizing in a negative way, for example when they prevent citizens from taking part in decision-making (2013). Brassett *et al.* argue that this points to the productive ambiguity of resilience, the politics of which are incomplete and ongoing (2013: 225). Resilience policies, so they argue, produce political communities on the one hand and foster anxiety and uncertainty on the other (ibid.: 222f.). Other critical scholars find that reflexivity and engagement are nearly impossible to instantiate through governmental strategies. Self-reflection cannot simply be demanded or measured in terms of impact. Rather, policies that seek to enhance reflexivity and self-organization cause a range of practical and ethical problems (cf. Grove 2014; Howell 2014; Oels and Methmann 2015). The less serious the political engagement with the inner workings of the system that is supposed to be resilient, the more resilience policies become a form of buck-passing, providing new possibilities of blame, leaving victims feeling left alone and reinforcing their self-image as weak, undesired and vulnerable (cf. Hagmann and Cavelty 2012).

Rather than enabling empowerment and bottom-up governance, political strategies to enhance resilience are marked by a rescaling of responsibility: "[s]ecurity is becoming more civic, urban, domestic and personal: security is coming home" (Coaffee and Wood 2006: 503). Such strategies move from "rings of steel" and the designing out of danger to the need for territorial participation through self-reflection (ibid.). What is politically framed as a form of social responsibility of empowered subjects is from a critical perspective understood as a technique of governing that "emphasises individual responsibility" (Joseph 2013: 38; Evans and Reid 2014). As a result, security becomes a problem of the vulnerable – and it reproduces vulnerability. Within war, Howell argues, individuals are being responsibilized for exhibiting resilience in the face of trauma (Howell 2012). When it comes to climate change, it is the victims who need to adapt their lifestyles (Oels and Methmann 2015). Approaching developmental and humanitarian issues through resilience equally implies a responsibilization of the local community which at best redefines, and in the worst case replaces the responsibility to protect (Chandler 2012; Duffield 2012).

Understood as self-organization, resilience leads to a remoteness of the sovereign, who not only values the responsible, enterprising and self-governing subject, but is also often spatially remote due to increasing technological mediation that replaces face-to-face interaction between state agencies and citizen. This remoteness has led to an increasingly accepted criticism of resilience as a neoliberalist mode of governing, much in the sense of Foucault's governmentality (2008; cf. Lentzos and Rose 2009; Zebrowski 2009, 2013; O'Malley 2009; Walker and Cooper 2011; Joseph 2013). The idea to enhance resilience would not only incorporate complexity thinking in general, but it would be indebted to Friedrich Hayek's understanding of the market in particular (Walker and Cooper 2011; Joseph 2013; Zebrowski 2013). Instead of following fixed norms, stable relations or the logic of equilibria, a neoliberal market opens itself up to unknowns. The only politics available are those of "optimising the conditions for

30 *Part I: Interconnectedness and emergencies*

self-organisation and adaptive evolution" (Zebrowski 2013: 169), while interventionism is discouraged. This principle of (neo)liberal economy to deliberately self-limit government or to govern from a distance in order to encourage free conduct, self-responsible decision-making, competitive practice and enterprise is nothing new. In fact, most critical analyses of neoliberal modes of governing refer to Foucault's formulation of laissez-faire governance, which is "legitimated through the liberal concern that one must not 'govern too much'" (Joseph 2013: 42; cf. Zebrowski 2013). Instead of "standardising, identificatory, hierarchical individualization" (Foucault 2008: 261) neoliberal governmentality would be the:

> image, idea, or theme-program of a society in which there is an optimization of systems of difference, in which the field is left open to fluctuating processes, in which minority individuals and practices are tolerated, in which action is brought to bear on the rules of the game rather than on the players, and finally in which there is an environmental type of intervention instead of the internal subjugation of individuals.
> (Foucault 2008: 259–260; cf. Zebrowski 2013: 169)

This modus of rendering the world governable is, as Joseph claims, also not unique to neoliberalism. It is in line with a range of other policies, philosophies or ontopolitical processes, such as new materialism, complexity theory, network analysis or reflexive approaches, or paradigms such as reflexive modernity, risk society, network society and information age, because they "share a set of ontological commitments" (Joseph 2013: 39). Similarly, O'Malley claims that

> the informatically-driven imaginaries of the biological and digital revolutions and the corresponding transformation of the military have co-evolved with advanced liberal politics. Advanced liberalism (...) had projected a neo-Darwinian requirement for adaptiveness and competitive "fitness landscapes" onto terrain of governance.
> (O'Malley 2009: 504; cf. O'Malley 2004; Rose 1999)

Walker and Cooper explain that these logics have become so all-encompassing that the dynamics of stressed systems, whether biospheres or financial markets, have been rendered virtually indistinguishable (2011). Resilience fits right into this logic as it follows neoliberalism's normative way of mobilizing social agents (Joseph 2013). Its discourse of nature and society promotes enterprising and risk-embracing subjects that exploit danger, turn contingency into opportunity and transform themselves to bounce back better (O'Malley 2009).

For many critics, this production of freedom and self-sufficiency through neoliberal modes of governing is opposed to the interventionist practices of liberal internationalism. Liberal interventionism would follow traditional epistemes of a distinction between subject (man) and object (the world around man), which enables human sovereignty and control of the environment with predictable effects (Rosenow 2012). Resilience would then be a shift away from this "Western securing or sovereign agency and towards a concern with facilitating [...] self-securing agency" (Chandler 2012: 213). Systems are believed to evolve most productively if they are freed from interventionist control (Walker and Cooper 2011), adapting to whichever contingency they face. This not only ties back to earlier discussed criticisms of depoliticization, as such modes of governing foreclose transformation, but it also abandons the liberal subject, whose autonomy and self-direction is defined by the "resistance to the will of others" (Evans and Reid 2014: 56) – not by the adaptation to it.

Other critics make the point that the idea of intervention still stands. Even though governments may step back to encourage free conduct, this conduct "is achieved through active intervention into civil society and the opening up of new areas to the logic of private enterprise and individual initiative" (Joseph 2013: 42). But even here agency remains an illusion, because autonomy and individual initiative are only constructed through ontopolitical discourses (ibid.). Rosenow argues slightly differently that elements of the liberal episteme become evident in the assumption that socio-ecological systems still need to be steered (Rosenow 2012):

> [I]t cautions against reductionism, but maintains the idea of the management of complexity; it recognizes the limits of knowledge, but does not dismiss the aim of increasing certainty; it advocates the inclusion of local knowledge and a wider range of participants in decisionmaking processes, but only as complementary to the structures of knowledge-gaining and regulation already in place.
>
> (Ibid.: 544–545)

Resilience is here likened to intervention at a distance, because the idea of governance is not abandoned completely. Governance is still exercised through a given set of norms and standards. Resilience would then promote a move away from hierarchical command and control policies, instantiating decentralized forms of governing marked by "consensual negotiations, partial self-regulation (with legal boundaries), and the use of market mechanisms and instruments" (Berger *et al.* 2001: 59). This inspires Grove to suggest that a complete withdrawal of governing bodies would be desirable in order to avoid technocratic management and promote resilience to "flourish in whatever direction it may take [...] where so-called "mutant rules" of resilience are possible, where resilience can be more than a process to simply avoid disturbance" (Grove 2014: 253).

Schmidt takes this idea of unrestrained adaptivity further and develops the argument that governing through resilience in fact goes beyond neoliberalism and intervention. From a Deweyan perspective, she argues, resilience conceptually allows for unmediated self-transformation and empowerment through learning. While neoliberal techniques of governing eventually lead to an impasse, since they focus on the governing of the external world in which uncertainty and complexity cannot be reduced, a pragmatist reading of complexity would

32 Part I: Interconnectedness and emergencies

identify resilience as that which can "unblock institutional stalemates and unleash unknown human potentialities" (Schmidt 2014: 7), creating "new states of being" (ibid.: 8). Because resilience conceptually enables a focus on the internal world, it engenders "a continuous process of self-transformation through experiencing and learning from life" (ibid.: 15). Through resilience, so she argues, agency is not restrained, because it is not a matter of will, but a matter of adaptation and indefinite transformation.

This book takes the vantage point from the discussion on self-governance to further differentiate between resilience as a governmental program and resilience as a spontaneous instance. This allows for a clearer distinction between those resilience practices that leave room for intervention and those that permit freely flourishing developments. Furthermore, it allows for a distinction between those forms of resilience that have depoliticizing effects and those that have potentially constitutive effects.

Resilience as critique

Similar to Schmidt's argument about self-transformation and learning, Chandler suggests that resilience-thinking eventually exceeds neoliberalism and the idea of intervention (Chandler 2014a,b). While the interventionist governance project of liberal universalism was based upon known knowns that follow assumptions of cause and effect, and policies were constructed top-down, neoliberalism accepted the market as a deus ex machina to capture and govern complex life. The market was

> the intermediary connecting local and specific knowledges through prices as indicators. Prices here played a fundamental role of revealing or giving access to the plural reality of complex life and also acting as a guide to future behaviour – how one should adapt to and learn through this reality.
>
> (Chandler 2014b: 53)

Through the market and the logic of prices, complexity became at least governable through known unknowns and states would focus on facilitating evolutionary adaptation, a form of intervening from below through "properly reading market signals" (Chandler 2014b: 54), as described and criticized by governmentality theorists. As such, neoliberalism extends the role of the state into many domains of socio-cultural life, intervening and directing through interactive processes and the lever of the market (cf. Chandler 2014a: 209). The principle of resilience annihilates this idea, because it presupposes that reality is never accessible *ex ante* in order to formulate policy goals – neither to the state, nor to the hidden hand of market price regulation. Reality is only ever accessible ex post facto through reflexive learning processes and can only be instantiated through multiplication instead of reduction. Resilience approaches governance through an ontology of the relational, not through epistemology, since it deals with unknown unknowns. As a result, policy-making necessarily becomes an ongoing process of relational understanding, binding the policy-makers with the problem which they seek to govern, rather than one of discrete decisions which are then implemented.

(Chandler 2014b: 58)

Resilience-thinking thus engenders a mode of governing through unknowability, rejecting the hubristic assumptions of the market and the state, as it works "'backwards' – from the problem – not forwards to achieve some collective policy-goal" (ibid.: 63). In its ideal form resilience would then allow for practices of governing in non-instrumental ways (Chandler 2014a,b).

Chandler thus suggests that on a conceptual level resilience is a consistent adaptation of "a postmodern ontology to the problematic of governing per se" (Chandler 2014b: 63). However, if that is the case what happens to critique? Critical scholars have evaluated this question in different ways. Rosenow, for example, emphasizes the power that lies in the understanding of life forwarded by resilience-thinking, which "escapes attempts to pin it down and make it comprehensible" (2012: 545), thereby imploding a variety of governmental regimes. Walker and Cooper, however, conclude that a system that "thrives upon disruptions," as the concept of resilience suggests, forces all critics to "inhabit the system they set out to challenge" (2011: 157). Their criticism refers back to Luhmann who formulated that "[t]he unity of the system is the self-reference of the system and its change will always require working within, not against the system" (1990: 183), which much reflects resilience-thinking. Thus, if any criticism or perturbation is merely a catalyst for self-differentiation, resilience thinking and any resilient system would "inoculate itself against critique" (Walker and Cooper 2011: 157). Chandler reinterprets this central notion of self-reflexivity as a mode of existence that defies representations and reductionist forms of thought that are inherent in liberal interventionist and market politics (2014a: 202ff.). As opposed to Walker and Cooper, who argue that critique is absorbed into systemic thought, Chandler argues that the ontology of resilience-thinking is the ontology of critique, which implies that "[w]e become critical as a mode of being, as a process of self-reflection" (Chandler 2014a: 224). Becoming "more aware of our affective and material attachments – is now the dominant framework for both governance and the critique of governance" (ibid.), but also a dominant discourse of power, "legitimizing and reproducing governing authority on the basis of the unknowability of the world" (ibid.: 226).

This suggested relationship between resilience and critique is further scrutinized and developed in the remainder of this book. While Schmidt and Chandler accept the idea of complexity as a given and utilize the analysis of resilience to theorize agency in a complex world, this book follows the premises of poststructuralism. Like complexity, poststructuralism also focuses on relationality, but it always explores relationality against that which is radically different, radically non-relational (Dillon 2000: 4f.). In the context of resilience discussions, this means that one must also consider the counterpoint to radical interconnectedness. This not only allows us to question the widely accepted complexity narratives, but it also shows that adaptation can hardly be considered a lifestyle of critique. Critique needs the radically different and the radically non-relational in order to spark transformation, which makes it different from mere adaptation. The following chapter will clarify and discuss this relationship between complexity, poststructuralism and relationality, which is crucial when studying resilience in interconnected societies.

The argument of this book was developed in parallel to what can be described as a decisive surge in critical resilience research. As such, it utilizes the discourses presented above as a starting point, to provide a more detailed and theoretically founded differentiation between the various workings and effects of resilience in an interconnected world. The book's contributions largely resonate with an understanding of resilience as a way of governing through insecurity, in which the self-organized subject plays a central role. Both of these aspects will be expanded on within this book, giving a more fine-grained analysis of the way in which this form of governing presupposes a specific ontology, spatiality, epistemology and temporality. It continues to discuss which kind of practices resilience as a way of governing entails and what kind of subject these practices involve.

The specific theoretical and empirical focus on resilience in interconnected societies does not, however, only include a discussion of conceptual premises reflected in resilience, but also an exploration of resilience within a domain that epitomizes connectedness: the Internet. Analyses on the relationship between resilience and technologies of interconnectedness are to date largely absent from the critical resilience discourse, even though there is a clear trend in governmental practices and discourses to utilize resilience in the context of Internet security (e.g., ENISA 2011), as well as to harvest data produced by social media users for the purposes of resilience planning (e.g., Meier 2011). In their introduction to a special issue on resilience, Brassett *et al.* emphasize the necessity to focus on the role that the Internet and social media can play here:

> [L]ike it or not, the stuff of security and risk is increasingly mediated through individuals on social networks, rather than through the editors of large media outlets. At present, of course, it is still too early to make any significant claims about what such changes mean in terms of politics and practice. However, it is fair to say that such developments are not being treated lightly by policymakers. Returning to the opening example of Boston, social media was not something that practitioners passively observed, but rather it formed a crucial site for the dissemination of strategic signals.
>
> (Brassett *et al.* 2013: 226)

This book addresses this gap in the critical resilience literature. It provides empirical insights and theoretical discussions on both resilience as a way of governing the Internet and as a way of governing through the Internet. It integrates themes and theories of complexity, interconnectedness and technology into resilience research. The aim is to examining parallels, interstices and patterns of mutual influence between resilience and the Internet as two concepts that speak to an interconnected world.

References

Adger WN (2000) Social and Ecological Resilience: Are They Related? *Progress in Human Geography* 24(3): 347–364.
Adger WN (2003) Building Resilience to Promote Sustainability: An Agenda for Coping with Globalisation and Promoting Justice. *IHDP Update* 2: 1–3.
Altheide DL (2002) *Creating Fear: News and the Construction of Crisis.* Hawthorne, NY: Aldine de Gruyter.
Amin M (2002) Toward Secure and Resilient Interdependent Infrastructures. *Journal of Infrastructure Systems* 8(3): 67–75.
Amoore L (2007) Vigilant Visualities: The Watchful Politics of the War on Terror. *Security Dialogue* 38(2): 139–156.
Amoore L (2009) Algorithmic War: Everyday Geographies of the War on Terror. *Antipode* 41(1): 49–69.
Aradau C (2014) The Promise of Security: Resilience, Surprise ond Epistemic Politics. *Resilience: International Policies, Practices and Discourses* 2(2): 73–87.
Aradau C, van Munster R (2008) Taming the Future: The Dispositif of Risk in the War on Terror. In: Amoore L, de Goede M (eds) *Risk and the War on Terror.* London: Routledge. 23–40.
Aradau C, van Munster R (2011) *Politics of Catastrophe. Genealogies of the Unknown.* Abingdon, Oxon: Routledge.
Australian Government (2011) *National Strategy for Disaster Resilience.* Available at: www.coag.gov.au/node/81 (accessed 11 August 2016).
Bahadur AV, Ibrahim M, Tanner T (2010) The Resilience Renaissance? Unpacking Resilience for Tackling Climate Change and Disasters. *Strengthening Climate Resilience Discussion Paper 1.* Brighton: Institute of Development Studies.
Baker T, Simon J (2002) *Embracing Risk: The Changing Culture of Insurance and Responsibility.* Chicago: University of Chicago Press.
Beck U (1986) *Risikogesellschaft. Auf dem Weg in eine andere Moderne.* Frankfurt am Main: Suhrkamp.
Berger G, Flynn A, Hines F, Richard J (2001) Ecological Modernization as a Basis for Environmental Policy: Current Environmental Discourse and Policy and the Implications on Environmental Supply Chain Management. *Innovation* 14(1): 55–72.
Bohle HG (2007) Leben mit Risiko – Resilience als neues Paradigma für die Risikowelten von morgen. In: Felgentreff C, Glade T (eds) *Naturrisiken und Sozialkatastrophen.* Heidelberg: Elsevier/Spektrum Akademischer Verlag. 435–441.
Bourbeau P (2013) Resiliencism: Premises and Promises in Securitization Research. *Resilience: International Policies, Practices and Discourses* 1(1): 3–17.
Bourbeau P (2015) Resilience and International Politics: Premises, Debates, Agenda. *International Studies Review* 17(3): 374–95.
Boy N (2015) *Report On the Theory of Risk as a Societal Security Instrument. Source Deliverable 5.1.* Available at: www.societalsecurity.net/sites/default/files/D5.1%20 Report%20on%20the%20theory%20of%20risk%20as%20a%20societal%20 security%20instrument_version2.pdf (accessed 31 August 2015).

Brassett J, Croft S, Vaughan-Williams N (2013) Introduction: An Agenda for Resilience Research in Politics and International Relations. *Politics* 33(4): 221–228.

Bundesamt für Bevölkerungsschutz und Katastrophenhilfe (n.d.) *Ratgeber für Notfallvorsorge und richtiges Handeln in Notsituationen. Meine persönliche Checkliste.* Available at: www.bbk.bund.de/DE/Ratgeber/VorsorgefuerdenKat-fall/Checkliste/Checkliste.html (accessed 11 August 2016).

Carpenter S, Walker B, Anderies JM, Abel N (2001) From Metaphor to Measurement: Resilience of What to What? *Ecosystems* 4: 765–781.

Challen A, Noden P, West A, Machin S (2010) *UK Resilience Programme Evaluation: Final Report.* Available at: www.gov.uk/government/uploads/system/uploads/attachment_data/file/182419/DFE-RR097.pdf (accessed 11 August 2011).

Chandler D (2012) Resilience and Human Security: The Post-interventionist Paradigm. *Security Dialogue* 43(3): 213–229.

Chandler D (2014a) *Resilience. The Governance of Complexity.* London and New York: Routledge.

Chandler D (2014b) Beyond Neoliberalism: Resilience and the New Art of Governing Complexity. *Resilience: International Policies, Practices and Discourses* 2(1): 47–63.

Coaffee J, Wood DM (2006) Security is Coming Home: Rethinking Scale and Constructing Resilience in the Global Urban Response to Terrorist Risk. *International Relations* 20(4): 503–517.

Cudworth E (2013) Armed Conflict, Insecurity and Gender: The Resilience of Patriarchy? *Resilience: International Policies, Practices and Discourses* 1(1): 69–75.

Davis JR (2004) *Tensile Testing.* Materials Park, OH: ASM International.

de Goede M (2008) Beyond Risk: Premediation and the Post-9/11 Security Imagination. *Security Dialogue* 39 (2/3): 155–176.

de Goede M (2012) *Speculative Security: The Politics of Pursuing Terrorist Monies.* Minneapolis, MN: University of Minnesota Press.

Dictionary.com (2014) *Anticipate.* Available at: http://dictionary.reference.com/browse/anticipate (accessed 11 August 2016).

Dillon M (2000) Poststructuralism, Complexity and Poetics. *Theory, Culture and Society* 17(5): 1–26.

Dillon M (2007) Governing Through Contingency: The Security of Biopolitical Governance. *Political Geography* 26(1): 41–47.

Dillon M, Reid J (2009) *The Liberal Way of War. Killing to Make Life Live.* London: Routledge.

Doherty GW (2010) *From Crisis to Recovery. Strategic Planning for Response, Resilience, and Recovery.* Laramie, WY: Rocky Mountain Region DMH Institute Press.

Donzelot J (1984) *L'Invention du Social: Essai sur le Declin des Pasions Politiques.* Paris: Fayard.

Duffield M (2012) Challenging Environments: Danger, Resilience and the Aid Industry. *Security Dialogue* 43(5): 475–492.

Duffield M (2016) The Resilience of the Ruins: Toward a Critique of Digital Humanitarianism. *Resilience – International Policies, Practices and Discourses.* 15 March: 1–19. Available at: http://dx.doi.org/10.1080/21693293.2016.1153772 (accessed 27 February 2017).

Dunn Cavelty M, Giroux J (2015) The Good, the Bad, and the Sometimes Ugly: Complexity as Both Threat and Opportunity in National Security. In: Kavalski E (ed.) *World Politics at the Edge of Chaos: Reflections on Complexity and Global Life.* Albany, NY: SUNY Press. 209–227.

ENISA (2011) *Inter-X: Resilience of the Internet Interconnection Ecosystem. Full Report.* Available at: www.enisa.europa.eu/publications/interx-report/at_download/fullReport (accessed 11 August 2016).

European Commission (2009) *Protecting Europe from Large Scale Cyber-Attacks and Disruptions: Enhancing Preparedness, Security and Resilience.* Available at: http://eur-lex.europa.eu/LexUriServ/LexUriServ.do?uri=COM:2009:0149:FIN:EN:PDF (accessed 11 August 2016).

European Commission (2010) *The EU Internal Security Strategy in Action: Five steps towards a more secure Europe.* Available at: http://ec.europa.eu/commission_2010-2014/malmstrom/pdf/news/internal_security_strategy_in_action_en.pdf (accessed 11 August 2016).

European Commission (2011) *Implementation Plan of the EU Strategy for Supporting Disaster Risk Reduction in Developing Countries 2011–2014.* Available at: http://register.consilium.europa.eu/doc/srv?l=EN&f=ST%206666%202011%20INIT (accessed 11 August 2016).

European Commission (2012) *The EU Approach to Resilience: Learning from Food Security Crisis.* Available at: http://ec.europa.eu/echo/files/policies/resilience/com_2012_586_resilience_en.pdf (accessed 11 August 2016).

European Commission (2013a) *Action Plan for Resilience in Crisis Prone Countries 2013–2020.* Available at: http://ec.europa.eu/echo/files/policies/resilience/com_2013_227_ap_crisis_prone_countries_en.pdf (accessed 11 August 2016).

European Commission (2013b) *Disaster Risk Reduction. Increasing Resilience by Reducing Disaster Risk in Humanitarian Action.* Available at: http://ec.europa.eu/echo/files/policies/prevention_preparedness/DRR_thematic_policy_doc.pdf (accessed 11 August 2016).

European Commission (2014a) *AGIR – Building Resilience to Food and Nutrition Crisis in the Sahel & West-Africa.* Available at: http://ec.europa.eu/echo/files/aid/countries/factsheets/sahel_agir_en.pdf (accessed 11 August 2016).

European Commission (2014b) *Building Resilience: The EU's Approach.* Available at: http://ec.europa.eu/echo/files/aid/countries/factsheets/thematic/EU_building_resilience_en.pdf (accessed 11 August 2016).

European Union Red Cross Office (2012) *Position Paper: Contribution to the Preparation of the European Commission Communication on Resilience, REF. RCEU 07/2012–001.* Available at: www.redcross.eu/en/upload/documents/pdf/2014Position_Papers/RCEU_EU_Resilience_Consultation_2012_ready.pdf (accessed 11 August 2016).

Evans B, Reid J (2013) Dangerously Exposed: The Life and Death of the Resilient Subject. *Resilience: International Policies, Practices and Discourses* 1(2): 83–98.

Evans B, Reid J (2014) *Resilient Life. The Art of Living Dangerously.* Cambridge: Polity Press.

Ewald F (1991) Insurance and Risk. In: Burchell G, Gordon C, Miller P (eds) *The Foucault Effect: Studies in Governmentality.* Hemel Hempstead, Herts: Harvester Wheatsheaf. 197–210.

Ewald F (2002) The Return of Descartes' Malicious Demon: An Outline of a Philosophy of Precaution. In: Baker T, Simon J (eds) *Embracing Risk. The Changing Culture of Insurance and Responsibility.* Chicago: University of Chicago Press. 273–302.

Folke C (2006) Resilience: The Emergence of a Perspective for Social-Ecological Systems Analysis. *Global Environmental Change* 16(3): 253–267.

Folke C, Colding J, Berkes F (2003) Synthesis: Building Resilience and Adaptive Capacity in Social-Ecological Systems. In: Berkes F, Colding J, Folke C (eds) *Navigating Social-Ecological Systems.* Cambridge: Cambridge University Press. 352–387.

Foucault M (2003) *Society Must Be Defended: Lectures at the Collège de France. 1975–76.* New York: Picador.
Foucault M (2008 [1979]) *The Birth of Biopolitics. Lectures at the Collège de France. 1978–1979.* Ed. Senellart M, Ewald F, Fontana A (general eds), Davidson AI (English ed.). Basingstoke, Hants and New York: Palgrave Macmillan.
Fujita Y (2006) Systems are Ever-Changing. In: Hollnagel E, Woods DD, Leveson N (eds) *Resilience Engineering. Concepts and Precepts.* Burlington, VT: Ashgate Publishing Company. 20–33.
Furedi F (1997) *The Culture of Fear. Risk Taking and the Morality of Low Expectations.* London: Cassell.
Furedi F (2006) *The Politics of Fear. Beyond Left and Right.* London: Continuum Press.
Garmezy N (1973) Competence and Adaptation in Adult Schizophrenic Patients and Children at Risk. In: Dean SR (ed.) *Schizophrenia: The First Ten Dean Award Lectures.* New York: MSS Information Corp. 163–204.
Garmezy NA (1990) Closing Note: Reflections on the Future. In: Rolf J, Masten A, Cicchetti D, Nuechterlein K, Weintraub S (eds) *Risk and Protective Factors in the Development of Psychopathology.* New York: Cambridge University Press. 527–534.
Garmezy N, Streitman S (1974) Children at Risk: The Search for the Antecedents of Schizophrenia. Part 1. Conceptual Models and Research Methods. *Schizophrenia Bulletin* 8(8): 14–90.
Gentry WD, Kobasa SC (1984) Social and Psychological Resources Mediating Stress-Illness Relationships in Humans. In: Gentry WD (ed.) *Handbook of Behavioral Medicine.* New York: Guilford. 87–116.
Grove K (2014) Agency, Affect, and the Immunological Politics of Disaster Resilience. *Environment and Planning D. Society and Space* 32(2): 240–256.
Grusin R (2004) Premediation. *Criticism* 46(1): 17–39.
Gunderson L (2000) Ecological Resilience – in Theory and Application. *Annual Review of Ecology and Systematics* 31(1): 425–439.
Gustavsson R, Ståhl B (2008) Self-healing and Resilient Critical Infrastructures. In: Setola R, Geretshuber S (eds) *Critical Information Infrastructures Security. Third International Workshop, CRITIS 2008.* Rome, Italy, October. Revised Papers. Berlin: Springer. 84–94.
Habermas J (1985): *Die Neue Unübersichtlichkeit.* Kleine Politische Schriften V. Frankfurt am Main: Suhrkamp.
Hacking I (1990) *The Taming of Chance.* Cambridge: Cambridge University Press.
Hagmann J, Cavelty M (2012) National Risk Registers: Security Scientism and the Propagation of Permanent Insecurity. *Security Dialogue* 43(1): 79–96.
Hale A, Heijer T (2006) Defining Resilience. In: Hollnagel E, Woods DD, Leveson N (eds) *Resilience Engineering. Concepts and Precepts.* Burlington, VT: Ashgate Publishing Company. 35–40.
Handmer JW, Dovers SR (1996) A Typology of Resilience: Rethinking Institutions for Sustainable Development. *Industrial and Environmental Crisis Quarterly* 9(4): 482–511.
Heath-Kelly C (2015) Securing Through the Failure to Secure? The Ambiguity of Resilience at the Bombsite. *Security Dialogue* 46(1): 69–85.
Holling CS (1973) Resilience and Stability of Ecological Systems. *Annual Review of Ecology and Systematics* 4: 1–23.
Holling CS (1995) What Barriers? What Bridges? In: Gunderson L, Holling CS, Light SS (eds) *Barriers and Bridges to the Renewal of Ecosystems and Institutions.* New York: Columbia University Press. 4–34.

Holling CS, Meffe GK (1996) Command and Control and the Pathology of Natural Resource Management. *Conservation Biology* 10(2): 328–337.
Home JF, Orr JE (1997) Assessing Behaviors that Create Resilient Organizations. *Employment Relations Today* 24(4): 29–39.
Howell A (2012) The Demise of PTSD: From Governing through Trauma to Governing Resilience. In: *Alternatives: Global, Local, Political* 37(3): 214–226.
Howell A (2014) Resilience, War, and Austerity: The Ethics of Military Human Enhancement and the Politics of Data. *Security Dialogue* 46(1): 15–31.
Howell A, Voronka J (2012) Introduction: The Politics of Resilience and Recovery in Mental Health Care. *Studies in Social Justice* 6(1): 1–7.
IFRC (2012) *The Road to Resilience: Bridging Relief and Development for a More Sustainable Future.* International Federation of the Red Cross and Red Crescent Societies. Available at: www.ifrc.org/PageFiles/96178/1224500-Road%20to%20resilience-EN-LowRes%20%282%29.pdf (accessed 11 August 2016).
IFRC (2013) *Options for Including Community Resilience in the Post-2015 Development Goals.* Available at: www.redcross.org.uk/What-we-do/~/media/BritishRedCross/Documents/What%20we%20do/Preparing%20for%20emergencies/Community%20resilience.pdf (accessed 11 August 2016).
Jontunen T, Hyvönen AE (2014) Resilience, Security and the Politics of Processes. *Resilience: International Policies, Practices and Discourses* 2(3): 195–209.
Joseph J (2013) Resilience as Embedded in Neoliberalism: A Governmentality Approach. *Resilience: International Policies, Practices and Discourses* 1(1): 38–52.
Kaplan HB (1999) Toward an Understanding of Resilience. A Critical Review of Definitions and Models. In: Glantz MD, Johnson JL (eds) *Resilience and Development. Positive Life Adaptations.* New York: Kluwer Academic/Plenum Publishers. 17–83.
Kaufmann M (2013) Emergent Self-organisation in Emergencies: Resilience Rationales in Interconnected Societies. *Resilience: International Policies, Practices and Discourses* 1(1): 53–68.
Kaufmann M (2015) Resilience 2.0: Social Media Use and (Self-)Care During the 2011 Norway Attacks. *Media, Culture & Society* 37(7): 972–987.
Kirk M, Theobald M (2010) Resilienz-Management. Einstieg in ein neues Konzept für die Krisen- und Katastrophenbewältigung. *Deutsche Feuerwehrzeitung Brandschutz* 9/10: 741–745.
Kobasa SC (1979) Successful Life Events, Personality and Health: An Inquiry into Hardiness. *Journal of Personality and Social Psychology* 37(1): 1–11.
Lash, S. (2006) Life (Vitalism). *Theory, Culture & Society* 23(2–3): 323–328.
Lentzos F, Rose N (2009) Governing Insecurity: Contingency Planning, Protection, Resilience. *Economy and Society* 38(2): 230–254.
Liddle H (1994) Contextualizing Resiliency. In: Wang MC, Gorton E (eds) *Educational Resilience in Inner City America: Challenges and Prospects.* Hillsdale, NJ: Lawrence Erlbaum. 167–77.
Longstaff PH, Armstrong NJ, Perrin K, Parker WM, Hidek MA (2010) Building Resilient Communities: A Preliminary Framework for Assessment. *Homeland Security Affairs* 6(3): 1–23.
Lösel F, Bliesener T, Köferl P (1989) On the Concept of "Invulnerability": Evaluation and First Results of the Bielefeld Project. In: Brambring M, Lösel F, Skowronek H (eds) *Children at Risk: Assessment, Longitudinal Research, and Intervention.* Berlin and New York: De Gruyter. 186–219.

40   Part I: Interconnectedness and emergencies

Lovins AB, Lovins HL (2001) *Brittle Power. Energy Strategy for National Security.* Andover, MA.: Brick House Publishing.

Luhmann N (1990) World Society as a Social System. In: Luhmann N (ed.) *Essays on Self-Reference.* New York: Columbia University Press. 175–190.

Luhmann N (1991) *Soziologie des Risikos.* Berlin/New York: de Gruyter.

Luthar SS, Zigler E (1991) Vulnerability and Competence: A Review of Research on Resilience in Childhood. *American Journal of Orthopsychiatry* 61(1): 6–22.

Luthar SS, Cicchetti D, Becker B (2000) The Construct of Resilience: A Critical Evaluation and Guidelines for Future Work. *Child Development* 71(3): 543–562.

Malcolm JA (2013) Project Argus and the Resilient Citizen. *Politics* 33(4): 311–321.

Mark G, Al-Ani B, Semaan B (2009) Resilience Through Technology Adoption: Merging the Old and the New Iraq. In: *Proceedings of the ACM Conference on Human Factors in Computing Systems* (CHI 2009). Boston, MA and New York: ACM.

Massumi B (1993) *The Politics of Everyday Fear.* Minneapolis, MN: University of Minnesota Press.

Masten AS, Powell JL (2003) A Resilience Framework for Research, Policy and Practice. In: Luthar SS (ed.) *Resilience and Vulnerability. Adaptation in the Context of Childhood Adversities.* Cambridge: Cambridge University Press. 1–28.

Masten AS, Best K, Garmezy N (1990) Resilience and Development: Contributions From the Study of Children Who Overcome Adversity. *Development and Psychopathology* 2(4): 425–444.

Meier P (2011) *Verifying Crowdsourced Social Media Reports for Live Crisis Mapping: An Introduction to Information Forensics.* Available at: http://irevolution.files.wordpress.com/2011/11/meier-verifying-crowdsourced-data-case-studies.pdf (accessed 2 July 2015).

National Geographic (2010) *Global Warming Fast Facts.* Available at: http://news.nationalgeographic.com/news/2004/12/1206_041206_global_warming_2.html (accessed 23 June 2016).

Nato (2002) *Nato Brief. Kurzbeiträge: Die Verwundbarkeit der vernetzten Gesellschaft.* Available at: www.nato.int/docu/review/2002/issue2/german/features2.html (accessed 2 July 2015).

Neocleous M (2012) "Don't Be Scared, Be Prepared": Trauma-Anxiety-Resilience. *Alternatives: Global, Local, Political* 37(3): 188–198.

Newlands M (2013) Contesting Capital in Neoliberal Times: Innovation, Resilience and Conformity in the Occupy Movement. *Resilience: International Policies, Practices and Discourses* 1(1): 76–81.

O'Malley P (2004) *Risk, Uncertainty and Government.* London: Routledge Cavendish.

O'Malley P (2009) "Uncertainty Makes Us Free": Liberalism, Risk and Individual Security. *Behemoth: A Journal on Civilisation* 2(3): 24–38.

Oels A, Methmann C (2015) From "Fearing" to "Empowering" Climate Refugees: Governing Climate-Induced Migration in the Name of Resilience. *Security Dialogue* 46(1): 51–68.

Online Etymology Dictionary (2012) *Resilience.* Available at: www.etymonline.com/index.php?allowed_in_frame=0andsearch=resilienceandsearchmode=none (accessed 12 March 2012).

Perelman LJ (2007) *Shifting Security Paradigm: Towards Resilience. GMU-CIPP Critical Thinking Series. CIPP Working Paper 10–06.* Arlington, VA: George Mason University.

Peron TKD, da Fontoura Costa L, Rodrigues FA (2012) The Structure and Resilience Of Financial Market Networks. *Chaos* 22(1): 013117.

Peters T (1987) *Thriving on Chaos: Handbook for a Management Revolution.* New York: Knopf.
Pimm SL (1984) The Complexity and Stability of Ecosystems. *Nature* 307: 321–326.
Pimm SL (1991) *The Balance of Nature? Ecological Issues in the Conservation of Species and Communities.* Chicago: University of Chicago Press.
Prigogine I (1997) *The End of Certainty.* New York: The Free Press.
Prior T, Eriksen C (2013) Wildfire Preparedness, Community Cohesion And Social–Ecological Systems. *Global Environmental Change* 23(6): 1575–1586.
Quinlan A (2003) Resilience and Adaptive Capacity: Key Components of Sustainable Social-Ecological Systems. *IHDP Update* 2: 4–6.
Rauh H (1989) The Meaning of Risk and Protective Factors in Infancy. *European Journal of Psychology of Education* 4(2): 161–173.
Rieger CG, Gertman DI, McQueen MA (2009): Resilient Control Systems: Next Generation Design Research. *Catania, Italy: 2nd IEEE Conference on Human System Interaction.* Available at: http://ieeexplore.ieee.org/xpl/login.jsp?tp=&arnumber=5091051&url=http%3A%2F%2Fieeexplore.ieee.org%2Fstamp%2Fstamp.jsp%3Ftp%3D%26arnumber%3D5091051 (accessed 11 August 2016).
Robin C (2004) *Fear: The History of A Political Idea.* New York: Oxford University Press.
Rogers P (2013) Rethinking Resilience: Articulating Community and the UK Riots. *Politics* 33(4): 322–333.
Rolf JE, Glantz MD (1999) Resilience. An Interview with Norman Garmezy. In: Glantz MD, Johnson JL (eds) *Resilience and Development. Positive Life Adaptations.* New York: Kluwer Academic/Plenum Publishers. 5–14.
Rose N (1999) *Governing the Soul.* Cambridge: Cambridge University Press.
Rosenow D (2012) Dancing Life into Being: Genetics, Resilience and the Challenge of Complexity Theory. *Security Dialogue* 43(6): 531–547.
Rosenzweig P (2010) The Organization of United States Government and Private Sector for Achieving Cyber Deterrence. In: National Research Council of the National Academies (ed.) *Proceeding of a Workshop on Deterring Cyberattacks. Informing Strategies and Developing Options for U.S: Policy.* Washington: The National Academies Press. 245–270.
Roylance D (2001) *Stress-Strain Curves.* Available at: http://ocw.mit.edu/courses/materials-science-and-engineering/3-11-mechanics-of-materials-fall-1999/modules/MIT3_11F99_ss.pdf (accessed 11 August 2016).
Rutter M (1990) Psychosocial Resilience and Protective Mechanisms. In: Rolf J, Masten AS, Chicchetti D, Nüchterlein KH, Weintraub S (eds) *Risk and Protective Factors in the Development of Psychopathology.* Cambridge: Cambridge University Press. 181–214.
Schipper L, Pelling M (2006) Disaster Risk, Climate Change and International Development: Scope for, and Challenges to, Integration. *Disasters* 30(1): 19–38.
Schmidt J (2014) Intuitively Neoliberal? Towards a Critical Understanding of Resilience Governance. *European Journal of International Relations* 21(2): 402–426.
Schoon M (2005) A Short Historical Overview of the Concepts Resilience, Vulnerability, and Adaptation. Workshop in Political Theory and Policy Analysis. Indiana University. Working Paper W05-4. Available at: https://michaelschoon.files.wordpress.com/2011/05/historical_critique-of-resilience-working-paper.pdf (accessed 11 August 2016).
Shih M (2004) Positive Stigma: Examining Resilience and Empowerment in Overcoming Stigma. *The ANNALS of the American Academy of Political and Social Science* 591(1): 175–185.

Siapno JA (2009) Living Through Terror: Everyday Resilience in East Timor and Aceh. *Social Identities* 15(1): 43–64.

Smithers J, Smit B (1997) Human Adaptation to Climatic Variability and Change. *Global Environmental Change* 7(2): 129–146.

The Economist (2005) *Predicting the Unpredictable*. Available at: www.economist.com/node/4161722 (accessed 23 June 2016).

Titus CS (2006) *Resilience and the Virtue of Fortitude. Aquinas Dialogue with the Psychosocial Sciences*. Washington, DC: Catholic University of America Press.

UN (2012a) *System Task Team on the post 2015 UN Development Agenda: "Disaster risk and resilience."* Available at: www.un.org/en/development/desa/policy/untaskteam_undf/thinkpieces/3_disaster_risk_resilience.pdf (accessed 11 August 2016).

UN (2012b) *Secretary-General's High-Level Panel on Global Sustainability: "Resilient People Resilient Planet: A Future Worth Choosing."* Available at: http://uscib.org/docs/GSPReportOverview_A4%20size.pdf (accessed 11 August 2016).

UN (2014) *United Nations: Plan of Action on Disaster Risk Reduction for Resilience*. Available at: www.preventionweb.net/files/33703_actionplanweb14.06cs1.pdf (accessed 11 August 2016).

UNDP (2011) *Towards Human Resilience: Sustaining Millennium Development Goals Progress in an Age of Economic Uncertainty*. Available at: www.undp.org/content/dam/undp/library/Poverty%20Reduction/Towards_SustainingMDG_Web1005.pdf (accessed 11 August 2016).

UNDP (2014a) *Sustaining Human Progress: Reducing Vulnerability and Building Resilience*. Available at: http://hdr.undp.org/sites/default/files/hdr14-report-en-1.pdf (accessed 11 August 2016).

UNDP (2014b) *Understanding Community Resilience: Findings from Community-Based Resilience Analysis (CoBRA) Assessments*. Available at: www.undp.org/content/dam/undp/library/Environment%20and%20Energy/sustainable%20land%20management/CoBRA/CoBRA_Assessments_Report.pdf (accessed 11 August 2016).

UNESCAP (2013) *Building Resilience to Natural Disasters and Major Economic Crisis*. Available at: www.unescap.org/sites/default/files/ThemeStudy2013-full2.pdf (accessed 11 August 2016).

UNISDR (2005) *Hyogo Framework for Action (2005–2015) "Building the Resilience of Nations and Communities to Disasters."* Available at: www.unisdr.org/2005/wcdr/intergover/official-doc/L-docs/Hyogo-framework-for-action-english.pdf (accessed 11 August 2016).

UNISDR (2010) Building Back Better for Next Time. Experiences and Lessons Learnt from the Project "Building Resilience to Tsunamis in the Indian Ocean." www.unisdr.org/files/14499_buildingbackbetterforthenexttime.pdf (accessed 11 August 2016).

UNISDR (2012a) *Making Cities Resilient Report 2012*. Available at: www.unisdr.org/files/28240_rcreport.pdf (accessed 11 August 2016).

UNISDR (2012b) *Making Cities Resilient Handbook*. Available at: www.unisdr.org/files/26462_handbookfinalonlineversion.pdf (accessed 11 August 2016).

UNISDR (2014) *A Catalyst for Change: How the Hyogo Framework for Action has Promoted Disaster Risk Reduction in South East Europe*. Available at: www.unisdr.org/we/inform/publications/39269 (accessed 11 August 2016).

US Department of Homeland Security (2013) Available at: www.dhs.gov/national-infrastructure-protection-plan *National Infrastructure Protection Plan*. (accessed 11 August 2016).

Walker B, Ludwig D, Holling CS, Peterman RM (1981) Stability of Semi-Arid Savanna Grazing Systems. *Journal of Ecology* 69(2): 473–498.

Walker B, Carpenter S, Anderies J, Abel N, Cumming G, Janssen MA, Lebel L, Norberg J, Peterson GD, Pritchard R (2002) Resilience Management in Social-Ecological Systems: A Working Hypothesis for a Participatory Approach. *Conservation Ecology* 6(1): Article 14.

Walker B, Holling CS, Carpenter SR, Kinzig A (2004) Resilience, Adaptability and Transformability in Social-ecological Systems. *Ecology and Society* 9(2): Article 5.

Walker J, Cooper M (2011) Genealogies of Resilience: From Systems Ecology to the Political Economy of Crisis Adaptation. *Security Dialogue* 42(2): 143–160.

Werner E, Smith R (1992) *Vulnerable but Invincible: A Study of Resilient Children.* New York: McGraw-Hill.

Woods DD (2006) Essential Characteristics of Resilience. In: Hollnagel E, Woods DD, Leveson N (eds) *Resilience Engineering. Concepts and Precepts.* Burlington, VT: Ashgate Publishing Company. 21–34.

Zebrowski C (2009) Governing the Network Society: A Biopolitical Critique of Resilience. *Political Perspectives* 3(1): 1–38.

Zebrowski C (2013) The Nature of Resilience. *Resilience: International Policies, Practices and Discourses* 1(3): 159–173.

3 Thinking for and from relationality

The study of resilience in *interconnected societies* may appear pleonastic at first, because relationships and interconnections constitute the very essence of *societas*, which derives from the Latin word for associated. While this book does not discuss the meaning of society as such, it does examine different facets of interconnectedness or relationality and the many ways in which resilience relates to them. The first facet of interconnectedness is a theoretical one. The analysis of resilience follows an understanding of the world as radically relational (cf. Dillon 2000) – an ontology that is embraced and expressed in the different theories and approaches of poststructuralism. Foucault's concepts of governmentality (Foucault 2004c [1978]) and subjectification (ibid.), Butler's theory of performativity (Butler 1993) and Deleuze's notion of the dividual (1992a), for example, recur throughout this book and share an understanding of language, bodies, spaces and human existence as marked by relations. As opposed to *mere* relationality, which describes the interplay of relations in general, *radical* relationality describes an ontological commitment. It represents the idea "that nothing is without being in relation, and that everything is – in the ways that it is – in terms and in virtue of relationality" (Dillon 2000: 4). Resilience is thus theorized and explored from a perspective of radical relationality. This theoretical angle overlaps, but also fundamentally differs from complexity theories. As we have seen in Chapters 1 and 2, the concept of resilience itself is embedded in discourses of complexity and draws on approaches that theorize the idea of interconnectedness from a systemic angle. A discussion of the way in which resilience speaks to complexity discourses, and what that entails for our understanding of security governance is here a second angle of interconnectedness. Finally, this book addresses a third, specific facet of interconnectedness: it is dedicated to the empirical study of resilience in societies that have incorporated the Internet into their daily activities. These are societies in which the issue of being and staying interconnected has become a central subject of security governance. These three facets of interconnectedness – theories of radical relationality, the study of resilience as embedded in complexity thinking, and the investigation of resilience in societies that have incorporated the Internet into their interactions – demarcate the vertices of this book.

The overarching aim of this book is thus to provide a critical conceptual and empirical analysis of resilience as a way of governing in interconnected societies.

Thinking for and from relationality 45

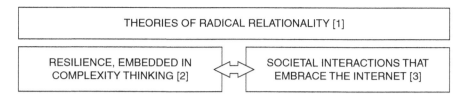

Figure 3.1 3 × interconnectedness: the three vertices of this book.

Part of this project is to explore to what extent resilience is indebted to an understanding of the world as interconnected and how that changes not only security practices, but also the overarching understanding of security and insecurity. Within that framework, the book shows how the growing presence of the Internet in societal interactions yields and influences resilience as a way of governing.

Thinking for and from relationality is, however, a process that first and foremost needs to be disentangled. Both poststructuralist theories, i.e., the analytical tools used to unlock and critically explore the concept of resilience, and complexity theories, i.e., the theoretical home of resilience, exhibit some striking similarities. The fact that the condition of interconnectedness applies to both the theories that have been used for the critical study of resilience and resilience itself (cf. Zebrowski 2009; Walker and Cooper 2011; Rosenow 2012; Joseph 2013; Aradau 2014; Chandler 2014a,b; Grove 2014; Schmidt 2014) has not yet gained enough traction in the academic discourse. This book will spend some time investigating the similarities and differences of complexity and poststructuralist theories. It does so in order to debunk the analytical fallacy that resilience eventually incorporates or consumes poststructuralist thinking (Chandler 2014a), mentioned in the section "Resilience as critique?" above. The following theoretical comparison of complexity studies and poststructuralism thus not only engage with an analytical challenge, but also set the stage for the theoretical argument of the book. It lays the foundation for a contribution to the critique of resilience, which builds upon a distinction of adaptation and transformation as two different forms of life, both of which speak to their respective theoretical genealogies.

Complexity theories meet poststructuralism

Complexity and uncertainty influence the choices taken across a wide range of security policies. A direct result of the rising acceptance of the complexity narrative is the integration of resilience into security strategies, as shown in Chapters 1 and 2. The same policies and strategies, however, have also become subject to critical investigation. A noteworthy aspect here is that some of these investigations equally use relationality as an implicit or explicit starting point for formulating their critique of resilience and complexity thinking. Relationality and interconnectedness, then, not only become the objects of critical study, for example, in asking how resilience is embedded in uncertainty thinking (cf. Aradau 2014) and neoliberalism (cf. Chandler and Reid 2016), but they are at the same time the theoretical vantage point for critical analyses. Taking a closer look at these two overlapping discourses, the shared commitment of complexity thinking and poststructuralist theories to the ontology of relationality seems perplexing. How can one critically study a phenomenon that shares its theoretical premise with the theories and methods used for its investigation? Chandler even goes one step further in suggesting that self-reference and reflexivity, championed by both traditions, would eventually obliterate a distinction between resilience and critique (2014a,b). This is why a brief juxtaposition of both research traditions is essential. A brief introduction into the main concepts and characteristics of each research tradition is followed by a discussion of their similarities and differences in order to make comprehensible how they arrive at different conceptualizations of life itself.

As a research tradition that subscribes to radical relationality poststructuralism collects a variety of theories and approaches under its label. What follows is a short introduction and by no means an attempt to discuss the accuracy of this label, or to equalize what are in fact quite distinct theoretical contributions with a difference "in their understanding of the project of thought itself" (Dillon 2000: 3). Dillon has exposed a range of commonalities within poststructuralist theories, the most significant of which are the "radical relationality of bodies" and the "emergent property of bodies" that again depend upon the different modes of relationality (2000: 2). Both relationality and emergence need to be understood vis-à-vis the "temporality of being and finitude of human existence" (ibid.; cf. Deleuze 1988; Foucault 1989; Agamben 1991; Heidegger 1962). To deepen this notion of radical relationality, which is central to this chapter's project, it is furthermore important to reference Derrida's notions of deconstruction and différance (1978a,b). Derrida develops his understanding of deconstruction through an extrapolation and radicalization of Lévi-Strauss' "valeur symbolique zero" (Derrida 1970: 10, quoting Lévi-Strauss). That is the floating signifier that sits at the center of any system, through which all societal structure can be constituted and upon which any societal meaning and symbolic content is dependent. This missing center of any structure, which can take on any required value and receive "different forms and names" (Derrida 1970: 2), necessarily leads to variation, multiplication and freeplay. It is a "non-locus in which an infinite number of sign-substitutions [come] into play" (Derrida 1970: 2). The result is that there is no guarantee for stability. Any system, also the societal system, is inherently instable. There is no closure, no total system, but only ever continuous relationships of exchange, which necessitate repetition to establish a sense of stability that can never be achieved (cf. Stäheli 2000a). Since no repetition can ever be identical, iterations and self-contaminations occur, re-opening the system and changing the structure over time. Any structure constantly re-invents itself: "the appearance of a new structure, of an original system, always comes about – and this is the very condition of its structural specificity – by a rupture with its past, its origin, and its cause" (Derrida 1970: 11). As a result, signs, structures and systems are emergent and radically relational, "the effect of deferred and differentiated meaning. Text then is differance, spacing, relationality, differentiation, deferral, delay" (Deutscher 2005: 34). The theme of relationality is also present in Butler's performativity theory that addresses the contingency of enunciation and the way in which identities are performed through acts of speech (1990, 1993). As already indicated, relationality is also reflected in many aspects of Foucault's work, most prominently in the way that relations, circulations and reflexivity are captured in the logic of the market and liberalism that inform the practices of governing in contemporary societies (cf. Foucault 1980a, 2004c, 2008 [1979]; Dean 2010; Bröckling *et al*. 2011).

Complexity sciences can equally not be summarized under one label without emphasizing the richness and differences that distinguish each project and approach. After all, complexity thinking has flourished in various fields, such as engineering and cybernetics (Wiener 1948; von Foerster 1974), biology (Maturana and Varela 1980 [1973]), chemistry and physics (Prigogine 1980), sociology (Luhmann 1984) and computation (Barabási 2003). It should be said here that complexity and network theories also relate to each other, most importantly through Wiener's theory of the feedback loop (1948) that translates into multiple feedback loops, which eventually form networks. This body of thought had, for example, been adopted into the complexity theories of biology (Maturana and Varela 1980 [1973]) and sociology (Luhmann 1984). The distinction of complexity from network theories is, however, a larger project since network theories can relate to Granovetter's (1973) and Barabási's (2003) focus on the science of networks or to Castell's Global Network Theory (1996). Network theories can furthermore include Cilliers' (2005) and Latour's (2005) different foci on the epistemology and ontology of objects that exist in and through networks, as well as Galloway and Thacker's (2007) argument about protocols as a modern, distributive way of governing, both of which are interestingly more often associated with poststructuralist approaches than complexity thinking. It is thus highly dependent on each network theory and the aspects they foreground to understand how they relate to and distinguish themselves from complexity theories. Nonetheless, it can be said here that a large part of network theories overlap with or relate to complexity thinking, which is why the remainder of this section now returns to the interests and assumptions that the different complexity theories have in common. The baseline of complexity thinking shared by each of the respective theories is that information exchange is understood as a mode of relating (von Foerster 1974), which again promotes self-reflexivity, autopoiesis and emergence (Maturana and Varela 1980 [1973]; Luhmann 1984), as well as adaptation and self-organization (Maturana 1987). Complexity theories accept that life is far from an equilibrium; it is constantly emergent and dynamic (Urry 2005). As such, complexity thinking inverts Newtonian Science with its arboreal logics of taxonomy, where pre-formed bodies can be assigned to categories and life is an instance of predictable, stable relationships. Following complex systems theory, life is contingent and relational. The role of time is no longer that of a parameter, but it is understood to be an operator that generates bodies in-formation, disorder, contingent assemblages and creativity in evolution (Dillon 2000). The logic of entities is substituted by mutable functions and modes of being related. Individuation, here, "is the process of change to which the component is subject in virtue of its very participation in a mode of relating" (Dillon 2000: 11).

Much more can be said about the respective research traditions of poststructuralism and complexity theories. However, in order to expose their relevance for an assessment of resilience the premises and theoretical vantage points of both traditions are best analyzed in detail in direct comparison. Poststructuralism and complexity theories have much in common. They share relationality as a mode of thought and as something they argue for and from (Dillon 2000: 4). Both traditions stress the dynamic, mobile and contingent nature of being. Dillon calls it "life-in-formation" (Dillon 2000: 12; cf. Dillon and Reid 2009) that with its unlimited play of forms creates diversity, polymorphality and polyphenomenality. This diversity is brought about by moments of invasion, colonization or contamination (cf. Deleuze 1988; Derrida 1970). As such, they do not subscribe to an epochal totality or a given rationality, but to a multiplication of knowledge. Poststructuralism and complexity theories favor assemblage (cf. Deleuze and Guattari 1980) over distinction, because having to relate is "invariant to all forms of life" (Dillon 2000: 13). This common appreciation of relationality leads to an analytic framework of instability, hybridity, ambiguity; it leads to one that investigates states of multiplicity and in-between-ness. There is no stable center or equilibrium, but only ever a constant interaction of disruption and re-opening of closure, endless differentiation and making of meaning. Boundaries, power and subjects are constantly negotiated. This is why both traditions emphasize emergence and coming into being rather than being as a total concept. In fact, they question the authority of being and of the present altogether. Poststructuralism and complexity theories embrace contingency and foreground the role of self-reflexivity to the extent that the notions of iteration (Stäheli 2000a on Derrida) and adaptation (cf. Maturana and Varela 1980 [1973]) could look quite similar if understood as mechanisms of dealing with contamination in their respective traditions. In the context of resilience this means that the response to emergencies or to a contamination will be met by what complexity theories would call adaptation and poststructuralism i.e., iteration or transformation. Both adaptation and iteration would then define the resulting form of life.

We shall see, however, that the notions of iteration and adaptation are not the same. While both traditions understand life as irreducible to the singular, straightforward or one-dimensional (Dillon 2000: 21), poststructuralism and complexity theories differ with regards to that which effectuates change and that which ultimately characterizes life in its entirety. And this difference is decisive when we assess what form of life resilience champions. Dillon argues convincingly that the main difference between complexity and poststructuralist theories lies in each tradition's ethos, which is intimately tied to their respective genealogies (ibid.). Ethos is "a mode of living, a way of life" (Deleuze 1988: 122), which is derived from the (varying) location of human existence in "an inescapable matrix of relationality that is both [...] temporal as well as spatial" (Dillon 2000: 2). It describes the guiding beliefs that characterize complexity thinking and poststructuralism as different schools of thought. The word ethos itself is etymologically close to rhetoric. It is a mode of persuasion that "like postmodern subjectivity, shifts and changes over time, across texts, and around competing spaces" (Reynolds 1993: 336). More concretely, it describes "[w]hat form of life is exemplified and championed" (Dillon 2000: 1). Ethos is not a matter of what we can know, but "a question of how we live, of how we may live and [...] how we may continue to live" (Dillon 2000: 1). What Dillon refers to as ethos then overlaps with and differs from Foucault's notion of ethos for whom it is also an attitude or a mode of relating (Foucault 1997; cf. Bernstein 1994: 215). This attitude, however, mainly concerns the relation of the subject to itself, the formation of subjectivity, which makes ethics the self-forming activities that transform oneself into an ethical being (Foucault 1988a, 1997). While Dillon does not address or foreground the self or the subject as such, his notion of ethos does speak to Foucault's telos, the ideal *state of being* toward which one strives (Foucault 1988a). The key question is then which different forms of life or being complexity thinking and poststructuralism seek to engender?

The ethos of complexity thinking may question the logic of arboreal taxonomies. However, at its core, Dillon argues that complexity theories remain "indebted to the modern project of science" (2000: 7) as they seek implicit orderliness. They stay preoccupied with that which can be signified, for example by engaging with relationality through mathematics of non-linearity (cf. Prigogine 1980): "[i]t has to be understood that what is not deterministic need not be random. The solution is the existence of a new type of causality" (Kempis 1991: 257). Within complexity thinking, processes of formation and change are still subject to causality. Interventions and disruptions occur, but they are steered and orchestrated through a strategy that aligns human life with the laws of becoming. This means that the ambition of complexity theories is to plan "how matters can be construed so that certain kinds of happenings are encouraged or discouraged" (Dillon 2000: 9) and to organize how bodies "come in and out of formation" (ibid.: 14). Whatever brings change has to be productive. To illustrate this point we need only to recall the latest resilience discourses. Resilience as a strategy to "bounce back better" (UNISDR 2010) embodies just that: an acknowledgment of relationality and disruption that is part of the modern, complex world we live in – paired with the idea that some strategic elements to organize emergencies remain. This association of the relational with the orchestrated constitutes the ethos of complexity theories, which advocates continuous survival, flexibility and "fitness for complexity" (Dillon 2000: 22). Adaptation is then also formation and organization in a closed system; learning is the orchestration of knowledge and autopoiesis here is not only self-reference, but also the maintenance of an *organized* structure (as Maturana and Varela 1980 [1973] argue with regards to cells). The overarching Darwinian logic of survival and adaptation that resilience embodies is one that incorporates disruption into a strategy that is driven by the attempt to closure, namely the perfection of the internal logics and workings of complex systems. Life, then, is based on alignment with given circumstances rather than transformation. With resilience, living in a complex world becomes a form of flexible, conformist survival.

The poststructuralist ethos, however, sees disruption as a call to consider the radically different. Its ethos always thinks relationality in connection with the radically non-relational, with that which resists relationality and which cannot be drawn into the logic of relation (Dillon 2000: 4f.). Non-relationality is expressed in the Other (Levinas 1998), alterity – a change of perspecitve, différance – the questioning of the authority of presence, the non-signifiable (Derrida 1970, 1993), that which escapes power (Foucault 1980b), the paradox or death (Heidegger 1962). Non-relationality is the disruptive moment, which

> continuously prevents the full realization or final closure of relationality, and thus the misfire that continuously precipitates new life and new meaning [...]. This persistence of the radically non-relational in the relational will always confound any notion of final order.
>
> (Dillon 2000: 5)

That which is intractable, so Dillon argues, continues to move us and exercises freedom from power-knowledge, as opposed to complexity's strategic use of freedom (ibid.). As such, poststructuralism accepts the presence of uncertainty, but it does not follow the rationality of perpetual survival. Poststructuralism understands life as finite. This disruptive moment of non-relationality allows for new life and meaning to emerge, not as a form of survival, of modulated, adapted old life, but as a new form of life and meaning. Poststructuralism thus subscribes to life as trans-formation. It is a form of life that can be fundamentally overhauled (as are the conditions of security and insecurity). Transformation implies the possibility of the political, because it allows for a break with the past, the cause of insecurity or disruption and as such favors the emergence of a something new. Being and life is qualified by constant repetition but, most importantly, iterations where the non-relational becomes the vantage point for political transformation and new meaning. This applies to both conditions for life and the subject itself. Allowing for transformation is, as discussed above and returned to below, largely absent from the ethos of resilience and complexity thinking. While complexity theories are inseparable from their natural scientific anchorage and their empirical pretense to document and scientifically substantiate complexity and interconnectedness, poststructuralism pays attention to those sensualities, discourses and narratives that establish something as complex and interconnected, but it also provides for the tools to fundamentally question the relational through the radically non-relational.

The differences in ethos, then, also leads to different forms of critique. The resilience discourse can, once again, illustrate this difference. Complexity theories consider the new that emerges from resilience processes as something that is based in relationality. Self-organization is here the main tool or strategy to bounce back better. Self-organization expresses the orchestrated aspect of complexity theories that champion life as productive adaptation. Complexity thinking indeed provides a powerful critique of the dominant paradigm of Newtonian and other positivist assumptions about the world: it renounces taxonomy and the arboreal structuring of life and understands life as multiple and emergent. The life that it envisions, however, is one that only ever continues in its adapted form. Life cannot be fundamentally re-thought and transformed. Poststructuralist theories, however, can question the relationality that adapted life is based upon; it can do so through the non-relational. Considering that which is radically different from relationality allows for transformation. By invoking the non-relational, the constant interplay of emergence and adaptation does not need to be taken as given, but it can be questioned. Complexity theories do not provide for such thinking tools to question the ethos of adaptation. Adaptation cannot be challenged as a mechanism of governance from within complexity thinking, because the moment of disruption is subsumed into the logic of the relational. This is why resilience cannot be understood as critique (cf. Chandler 2014a). Dewey's pragmatism (cf. Schmidt 2014), which would recast resilience through *learning as a way of life*, is then merely a positive take on the limit of complexity thinking, but pragmatism – like complexity thinking – can equally not question or transform the conditions for life itself. This goes to show that despite its commitment to the relational, fluid and emergent, the logic of complexity thinking and resilience is totalizing. The poststructuralist ethos is here fundamentally different as it does not subscribe to this form of closure (cf. Stäheli 2000b: 309ff.). Thus, poststructuralism offers a different critique than complexity thinking can. It seeks to uncover the hidden mechanisms and the strategic use of power and orchestration by questioning the authority of presence and by invoking that which is radically different from the relational.

This difference in the form of life that each research tradition values also brings us back to the initial question: it explains why one can study a phenomenon critically that shares its theoretical premise of relationality with the theories and methods used for its investigation. The difference in *ethos* allows us to study complexity narratives and resilience from a perspective of radical relationality as expressed in poststructuralism. While complexity thinking and resilience answer emergencies with strategic interventions, orchestration and productive adaptation, poststructuralist approaches seek to deconstruct and destabilize these modes of governing by asking, for example, what it means that adaptation and resilience are a new form of security politics and which kind of life they instantiate.

Now that the main differences between complexity thinking and poststructuralism are clarified, this section will move the theoretical engagement from the abstract level to the more concrete. At this point, it is useful to take a closer look at some of the methodological tools, themes and concepts used throughout this book, since all of them closely interlink with the subject matter.

Investigating relationality

Due to their engagement with interconnectedness and interrelations all chapters share a certain theoretical commitment to assemblage theory (Deleuze and Guattari 1980). The chapters reflect, however, only the premises of assemblage theory. None of them deploy assemblage as a key concept. For that reason, assemblage theory is not presented as a methodological tool in this section, but only with regards to its stance on relationality. In a similar vein, theories of relational space (cf. Massey 1994, 2011), performativity (Butler 1993) and affect (Massumi 1995; Negri 1999; Seyfert 2012) are central for the development of specific arguments within this book and will be presented in the respective chapters rather than at this point. The aim of this section is to integrate these various tools, themes and concepts into reflections about the recurring and overarching methodological assumptions of this book. Moreover, this section aims to draw out how each of them incorporates relational accounts of the world. After introducing those, two analytical lenses are expanded on in particular: governmentality and subjectification, as used in Foucault's work (cf. 1980a, 1988b, 2003a, 2004a,b,c, 2008) and in that of many of his scholars. They recur throughout the different chapters as a way to theorize and study instances of resilience. They address the various aspects of governing in interconnected societies in a way that distinguishes itself from complexity thinking, since they provide for a critical stance toward resilience's strategic use of relationality.

Each of the theories and analytical lenses mentioned above, whether that is relational space or governmentality, share a view of the world that opposes essentialism, realism and assumptions about stability. Cilliers calls these "modest positions" (2005: 256), since they highlight the limitations to our understanding of the world. These positions recognize that neither the political, nor bodies themselves are a given; they are not pre-formed or exist independent of observers (Dillon and Reid 2009; Bröckling et al. 2011). Instead, these theories focus on how things come into being, how the political is produced, and how technologies of government create particular subjects. Phenomena and meaning are understood to be what they are because they are situated in a network of relations. Butler's performativity theory, for example, stresses that meaning does not merely exist, but it is contingent and can only ever become present in relation to other elements and discourses (Butler 1990, 1993). Discourses are thus very powerful, because they can bring meaning to life. In a similar vein, theories of relational space express this sense of being interconnected:

> Instead, then, of thinking of places with boundaries around, they can be imagined as articulated moments in networks of social relations and understandings, but where a larger proportion of these relations, experiences and understandings are constructed on a far larger scale than what we happen to define for that moment as the place itself.
>
> (Massey 1994: 154)

One of the first times Foucault reflected about the relevance of relationality was in his early work on political anatomy:

> As a matter of fact, this technique of indications does not necessarily work from the visible periphery to the grey forms of organic interiority: it can establish necessary networks connecting any point in the body with any other.
> (Foucault 2004a [1966]: 294)

Later, when he developed his notions of dispositif and apparatus he expanded this relational logic to virtually anything. A critical methodology of relationality would thus not explore isolated

> discourses, institutions, architectural forms, regulatory decisions, laws, administrative measures, scientific statements, philosophical, moral, and philanthropic propositions – in short, the said as much as the unsaid.
> (Foucault 1980a: 194)

What matters is the "the network [le réseau] that can be established between these elements" (Foucault 1977: 298; Agamben 2009: 7). Thus, relationality rises as a mode of studying phenomena, mainly because "the dissection of a system into its components, either physically or theoretically, destroys that system and precludes a full understanding of its dynamics and properties" (Capra 1996: 29; cf. Bousquet and Curtis 2011). As such, relationality always implies a key research statement, namely not to avoid, but to face heterogeneity.

While Foucault's notion of dispositive (or Agamben's interpretation of it as apparatus, cf. Agamben 2009) does fulfill strategic functions – a *positive* in the sense of its instrumental role within the practice of governing, Deleuze's notion of assemblage emphasizes multilinearity:

> Each has lines of different natures, which break and change direction: Untangling these lines within a social apparatus is, in each case, like drawing up a map, doing cartography, surveying, unknown landscapes, and this is what [Foucault] calls "working on the ground."
> (1992b: 159)

He concludes that

> [r]ather than ordering and capturing with omniscient foresight, apparatuses get muddled and mix things up, producing subjectivities which escape and need to be reinserted into a different "multiplicity," forcing a constant reconsideration of the "new."
> (Ibid.: 162–163)

As a response to apparatus he introduces the term assemblage, allowing for continuous deconstruction and re-assemblage. Tampio summarizes that a "political assemblage [...] has some coherence in what it says and what it does, but it continually dissolves and morphs into something new" (Tampio 2009: 394). Assemblages graft new elements and forge new ones, they employ existing discourses to new ends and transpose the meaning of key terms (Murray Li 2007).

A perspective of relationality will thus necessarily lead to a focus on multiplicity. Most importantly, relational accounts of the world embrace hybridity, ambiguity and states of in-between, which are bypassed by essentialist positions. In contradistinction to essentialist accounts of being, relational theories foreground processes of coming into being. Performativity theory reflects this position as it states that concepts are always in the making. Deleuze's assemblages affix "sociotechnical networks, hybrid collectivities and alternative topologies" in a constant "process of becoming" (Farías and Bender 2010: 2). The assemblage forwards the idea of the open-ended, fluid system, the properties of which emerge through the interaction of its elements (Bousquet and Curtis 2011: 58). This understanding becomes particularly relevant in the study of resilience, which is itself considered as processual and emergent. The notion of affect also reflects this idea of processuality. Affect does, in the broadest sense, commit to relationality, since it emerges at the encounter as an inter-corporeal and social instant (Seyfert 2012). For that reason, it is strictly situational, processual, transitional, and heterogeneous. Most importantly, since it is transformative at its core, affect is also constitutive of the subject (ibid.).

In order to study multiplicity, hybridity and ambiguity, but also instability and breakdown this book takes radical relationality – the ontological claim that everything exists in and through relations – as a vantage point. Theories of radical relationality embrace that which is in-between, emergent and processual as they understand phenomena through a logic of becoming. Analytical conclusions that can be drawn from the commitment to relationality are that phenomena can only be understood through the heterogeneous networks they are situated in. This includes an investigation of those elements that contribute to the stabilization of the phenomenon (as reflected in apparatus, or performativity), but also to its multiple forms (as reflected in assemblage and différance), or to its breakdown and transformation (as investigated through the radically non-relational), which, as discussed above, is what allows us to distinguish between the notions of resilient adaptation and transformation.

Most importantly, does this framework acknowledge that any such analyses also contribute to the making and un-making of the studied phenomenon? Knowledge about a phenomenon is not only situated, but it is tied to power, because the formulation and the repeated enunciation of knowledge has the power to bring phenomena into being (cf. Butler 1990; Foucault 1980a). This also means that writing critically about resilience leads to the stabilization of the resilience discourse – a fact that prompts Neocleous to refrain from writing about resilience altogether (2013). Instead of joining him, this book chooses a stance of reflexivity. For those who produce and enunciate knowledge, this circularity between cause and effect must serve as a reflexive and self-critical mechanism. Reflexivity is a means to acknowledge partiality and to create transparency about

Thinking for and from relationality 55

the research process and the conditions it is tied to wherever possible, which also gives a reason for why an explication of the themes, tools and concepts used throughout this book is so important.

As discussed in the previous section, resilience and complexity theories share the commitment to relationality and many of the associated analytical concepts up to and including reflexivity. However, since one of their main differences is that complexity theories (and resilience) are orientated toward orchestration and strategy (Dillon 2000; Dillon and Reid 2009), the following paragraphs will expand on governmentality as a methodological concept that captures how relationality, circulation and freedom are enframed into a strategy of governing. Governmentality is at the same time utilized as a way of problematizing the effects of complexity thinking in general and resilience as a form of governing interconnected societies in particular. For Foucault,

> [p]roblematization doesn't mean the representation of a pre-existing object, nor the creation by discourse of an object that doesn't exist. It is the totality of discursive and non-discursive practices that introduces something into the play of true and false and constitutes it as an object for thought (whether under the form of moral reflection, scientific knowledge, or political analysis, etc.).
>
> (1988b: 257)

The problematization of resilience through the analytical lens of governmentality thus begins with the basic, but important insight that "rationalities and technologies of government, modes of thinking and forms of intervention, are inextricably interconnected and co-produce one another" (Bröckling *et al.* 2011: 11; cf. Miller and Rose 2008). They condition each other through claims of plausibility, legitimacy and acceptability. Within the context of this book, this means that resilience as a way of governing is embedded in the scientific inventory of complexity thinking that has gained considerable authority within many societal discourses. We have seen that complexity thinking, in turn, embodies the basic elements of liberalism, such as circulation, freedom and emergence, at the same time as it embraces uncertainty and contingency. They condition each other. Foucault conceptualized how these processes and premises, which are traditionally thought to be external to political authority (Dean 2010), have increasingly been incorporated into practices of governing. Foucault describes the relation between liberalism and practices of governing as follows:

> These individuals who are still subjects of rights as well as being economic actors, but who are not "governmentable" as one or the other, are only governable insofar as a new ensemble can be defined which will envelop them both as subjects of rights and as economic actors, but which will bring to light not just the connection or the combination of these two elements, but a series of other elements in relation to which the subject of right and the economic subject will be aspects, partial aspects, which can be integrated

insofar as they belong to a complex whole. And I think it is this new ensemble that is characteristic of the liberal art of governing.

(Foucault 2008 [1979]: 295)

The liberal art of governing is thus to guide individuals through their freedom and prompt them to govern themselves, for example through incentives. This "way in which one conducts people's conduct" (Foucault 2004c: 192) is what Foucault calls governmentality. In order to understand itself as a free subject, "the subject must first be shaped, guided and moulded into one capable of responsibly exercising that freedom through systems of domination" (Dean 2010: 193). For that reason governmentality is also an "analytical perspective for relations of power" (Foucault 2004c: 192), that makes it possible "to study how techniques of rule are tied to "technologies of the self" [...] and how forms of political governance have recourse to 'processes by which the individual acts upon himself'" (Bröckling *et al*. 2011: 2; cf. Foucault 1988a; 1993). Resilience is one such technology of the self. Through its legacy of complexity the concept explicitly stresses both the fundaments of liberalism – circulation, freedom, emergence – and the related need to adapt to insecurities in a self-organized fashion. Given the increased acknowledgment of complexity thinking within political discourses it is no surprise that resilience has grown into a pervasive mode of governing throughout the past decade.

Governmentality captures many aspects of resilience. One of them is the increased responsibilization of the individual, as is also expressed in the conceptual focus on self-organization. In general, governmentality operates through diverse practices of liberty, most of which are "concerned with structuring, shaping, predicting and making calculable the operation of our freedom" (Dean 2010: 194). Cost–benefit analysis, for example, is a tool that engages citizens in the calculation of danger – and "[t]here is no liberalism without a culture of danger" (Foucault 2008: 67). Later analyses of governmentality also discuss governmental techniques of optimizing performance (Miller 1992; Dean 2010). Calculation and entrepreneurship is, however, not only a basic pillar of risk technologies, but the ideas of new prudentialism also sit at the heart of the resilience concept, as the active citizen is now capable of managing its own disruptions. The responsible subject optimizes its ultimate independence from the state, because it not only enacts the prevention of dangers through risk, but also the response to disorder through resilience. How the rationalities of calculation and algorithmic forms of governing influence resilience is, for example, a theme explored in the chapter on the digitization of resilience.

The ideal of the self-managing community is, for example, also embraced by recent resilience models for the development and aid sector (cf. Duffield 2012). They equally include rather inconspicuous techniques of self-esteem, empowerment and consultation (Cruikshank 1993, 1994) to create responsible citizens, using "the instruments of voice and representation by which the claims of user groups can enter into the negotiation over needs" (Yeatman 1994: 110; cf. Dean 2010: 196). Even the very notion of community as such can be considered an instance of governmentality:

Community, as much as the autonomous citizen, is a resultant of a detailed work of political construction. It is an attempt to stabilize and normalize particular sets of relations and practices and to establish relatively continuous regimes of authority. It works on the much more open and fluid identifications that characterize contemporary forms of sociality.

(Dean 2010: 199)

One of the major effects of responsibilization, entrepreneurship and self-organization, is that governance moves from direction to coordination and facilitation (cf. Dean 2010). This leaves us with the question as to whether "governing at a distance" (Rose and Miller 1992) enables agency (Dean 2010) or expresses indirect domination; a question that is still central in the resilience discourse and will be discussed below.

This question is linked to another debate that governmentality inspires and that is whether the responsibilization of the citizen results in a disappearance of real (not ordered) solidarity and the welfare state, which would eventually lead to the death of the social. Dean argues here that what is transformed is not the social itself, but its welfarist form that no longer exists in the shape of a centralized state:

[I]t will be reconfigured as a set of constructed markets in service provision and expertise, made operable through heterogeneous technologies of agency, and rendered calculable by technologies of performance that will govern at a distance.

(Dean 2010: 223)

While Foucault traced a trajectory toward the governmentalization of the state, Dean suggests a governmentalization of government, a turning of the government upon itself. This reflexive government has as its aim the securing of governmental mechanisms that provide efficiency. This means that it renders "the social itself, efficient, accountable, transparent and democratic by the employment of technologies of performance" (Dean 2010: 223), as can, for example, be seen in technologies of active citizenship. However, the debate about the social not only moves the critical discourse on resilience, but this debate is also linked to the question as to whether practices of self-organization, one example of it being resilience, leave room for sovereignty and intervention, for example through a "democratization of sovereignty" (ibid.: 130) or "indirect intervention" (Bröckling *et al.* 2011: 5). Foucault himself argues about practices of governing and the exercise of power that

it incites, it induces, it seduces, it makes easier or more difficult; it releases or contrives, makes more probable or less [...] but it is always a way of acting upon one or more acting subjects by virtue of their acting or being capable of action. A set of actions upon other actions.

(Foucault 2003b: 138)

Governmentality then means that governmental actors organize the conditions under which individuals can use freedoms or act freely. As such, inciting the self-organization of citizens is still a form of intervention. It prompts, however, a reformulation of the question about intervention, namely as to whether the notion of freedom is what it promises and whether it can give rise to true agency. This point is crucial to the whole project of this book. While all of these chapters take a critical, deconstructive stance toward resilience, it is important to note that the aim of this book is not to provide a sweeping, annihilating argument of resilience as intervention, but one that aims at a careful distinction of those forms of resilience that are depoliticizing, where resilience becomes the result of a strategy of incited self-organization, from those moments of spontaneous response and agency. These differences are further discussed in the chapters on resilience and affect, resilience and the network, as well as in the final chapter that theorizes resilience.

In sum, governmentality is a form of power that is typical for liberal societies. It has

> pre-eminence over all other types of power – sovereignty, discipline, and so on – of the type of power we can call "government" and which has led to the development of a series of specific governmental apparatuses (appareils) on the one hand, [and on the other] to the development of a series of knowledges (saviors).
>
> (Foucault 2004b: 108)

The government Foucault evokes here concerns any social relation (Bröckling *et al.* 2011) and, as a result, it exercises the practice of intervention by inciting self-constitution.

Because self-constitution plays such a central role in liberal modes of governing, governmentality is also an analytical entry point for processes of subjectification, the making of the subject. In the context of this book, the analytic concept of subjectification addresses how governments unfold their effects, legitimize images of the self and create self-organizing, active resilient subjects. Agamben formulates that "literally anything that has in some way the capacity to capture, orient, determine, intercept, model, control, or secure the gestures, behaviors, opinions, or discourses of living beings" (Agamben 2009: 14) would always entail the study of processes of subjectification. Subjectification refers to the relations between human beings and the instruments, tools, objects and gadgets that are being used to govern (ibid.: 17). Subjectification entails "being addressed in a certain way as a subject, understanding oneself as a subject, and working on oneself in alignment with this self-understanding" (Bröckling *et al.* 2011: 14).

The many ways in which resilience seeks to create self-organized, responsible subjects are discussed in this book with reference to concrete practices in Chapters 5–8. Chapter 5 explores the role of protocol and *self x*, meaning the self-governance of local actors, in the organization of resilience within the Internet interconnection ecosystem. The chapter on resilience and affect, for example, investigates processes of subjectification through the instrument of cyber-emergency exercises, and the chapter on resilience and the digital discusses practices of remote governing and the creation of resilient subjects through the use of digital information. The chapter on resilience and networks studies the use of social media for self-organized crisis management, as an instance of the way in which subjects conduct themselves in alignment with responsibilizing discourses. That being said, subjects are not just the effect of power, but "in articulating themselves as subjects they take part in power relations, thus reproducing and transforming them" (Foucault 2003a: 29–30). Subjectification is thus not a singular process, but individuals always have multiple relations to themselves and are subjectified in manifold ways (Stäheli 2000a). For the study of resilience, this means that the intent to create resilient subjects is not summarized in one form of subjectification, but it includes a multiplicity of subjectification processes, dependent on each context.

As the word indicates, subjectification is constantly in the making, because any individual is situated in a multitude of relations and is characterized by flexible demarcations of inclusion and exclusion (Stäheli 2000a). Each individual is part of different processes of subjectification, because it is situated in different discourses, whether literal, emotional or practical (ibid.). Butler describes a particular hybridity that is inherent to the concept of subjectification, namely that subject positions empower individuals, while subjecting them at the same time (Butler 1997). This logic is also reflected in governmentality (especially as expressed in Dean 2010). Using the lenses of governmentality and subjectification, this book reflects this tension between constitutive and disciplining power. It argues that the majority of resilience discourses aim to legitimize the self-sufficient subject, whereby they perpetuate the focus on the self and – not to forget – a subject that contributes to the idea of being in-formation, an ever-emergent and adaptive subject that can continuously cope with exposure to harm.

Finally, when using governmentality and subjectification as analytical concepts, one also explores the technological aspect of governing. This aspect refers to practices and artifacts of governing that establish a new relationship between the citizen and the state, which include technologies of the self or self-regulation (cf. Foucault 1988c), but also technology in the sense of technical artifacts (cf. Bröckling *et al*. 2011: 12). Such artifacts could be "arrangements of machines, medial networks, recording and visualization systems, [... and] a range of procedural devices through which individuals and collectives shape the behavior of each other or themselves" (ibid.). The role that digital and networked artifacts, in particular, play for resilience as a way of governing, that is for the creation of resilient subjects through governmental practices of calculating, responsibilizing and empowering, are addressed in the following chapter.

References

Agamben G (1991) *Language and Death: The Place of Negativity*. Minneapolis, MN: University of Minnesota Press.

Agamben G (2009) *What is an Apparatus? And Other Essays*. Stanford, CA: Stanford University Press.

Aradau C (2014) The Promise of Security: Resilience, Surprise and Epistemic Politics. *Resilience: International Policies, Practices and Discourses* 2(2): 73–87.

Barabási AL (2003) *Linked: How Everything is Connected to Everything Else and What it Means for Business, Science, and Everyday Life*. New York: Plume.

Bernstein R (1994) Foucault: Critique as a Philosophical Ethos. In: Kelly M (ed.) Critique and Power: *Recasting the Foucault/Habermas Debate*. Cambridge: MIT Press. 211–242.

Bousquet A, Curtis S (2011) Beyond Models and Metaphors: Complexity Theory, Systems Thinking and International Relations. *Cambridge Review of International Affairs* 24(1): 43–62.

Bröckling U, Krasmann S, Lemke T (2011) From Foucault's Lectures at the Collège de France to Studies of Governmentality. An Introduction. In: Bröckling U, Krasmann S, Lemke T (eds) *Governmentality. Current Issues and Future Challenges*. New York/Abingdon, Oxon: Routledge. 1–33.

Butler J (1990) *Gender Trouble: Feminism and the Subversion of Identity*. New York: Routledge.

Butler J (1993) *Bodies that Matter. On the Discursive Limits of Sex*. London and New York: Routledge.

Butler J (1997) *The Psychic Life of Power. Theories of Subjection*. Palo Alto, CA: Stanford University Press.

Capra F (1996) *The Web of Life: A New Synthesis of Mind and Matter*. London: Harper Collins.

Castells M (1996) *The Rise of the Network Society*. Cambridge, MA: Blackwell Publishers.

Chandler D (2014a) *Resilience. The Governance of Complexity*. London and New York: Routledge.

Chandler D (2014b) Beyond Neoliberalism: Resilience and the New Art of Governing Complexity. *Resilience: International Policies, Practices and Discourses* 2(1): 47–63.

Chandler D, Reid J (2016) *The Neoliberal Subject. Resilience, Adaptation and Vulnerability*. London: Rowman & Littlefield.

Cilliers P (2005) Complexity, Deconstruction and Relativism. *Theory Culture & Society* 22(5): 255–267.

Cruikshank B (1993) Revolutions Within: Self-government and Self-esteem. *Economy and Society* 22(3): 327–344.

Cruikshank B (1994) The Will to Empower: Technologies of Citizenship and the War on Poverty. *Socialist Review* 33(4): 29–55.

Dean M (2010) *Governmentality. Power and Rule in Modern Society*. London: Sage.

Deleuze G (1988) *Spinoza: Practical Philosophy*. San Francisco: City Lights.

Deleuze G (1992a) Postscript on the Societies of Control. *October* 59 (Winter 1992): 3–7.

Deleuze G (1992b) What is a Dispositive? In: T.J. Armstrong (ed.) *Foucault: Philosopher*. New York: Harvester Wheatsheaf. 159–168.

Deleuze G, Guattari F (1980/1987) *A Thousand Plateaus. Capitalism and Schizophrenia*. London: Athlone.

Derrida J (1970) *Structure, Sign, and Play in the Discourse of the Human Sciences.* Translated from: "La Structure, le signe et le jeu dans le discours des sciences humaines." Available at: www.csudh.edu/ccauthen/576f13/DrrdaSSP.pdf (accessed 11 August 2016).
Derrida J (1978a [1963]) *Cogito and the History of Madness. From Writing and Difference.* London and New York: Routledge.
Derrida J (1978b [1967]) *Of Grammatology.* Baltimore, MD and London: Johns Hopkins University Press.
Derrida J (1993) *Aporias.* Stanford, CA: Stanford University Press.
Deutscher P (2005) *How to Read Derrida.* London: Granta Books.
Dillon M (2000) Poststructuralism, Complexity and Poetics. *Theory, Culture & Society* 17(5): 1–26.
Dillon M, Reid J (2009) *The Liberal Way of War. Killing to Make Life Live.* London: Routledge.
Duffield M (2012) Challenging Environments: Danger, Resilience and the Aid Industry. *Security Dialogue* 43(5): 475–492.
Farías I, Bender T (2010) *Urban Assemblages: How Actor Network Theory Changes Urban Studies.* London: Routledge.
Foucault M (1977a) *Le Jeu de Michel Foucault. Dits et écrits, Vol. III (2001).* Paris: Quarto Gallimard. 298–329.
Foucault M (1980a) *Power/Knowledge: Selected Interviews and Other Writings. 1972–1977.* Ed. C Gordon. New York: Pantheon.
Foucault M (1980b) *Herculine Barbin: Being the Recently Discovered Memoires of a Nineteenth Century French Hermaphrodite.* New York: Random House.
Foucault M (1988a) *The History of Sexuality. Volume 3: The Care of the Self.* New York: Vintage Books.
Foucault M (1988b) The Concern for Truth. In: Kritzman LD (ed.) *Politics, Philosophy, Culture. Interviews and Other Writings 1977–1984.* New York: Routledge. 255–267.
Foucault M (1988c) Technologies of the Self. A Seminar with Michel Foucault at the University of Vermont, October 1982. In: Martin LH, Gutman H, Hutton PH (eds) *Technologies of the Self: A Seminar with Michel Foucault.* Amherst, MA: University of Massachusetts Press. 16–49.
Foucault M (1989) *The Order of Things.* London: Routledge.
Foucault M (1993) About the Beginning of the Hermeneutics of the Self. *Political Theory* 21(2): 198–227.
Foucault M (1997) *The Essential Works of Michel Foucault, Vol. 1: Ethics: Subjectivity and Truth.* Ed. P Rabinow. New York: New Press.
Foucault M (2003a) *Society Must Be Defended: Lectures at the Collège de France. 1975–76.* New York: Picador.
Foucault M (2003b) The subject and power. In: Rabinow P, Rose N (eds) *The Essential Foucault: Selections from Essential Works of Foucault. 1954–1984.* New York: New Press. 126–144.
Foucault M (2004a [1966]) *The Order of Things.* London and New York: Routledge.
Foucault M (2004b) *Security, Territory, Population. Lectures at the Collège de France 1977–1978.* Ed. Senellart M, Ewald F, Fontana A (general eds), Davidson AI (English ed.). Basingstoke, Hants and New York: Palgrave Macmillan.
Foucault M (2004c) *Naissance de la biopolitique. Cours au Collège de France. 1978–1979.* Ed. M Senellart. Paris: Gallimard-Le Seuil.

Foucault M (2008 [1979]) *The Birth of Biopolitics. Lectures at the Collège de France. 1978–1979*. Ed. Senellart M, Ewald F, Fontana A (general eds), Davidson AI (English ed.). Basingstoke, Hants and New York: Palgrave Macmillan.

Galloway AR, Thacker E (2007) *Exploit: A Theory of Networks*. Minneapolis, MN: University of Minnesota Press.

Granovetter MS (1973) The Strength of Weak Ties. *American Journal of Sociology* 78(6): 1360–1380.

Grove K (2014) Agency, Affect, and the Immunological Politics of Disaster Resilience. *Environment and Planning D. Society and Space* 32(2): 240–256.

Heidegger M (1962) *Being and Time*. Oxford: Blackwell.

Joseph J (2013) Resilience as Embedded in Neoliberalism: A Governmentality Approach. *Resilience: International Policies, Practices and Discourses* 1(1): 38–52.

Kempis GK (1991) *Self-Modifying Systems in Biology and Cognitive Sciences*. Oxford: Pergamon.

Latour B (2005) *Reassembling the Social: an Introduction to Actor-Network-Theory*. Oxford: Clarendon.

Levinas E (1998) *Of God Who Comes to Mind*. Stanford, CA: Stanford University Press.

Luhmann N (1984) *Soziale Systeme: Grundriß einer allgemeinen Theorie*. Frankfurt am Main: Suhrkamp.

Massey D (1994) A Global Sense of Place. In: Massey D (ed.) *Space, Place and Gender*. Minneapolis, MN: University of Minnesota Press. 146–156.

Massey D (2011) A Counterhegemonic Relationality of Place. In: Ward K, McCann E (eds) *Globalization and Community. Mobile Urbanism: Cities and Policymaking in the Global Age*. Minneapolis, MN: University of Minnesota Press. 1–14.

Massumi B (1995) The Autonomy of Affect. *Cultural Critique* 31(2): 83–109.

Maturana H (1987) Everything is Said By an Observer. In: Thompson W (ed.) *Gaia, a Way of Knowing*. Great Barrington, MA: Lindisfarne Press. 65–82.

Maturana H, Varela F (1980 [1973]) Autopoiesis and Cognition: The Realization of the Living. In: Cohen RS, Wartofsky MW (eds) *Boston Studies in the Philosophy of Science 42*. Dordrecht, Netherlands: D. Reidel Publishing Co.

Miller P (1992) Accounting and Objectivity: The Invention of Calculating Selves and Calculable Spaces. *Annals of Scholarship* 9(1/2): 61–86.

Miller P, Rose N (2008) *Governing the Present. Administering Economic, Social and Personal Life*. Cambridge: Polity Press.

Murray Li T (2007) Practices of Assemblage and Community Forest Management. *Economy and Society* 36(2): 263–293.

Negri A (1999) Value and Affect. *Boundary* 2: 26–86.

Neocleous M (2013) Resisting Resilience. *Radical Philosophy* 178 (March/April). Available at: www.radicalphilosophy.com/commentary/resisting-resilience (accessed 11 August 2016).

Prigogine I (1980) *From Being to Becoming*. San Francisco, CA: Freeman.

Reynolds N (1993) Ethos as Location: New Sites for Discursive Authority. *Rhetoric Review* 11(2): 325–338.

Rose N, Miller P (1992) Political Power Beyond the State: Problematics of Government. *British Journal of Sociology* 43(2): 173–205.

Rosenow D (2012) Dancing Life into Being: Genetics, Resilience and the Challenge of Complexity Theory. *Security Dialogue* 43(6): 531–547.

Schmidt J (2014) Intuitively Neoliberal? Towards a Critical Understanding of Resilience Governance. *European Journal of International Relations* 21(2): 402–426.

Seyfert R (2012) Beyond Personal Feelings and Collective Emotions: Toward a Theory of Social Affect. *Theory, Culture & Society* 29(6): 27–46.
Stäheli U (2000a) *Poststrukturalistische Soziologien*. Bielefeld, Germany: Transcript Verlag.
Stäheli U (2000b) *Sinnzusammenbrüche. Eine dekonstruktive Lektüre von Niklas Luhmanns Systemtheorie*. Weilerswist, Germany: Velbrück Wissenschaft.
Tampio N (2009) Assemblages and the Multitude: Deleuze, Hardt, Negri, and the Postmodern Left. *European Journal of Political Theory* 8(3): 383–400.
UNISDR (2010) *Building Back Better for Next Time. Experiences and Lessons Learnt from the Project "Building Resilience to Tsunamis in the Indian Ocean."* Available at: www.unisdr.org/files/14499_buildingbackbetterforthenexttime.pdf (accessed 11 August 2016).
Urry J (2005) The Complexity Turn. *Theory, Culture & Society* 22(1): 1–14.
von Foerster H (1974) *Cybernetics of Cybernetics*. Urbana, IL: University of Illinois.
Walker J, Cooper M (2011) Genealogies of Resilience: From Systems Ecology to the Political Economy of Crisis Adaptation. *Security Dialogue* 42(2): 143–160.
Wiener N (1948) *Cybernetics: Or Control and Communication in the Animal and the Machine*. Paris and Cambridge, MA: MIT Press.
Yeatman A (1994) *Postmodern Revisionings of the Political*. New York: Routledge.
Zebrowski C (2009) Governing the Network Society: A Biopolitical Critique of Resilience. *Political Perspectives* 3(1): 1–38.

4 From program to programming

Foucault's governmentality is not a critique on the kind of power that the state does or should exercise. In fact, it does not take the state as a given origin or a "terminal point of power" (Rose *et al.* 2006: 86). Rather, it is a critical analysis of the way in which power operates. As an analytic lens, its intention is to identify governmental strategies and programs. Like any governmental program, resilience is subject to specific rationalizations and problematizations, and it is directed to certain ends (ibid.) that governmentality analyses seek to identify. One dominant rationale within the resilience program is, for example, that it speaks to an epistemology of uncertainty. This means that shape, form and time of insecurity are unknown and in some cases considered unknowable. As a result, emergencies are problematized as an essential part of societal life. Some of the program's aims are thus to instill self-organization and adaptation in order to govern populations vis-à-vis such fundamental insecurities. Resilience can then be considered as a new way of making emergencies administrable, of making them "thinkable" and "practicable" (cf. ibid.). It can be argued that resilience shares many of its rationales, problematizations and aims with a range of other governmental programs and techniques that are close to neoliberalism (Chandler and Reid 2016). This doesn't mean, however, that resilience can be placed exclusively in a neoliberal discourse. The analytic pretense of governmentality is rather to draw out the specificity of each governmental program. But what exactly makes a program and what does its analysis involve?

Identifying a governmental program is to analyze:

> different styles of thought, their condition of formation, the principles and knowledges they borrow from and generate, the practices that they consist of, how they are carried out, their contestations and alliances with other arts of governing.
>
> (Rose *et al.* 2006: 84)

Governmental programs are strictly situational, which means that they are closely tied to the idea of who is to be governed. Government is here not only what the program seeks to make of the subject to be governed, but also what it implies for how life in general is to be led (ibid.: 95). For example, the prominence of

From program to programming 65

adaptation as a specific form of leading one's life is typical for the resilience program. The governmental discourse of *bouncing back better* presents adaptation as a form of life that is best suited to meet the insecurities of complex societies and that utilizes the constant work of reestablishing security as opportunity to evolve. The analysis of programs means, furthermore, that the technologies which are used to govern have their own characteristics and requirements (ibid.: 86); for example, a specific way of involving the citizen into emergency management tasks. A major aspect of governmentality as an analytic lens is, in fact, to emphasize the role of the population in the process of governing. The population is considered a reality of its own. This focus couldn't be more relevant in the analysis of resilience. The emphasis on the population's role is particularly strong because self-organization during disasters and crises becomes an outspoken aim of the governmental program of resilience.

Studying the body, role and actions of populations, however, is currently undergoing important changes that need to be reflected upon. The attention that this book pays to the role of digital interconnections, as well as to the use of digital data and social media within emergency management strategies, adds a new dimension to the role of the population. Chapters 6, 7 and 8 describe how the population becomes a provider and analyst of data: how its actions are being translated into digital information, which then becomes part of evaluations and governmental programming efforts. In a different way, Chapter 5 explores how many digitized societal connections tied via the Internet are subject to both resilience programs and programming efforts in order to accommodate for what is understood as network-internal insecurity.

In the analysis of governmental programs, Rose *et al.* point to the importance of the language of programs, which is not merely a "gloss on the practices of rule" (Rose *et al.* 2006: 88), but an intellectual technology. It is "a mechanism for rendering reality amenable to certain kinds of action" (ibid.: 89; Miller and Rose 1990: 7). This book takes this focus on language seriously by examining how the language of the resilience program is turned into a language of programming, and meaning into concrete digital practices. It explores how the inclusion of digital technologies in the resilience program enables a new set of practices. The book discusses both the art and the program of governing that such technologies are expressive of. In order to analyze this move from programs to programming from a perspective of governmentality, it is important to better understand the notion of *technologies*, which refers to both modes of governing as well as the materiality and workings of machines.

Technologies of the self and technologies off-the-shelf

Foucault's notion of technologies has been described as the collection of

> complex practical processes, instruments, programs, calculations, measures, and apparatuses making it possible to form and to control forms of action,

structures of preference, and premises for decisions by societal agents in view of certain goals.

(Bröckling *et al*. 2011: 12)

Such a description includes, for example, cultural technologies of habits, morals and ethics that are applied to govern subjects (Rose *et al*. 2006). Most importantly, however, technologies always relate to a combination of artifacts and actions that together constitute the process of governing. That makes technology

not simply an ethically neutral set of artifacts by which we exercise power over nature, but also always a set of structured forms of action by which we also inevitably exercise power over ourselves.

(Gerrie 2007: 1)

Technologies of governing associate power that is exercised over subjects with the power that subjects exercise over themselves. Technologies of governing thus describe a dispersion of a specific mentality of government amongst the population and the subjects that are to be governed. *Technologies of the self* are thus an inflection of governance into the subject, but they exist together and alongside with technologies of domination. Many technologies of self-government are based on the creation of freedom – a condition under which choice, autonomy, efficiency and responsible conduct become the tasks of the population (Rose 1992). Subjects then "produce the ends of governments by fulfilling themselves rather than being merely obedient"; they are "obliged to be free in specific ways" (Rose *et al*. 2006: 89).

However, as the above quotes indicate, technologies of the self are not only about the internalization and realization of a program's principles, processes and actions by the population. The exercise of self-governing includes instruments, concrete artifacts, machines – in short: material structures, some of which create effects that are beyond the intention of those controlling them (Rose *et al*. 2006). Particularly in the resilience programs that are discussed in this book, technologies of the self are entangled with and redefined by *technologies off-the-shelf*. Off-the-shelf refers here not only to machines that follow specific technical characteristics and (changing) standards, such as digital technologies do (Chapter 7 will expand upon this), but also that these artifacts have become a standard technology in specific populations. The remainder of this book discusses how "connectivity has allowed resilience to come of age as an operational tool" (Duffield 2016: 15). It investigates technologies that have become a new standard with the explosive dispersion of mobile phones and personal computers over the past years, both of which feature different digital services and provide access to the Internet, but also foster specific technologies of the self. Even though a strong relationship between per capita income, Internet access and smartphone ownership continues to exist (Pew 2016), which describes just one of many persisting digital divides (cf. Chapter 5), the number of smartphone users worldwide is estimated to grow from 1.5 billion in 2014 to around 2.5 billion in 2019 (Statista

From program to programming 67

2016). This also means that over 35 percent of the world's population is expected to own a smartphone by 2018 (ibid.).

This book looks at societies in which computer and smartphone ownership, as well as almost continuous access to the Internet is already shaping everyday activities. More specifically, it examines how digital technologies off-the-shelf and technologies of the self begin to shape each other in the context of resilience programs, and how these two technologies express and instantiate practices and rationalities of choice, autonomy and efficiency. The access to digital and Internet-based services has begun to influence the fulfillment of oneself as a free, self-organized and emergency-managing subject. Emergency populations have become entrepreneurs of themselves and have begun to participate in the production and restoration of security by using digital services and by voluntarily providing information, for example, via social media. Through this use of digital information, emergencies have become a new form of calculable and manageable space. This trend extends what has already long been a subject of governmentality studies: technologies of risk were, for example, "crucial for the operationalization of programs of governing at a distance" (Rose *et al.* 2006: 95; cf. Duffield 2001, chapter 2). Such technologies have now been conjoined by digitized resilience practices that seek to render uncertainty thinkable and governable after and before the event, whether that is through digital mapping practices, digital relief actions or digital coordination efforts that take effect in case of emergency (cf. Chapter 7). This is where technology as a program and technology as programming meet – an alliance which will be expanded upon by the end of this chapter.

The presence of digital technologies in everyday activities not only affords specific technologies of governing, but it also nurtures the very discourses about being and knowledge that resilience programs are based upon: complexity and interconnectedness. These discourses take the material or machinic aspect of technology as a vantage point when they address, for example, how the Internet and the many Internet-based services raise complexity within society. Not only do these discourses include narratives about how physical networks and digital technologies *raise* complexity and therewith emergencies, for example, through infrastructure breakdown and cascade effects in case of cyber-attacks. The same technologies are also discussed as an opportunity to *administer* complexity and emergencies. Let's first take a look at the way in which digital technologies inspire narratives and imaginaries of heightened complexity.

Once they have become integrated into everyday activities, digital technologies seem to be ubiquitous and universal. According to Galloway and Thacker, this impression can be explained by the way in which they affect many domains. They have become foundational to "everything from cultural identity to war" (2007: 10). Within highly developed nations, it is the everydayness of the digital, such as email, mobile phones and the Internet that produces the effect that the digital seems to be "everywhere" (ibid.). This does not imply, however, that digital technologies are the bedrock of society:

> We note a difference, then, between the ways in which new technologies can be constitutive of social, cultural, and political phenomena, and the notion that digital technologies are the foundation on which society is constructed.
>
> (Galloway and Thacker 2007: 10)

To appreciate the argument that digital technology and complexity thinking influence each other, it is critical to understand the distinction that Galloway and Thacker make here. This requires a brief reflection about the role that technology plays in and for society. The latter, essentialist view on technology, as, for example, forwarded by Heidegger (1977), would argue that technology reveals *being as such* and thus privileges function over all other aspects of technology (Feenberg 2000: 305). This view grants technology a powerful position that overrides or underrates the influences of society on the development of technology. A similar argument is made by what Latour critically calls the materialist position, which assumes that we are what we have because technology does shape society (2009). The opposite argument is one that conceptualizes technologies as diligent and merely mediating, implying that society can master technologies. Both positions, Latour suggests, cannot take account of the role and responsibility that technology and societal actors actually assume. According to him, they have entered into a relationship, defying any essence of subject or object, but creating a new entity together (ibid.).

Less dedicated to the idea of a new entity, but yet emphasizing the interrelationship between the two, Feenberg proposes that "technology is a scene of struggle, a parliament of things" (2009: 144). Rather than revealing being as such, technology is "an environment within which a way of life is elaborated" (ibid.: 145), because "social meaning and functional rationality are inextricably intertwined dimensions of technology" (ibid.: 147). As a result, "[m]achine design mirrors back the social factors operative in the prevailing rationality" (ibid.: 146). Or as Deleuze puts it: "[t]ypes of machines are easily matched with each type of society – not that machines are determining, but because they express those social forms capable of generating them and using them" (Deleuze 1992: 6). The functions of technology, then, are societally imbued. Following this line of thinking, digital technologies are not fundamental to the organization of society, governance or a mode of being as such. Rather, governmental discourses and practices have an influence on the design of digital technologies[1] at the same time as the presence of digital technologies expresses, inspires and brings about discourses and practices of governing.

The book discusses, for example, how the apparent ubiquity of digital technologies amplifies complexity discourses within different governmental domains. Particularly in the political discourse about the security of information and communication technology (ICT), notions of emergence, self-organization and interconnectedness beyond comprehension have grown over the past decades (cf. Chapter 5). Being interconnected, then, not only allows for new practices of governing and generating security, but it is also understood to bear threats (Galloway and Thacker 2007), because viruses and hacks can equally thrive upon interconnectedness. In a similar vein, Deleuze sees the advent of a society the characteristic machine of which is the computer "whose passive danger is jamming and whose active one is piracy or the introduction of viruses" (Deleuze 1992: 6). Concepts of dark networks and computer viruses alone, however, do not reflect the deep-seated role that insecurity plays in the discourse of governing interconnected societies. It is, rather, reflected in the way in which security-oriented practices in the ICT sector concretely embrace complexity thinking by theorizing the freedom of information circulation and insecurity as two sides of the same coin (cf. Chapter 5). Such narratives of complexity entail an important change in the way technology and technical artifacts are conceptualized. Since technology is understood to reflect and enhance complexity, distinctions between the organic and non-organic are broken down. Digital technologies are understood to exhibit adaptation and transcend "the boundaries once confined to the mortal biological body" (Dillon and Reid 2009: 65). Galloway and Thacker also observe that there is a sense of vitality in digital technologies and the language that surround it:

> [C]omputer "viruses," Internet "worms," and "computer immunology." These [...] examples tell us already a number of things about the naming of networks, least of which that naming often takes place in proximity to vital forms.
>
> (Galloway and Thacker 2007: 12)

The response to such vital forms of threats are then, not surprisingly, also security strategies or technologies of governing that are based on vitality: resilience which stands for ongoing adaptation. The fact that digital technology, specifically the Internet, is increasingly understood in terms of complexity and vitality entails not only important consequences for the way in which technology, too, is understood, but also how the interplay of insecurity and security is conceptualized in societies that embrace digital technologies. In the Internet, contingency and insecurity are not only brought about by disruptive usage of digital connectivity, such as hacks, but insecurity is framed to be an integral part of the complex system of interrelations. Complexity thinking, then, allows governmental discourses to reframe breakdown and disruption in digital technologies as an information-rich site for analysis (Dillon and Reid 2009: 62), which enables spontaneous local learning, creativity through adaptation and evolution. Like any other complex system, the Internet would do both invoke disruption, but also adapt to disruption (cf. Chapter 5). Digital technologies and specifically the Internet, here, embody and express not only this key assumption of complexity thinking. Chapter 5 explains how Internet protocols (cf. Galloway and Thacker 2007) express the way in which governance in complex systems is sought to be organized: dispersed, locally, through self-organization and learning process – all of which are characteristic of resilience.

For analytical reasons, it is crucial here to distinguish between the fact that technology is increasingly framed in terms of complexity – which reflects a specific discourse in a given society and inspires a particular set of governmental practices, and the ontology of complexity itself, which is one that considers interconnectedness as a condition for life to exist. Consequently, the above does not mean that the analytical lens used in this book is an essentialist one, claiming that technology is a way of being and existing. Rather, this book considers digital technologies, and the Internet in particular, to express, reflect and reinforce a discourse of complexity that is already prominent in interconnected societies.

The fact that digital technologies are increasingly paired with a governmental discourse of complexity thinking has concrete effects on technologies of the self, meaning the actual practices of governing. The program of resilience reflects this discursive overlap as it employs concepts of freedom, circulation, emergence and evolution in order to govern insecurity. Moreover, technologies not only express and afford these strategies, but they also change the way in which, for example, processes of subjectification, of creating resilient subjects, take place. This brings us to the second aspect of how technology is also used to administer complexity and emergencies, which is developed throughout the next few pages.

When governmental programs turn to programming

As an important artifact in contemporary forms of governing, digital technologies not only enable information exchange, but they also mediate social interaction. As early as the 1950s, Innis wrote that:

> A medium of communication has an important influence on the dissemination of knowledge over space and over time. [...] The relative emphasis on time or space will imply a bias of significance to the culture in which it is embedded.
>
> (Innis 1951: 33)

It means that digital technologies temporalize and spatialize information exchange and the dissemination of knowledge. They set apart and delay, but they also compress and accelerate processes that are fundamental to the art of governing (van Loon 2008). What is particular about digital technologies is that they additionally are:

> encouraging, opening up, or enabling physical transactions and social interactions, with the aim of generating data which can be mined to govern effectively the flow of populations, commodities, and cultural productions.
>
> (Grusin and Cox 2010: 4)

It goes to show that digital technologies not only temporalize and spatialize the dissemination of knowledge, which influence practices of governing (cf. Chapter 8). They also modulate collective affect, as has been studied with regards to media as a specific form of digital technology (Grusin 2004; Grusin and Cox

2010; cf. Chapter 6). Even more importantly, the increased deployment of digital technologies leads to a digitization of the information exchange that characterizes societal interaction and thus to new ways of organizing social life. This is the part where governmental programs turn to programming.

The Internet, for example, allows stories about societal processes to circulate. At the same time, it makes these stories accessible for governing through the form of code. Governmental programs have, in fact, begun to incorporate digital information into their practices and as a result, new technologies of (self-)governing have emerged. In the context of emergency management, particularly, the harvest and use of digital information is mainly identified as an opportunity to render response more efficient. The trend is met with "an affirmatory rhetoric that celebrates the restorative powers of smart technologies and fast machine thinking" (Duffield 2016: 3; cf. Meier 2015). Established in 2007, for example, platforms like Ushahidi suggested that the emergency management of the 21st century is going digital (Leson 2012). On his website iRevolutions, a hub for digitized disaster and emergency management solutions, owner Patrick Meier proclaims that his "mission is to pioneer Next Generation Humanitarian Technologies" (iRevolutions.org 2016). The European Commission funds projects that explore how social media can be integrated into emergency management (Cordis 2016) and the UK government explored in 2012 the usefulness of social media for emergency management (UK Government 2012). These are just a few of the many fields where digital technologies have begun to shape the governance of emergencies.

The inclusion of digital information into the program of resilience concerns any step, from accessing the information to analyzing information and translating it into actions and advice. While accessing information is a big debate and research topic in its own right (Bennet and Raab 2006; Tavani 2008; Boyd and Crawford 2012; Andrejevic and Gates 2014) the remainder of this book will focus on the analysis and translation of digital information into concrete actions. It should be clear, however, that the turn from programs to programming is – like the process of rationalization itself – never a finished, top-down process. Rather, programming here refers to a negotiation process, a specific form of rationalizing government using digital information. The question here is not whether the disaster population needs to match the programming models or whether populations actually contribute to writing programs and creating solutions to their problems. The aim is rather to describe how populations, the digital and governmental programs influence each other, as well as to understand the role of digital information in rendering various elements of government consistent (cf. Rose *et al.* 2006). In the spirit of governmentality analyses, the aim is not to identify an ideal practice or to give advice on how programming efforts should be exercised (ibid.: 99). The aim is rather to discuss what kind of governmental principles digital practices reflect and to map the guiding rationalities of digital practices of governing. Digital technologies are explored as means and processes that can open up for political as well as anti-political acts (cf. Bellanova forthcoming; Barry 2002). They can be used for spontaneous, political expressions, as was the case in the aftermath of the 2011 terror attacks in Norway, which will be discussed in Chapter 8. At the same time, the workings of programming foreclose debate, for example, when social difference is folded into simplified machine interfaces, when human behavior is abstracted and translated into patterns instead of relying on ground truths, and when characteristics, such as race, class, gender and developmental differences that constitute the human terrain, are mathematically encoded (Duffield 2016: 11). Duffield continues to explain:

> Whereas these differences were once open to political contestation and readjustment, with the rise to dominance of remote sensing and algorithmic behavioural surveillance, ideologically defined social, economic and security fault lines easily blur into scientifically verified objective differences.
> (Ibid.; cf. Chamayou 2015; Magnet 2011)

Programming thus has concrete effects on the way in which programs work. While Duffield claims that "the roll-out of an embedded digital infrastructure transforms the desired qualities of resilience into a cybernetic command and control function" (Duffield 2016: 15), this chapter suggests that command-and-control does not capture the full logic of the digital. At the same time as programming indeed locks disaster populations "into digital interfaces" (ibid.: 10), the digital also incentivizes populations in its very own modus of operation. Entrepreneurial norms and practices and the incentive to self-organize, for instance, do take a new shape. The "connectivity, ubiquity, mobility and affectivity" (Grusin and Cox 2010: 3) of digital technologies enable circulation and inspire a new idea of freedom, through which advanced liberal modes of governing work. Internet protocols (cf. Galloway and Thacker 2007), for example, become expressive of a new form of conducting the conduct of populations, where the subject is both self-organized and free, meaning that it doesn't follow top-down orders, and yet is subject to power. This is possible, because organization in protocols is decentralized and power works through mechanisms of instigation, animation, negotiation and the creation of incentives rather than discipline or command-and-control. Chapter 5 will expand on resilience programs that have turned to programming by discussing this modus of exercising power through protocols.

Another aspect of the turn from programs to programming is that digital technologies reflect the assumptions about being, knowing and time that underly resilience programs at the same time as they bring about new resilience practices. Through their apparent ubiquity, digital technologies translate global problems of emergency into mundane practices, bringing them home and making them part of everyday life (Galloway and Thacker 2007). At the same time, digital technologies evoke discourses of complexity that deliver not only the necessary vocabulary, but also the ontological, spatial and epistemological narratives that legitimize such practices of governing (cf. Chapters 5, 7 and 9). Analyzing programming, then, means to identify the rationalities and to trace the power-knowledge system that digital technologies and the Internet reflect and reinforce. It means to study practices of instigating self-organization that are based on information sharing, circulation and codification. A crucial aspect to understand here is how the digital makes new objects, for example, interrelations themselves, "accessible for investigation" (Dillon and Reid 2009: 57), and how it creates new modes of knowledge production through calculation. Algorithms, for example, have now become the calculable means to trace patterns and correlations (cf. Amoore 2007, 2009, 2013; Andrejevic and Gates 2014). Programming, then, instigates new forms of knowledge-production and reflexivity that are available to the active, planning, calculating and rational subject.

This in itself is not a new trend. As Duffield writes: "Finding an effective tool or set of inducements that encourage people to self-organise independent of the state has been a liberal Holy Grail since the industrial revolution" (Duffield 2016; cf. Cowen and Shenton 1996). The availability of digital information was, for example, a crucial factor in the development of new risk practices. The rise of digital information nurtured the calculation of future insecurities through probability calculation. This knowledge would then be translated into preventative technologies, designed to keep insecurity outside of society (cf. Chapter 2). Grusin argues in this context that the digital enabled new forms of voluntary self-policing that internalize the panopticon and make citizens monitor their own behavior without outer surveillance (Grusin and Cox 2010). An illustration of the way in which digital technologies have recently influenced the conduct of conduct are, for example, smart watches that allow for voluntary personal fitness tracking, thus lowering medical risks and potentially insurance costs. Not all forms of prevention, however, are based on calculation – particularly not in a society that believes itself exposed to rising complexity. This is why preventative efforts have begun to involve techniques that are not based on calculation, but also imagination (Aradau and van Munster 2008, 2011). Vice versa, not all forms of calculation necessarily feed into techniques of prevention. Digital resilience practices, for example, embrace the logics of algorithms as a means to bring about survival, adaptation and evolution once emergencies have occurred (cf. Chapter 7). A prominent digital resilience practice is here the mapping of emergencies and the translation of such maps into concrete behavioral guidelines, indicating where safe and dangerous locations can be found, which kinds of capacities are needed in a specific space, and where resources can be accessed. Calculation of digital information is furthermore used to identify resilience patterns and create resilience indexes in order to measure how a population performed during emergencies, to optimize learning processes and to determine successful, desirable and sensible designs for adaptation. Such instances of governmentality are further discussed in Chapters 7 and 8, where social media are explored as means to enhance self-organization and learning processes that seem to rise out of the emergency population.

With the turn from programs to programming governance becomes a form of code (cf. Dillon and Reid 2009). This leads to a new combination of calculation, responsibilization and remote management that exceeds preventative and risk-oriented practices: resilience programming efforts measure and calculate desired forms of emergency response, in order to optimize performance after disruption has hit. Programming resilience is to use digital means to shape opportunities for self-organization during emergencies. But what does that mean for our understanding of the subject that is to be rendered resilient? The very fact that the digital presents information in the form of numerical code is central here:

> The numerical language of control is made of codes that mark access to information or reject it. We no longer find ourselves dealing with the mass/individual pair. Individuals have become "dividuals" and masses, samples, data, markets, or "banks."
>
> (Deleuze 1992: 5)

The pairing of constant information exchange and calculation based on big data is what creates subjectifications that follow the logic of mass on the one hand and the principle of constant transformation on the other:

> The family, the school, the army, the factory are no longer the distinct analogical spaces that converge towards an owner – state or private power – but coded figures – deformable and transformable – of a single corporation that now has only stockholders. Even art has left the spaces of enclosure in order to enter into the open circuits of the bank.
>
> (Deleuze 1992: 6)

This means that resilience programming is not interested in disciplining the individual, neither in the steering of populations via statistical techniques (as was the case with risk), but in the individual or the population whose conduct is determined through mass and collectivity (cf. Aradau and Blanke, 2016). The subject to be governed is determined through patterns, correlations and associative reasoning, following motifs of, for example: *Who is exposed to A is also exposed to B.* Governmental bodies co-determine these patterns, correlations and associations, together with those providing the hardware, those who write programs and those who share information, which is most likely the population itself.

The turn from programs to programming, then, has a fundamental principle in common with the idea of resilience itself, namely a shift in the focus of governance from causes to effects. As a concept, resilience does not seek to address causes (unlike prevention), but its aim is to steer the effects of emergencies. Resilience is inherently about the reaction to disruptions and disasters, whether they lie in the past, the present or the future. The associative reasoning that the digital provides for increases the focus on effects, as it lends itself more easily to the detection of correlations. This has to do with the fact that the digital is not merely binary, but also networkable: it exists in a network, where items of information can be traced and associated with each other. The networkability of digital information, or big data, is that which allows for relational and associative reasoning. As that, resilience programming becomes expressive of governmental techniques that are no longer based on subject–object binaries and distinctions between cause and problem, but that are characterized by governance *through* effects, being in-formation and ex post facto activity.

Note

1 This aspect has so far not been a core focus of governmentality studies (Bröckling *et al.* 2011: 12).

References

Amoore L (2007) Vigilant Visualities: The Watchful Politics of the War on Terror. *Security Dialogue* 38(2): 139–156.

Amoore L (2009) Algorithmic War: Everyday Geographies of the War on Terror. *Antipode* 41(1): 49–69.

Amoore L (2013) *The Politics of Possibility. Risk and Security Beyond Probability.* Durham, NC: Duke University Press.

Andrejevic M, Gates K (2014) Big Data Surveillance: Introduction. *Surveillance and Society* 12(2): 185–196.

Aradau C, Blanke T (2016) *Politics of prediction.* Security and the time/space of governmentality in the age of big data. European Journal of Social Theory. DOI: 10.1177/1368431016667623 (accessed 25 March 2017).

Aradau C, van Munster R (2008) Taming the Future: The Dispositif of Risk in the War on Terror. In: Amoore L, de Goede M (eds) *Risk and the War on Terror.* London: Routledge. 23–40.

Aradau C, van Munster R (2011) *Politics of Catastrophe. Genealogies of the Unknown.* Abingdon, Oxon: Routledge.

Barry A. (2002) The Anti-political Economy. *Economy and Society* 31(2): 268–284.

Bellanova R (forthcoming) *Politics and the Digital* Special Issue.

Bennett CJ, Raab CD (2006) *The Governance of Privacy. Policy Instruments in Global Perspective.* Cambridge, MA: MIT Press.

Boyd D, Crawford K (2012) Critical Questions for Big Data. *Information, Communication & Society* 15(5): 662–679.

Bröckling U, Krasmann S, Lemke T (2011) From Foucault's Lectures at the Collège de France to Studies of Governmentality. An Introduction. In: Bröckling U, Krasmann S, Lemke T (eds) *Governmentality. Current Issues and Future Challenges.* New York/Abingdon, Oxon: Routledge. 1–33.

Chamayou G (2015) *Drone Theory.* London: Penguin.

Chandler D, Reid J (2016) *The Neoliberal Subject. Resilience, Adaptation and Vulnerability.* London: Rowman & Littlefield.

Cordis (2016) *How Social Media Can Improve Emergency Service Responses.* Available at http://cordis.europa.eu/news/rcn/122383_en.html (accessed 8 July 2016).

Cowen MP, Shenton RW (1996) *Doctrines of Development.* London: Routledge.

Deleuze G (1992a) Postscript on the Societies of Control. *October* 59 (Winter 1992): 3–7.

Dillon M, Reid J (2009) *The Liberal Way of War. Killing to Make Life Live.* London: Routledge.

Duffield M (2001) Governing the Borderlands: Decoding the Power of Aid. *Disasters* 25(4): 308–320.

Duffield M (2016) The Resilience of the Ruins: Toward a Critique of Digital Humanitarianism. *Resilience: International Policies, Practices and Discourses.* 15 March: 1–19. Available at: http://dx.doi.org/10.1080/21693293.2016.1153772 (accessed 27 February 2017).

Feenberg A (2000) From Essentialism to Constructivism: Philosophy of Technology at the Crossroads. In: Higgs E, Light A, Strong D (eds) *Technology and the Good Life.* Chicago and London: University of Chicago Press. 294–315.

Feenberg A (2009) Democratic Rationalization: Technology, Power, and Freedom. In: Kaplan DM (ed.) *Readings in the Philosophy of Technology.* Plymouth, UK: Rowman & Littlefield Publishers Inc. 139–155.

Galloway AR, Thacker E (2007) *Exploit: A Theory of Networks.* Minneapolis, MN: University of Minnesota Press.

Gerrie J (2007) Was Foucault a Philosopher of Technology? *Techné: Research in Philosophy and Technology* 7(2): 1–7.

Grusin R (2004) Premediation. *Criticism* 46(1): 17–39.

Grusin R, Cox G (2010) *On Premediation. Interview with Richard Grusin led by Geoff Cox.* Available at: www.academia.edu/4754419/Grusin-Interview_With_Geoff_Cox_2010_ (accessed 11 August 2016).

Heidegger M (1977) The Question Concerning Technology. In: Heidegger M (ed.) *The Question Concerning Technology and Other Essays.* New York: Harper & Row Publishers. 3–35.

Innis HA (1951) *The Bias of Communication.* Toronto: University of Toronto Press.

iRevolutions.org (2016) Bio. Available at: https://irevolutions.org/bio (accessed 8 July 2016).

Latour B (2009) A Collective of Humans and Nonhumans: Following Daedalus's Labyrinth. In: Kaplan DM (ed.) *Readings in the Philosophy of Technology.* Plymouth, UK: Rowman & Littlefield Publishers Inc.156–167.

Leson H (2012) *Going Digital: Emergency Management in the 21st Century, The ICT in Conflict & Disaster Response and Peacebuilding Crowdmap.* Available at: www.ushahidi.com/blog/2012/12/20/going-digital-emergency-management-in-the-21st-century-the-ict-in-conflict-disaster-response-and-peacebuilding-crowdmap (accessed 8 July 2016).

Magnet SA (2011) *When Biometrics Fail: Gender, Race and the Technology of Identity.* Durham, NC: Duke University Press.

Meier P (2015) *Digital Humanitarians: How BIG DATA is Changing the Face of Humanitarian Response.* Boca Raton, FL: CRC Press.

Miller P, Rose N (1990) Governing Economic Life. *Economy and Society* 19(1): 1–31.

Pew (2016) *Smartphone Ownership and Internet Usage Continues to Climb in Emerging Economies* Available at: www.pewglobal.org/2016/02/22/smartphone-ownership-and-internet-usage-continues-to-climb-in-emerging-economies (accessed 6 July 2016).

Rose N (1992) *Towards a Critical Sociology of Freedom. Inauguration Lecture.* Goldsmith College, London, 5 May 1992; Folio paper, Goldsmiths College, University of London, 1993.

Rose N, O'Malley P, Valverde M (2006) Governmentality. *Annual Review of Law and Social Science* 2(1): 83–104.

Statista (2016) *Number of Smartphone Users Worldwide from 2014 to 2019 (in Millions).* Available at: www.statista.com/statistics/330695/number-of-smartphone-users-worldwide (accessed 6 July 2016).

Tavani H (2008) Informational Privacy: Concepts, Theories, and Controversies. In: Himma K, Tavani H (eds) *The Handbook of Information and Computer Ethics.* Hoboken, NJ: Wiley. 131–164.

UK Government (2012) *Using Social Media in Emergencies: Smart Practices.* Available at: www.gov.uk/government/uploads/system/uploads/attachment_data/file/85946/Using-social-media-in-emergencies-smart-tips.pdf (accessed 8 July 2016).

van Loon J (2008) *Media Technology. Critical Perspectives.* Maidenhead, Berks: Open University Press.

Part II
Resilience as a way of governing the Internet

5 Resilience and spatiality

The Internet is a complex space. Making and keeping it secure is a challenge. Infrastructural disconnections, for example, can lead to local disruptions. Connectivity here is often the solution to the problem, because disrupted spaces can simply be circumvented. Complexity theory finds, however, that connectivity itself is not only the solution to, but can also be the cause of insecurity. Vital forms of insecurity, such as viruses, worms and DDOS attacks thrive on connectivity as they work through mechanisms of blockage and overload. Complexity theories suggest, furthermore, that too much connectivity can lead to emergences, to sudden, unplanned and local changes, which can cascade and grow throughout entire parts of a network – precisely because connectivity allows for negative feedback loops. In the Internet, insecurity is then not only the interruption or absence of connectivity, but also the overload and exploitation of connectivity by malware. Insecurity is a disturbance, something that can disrupt, challenge or fundamentally change the flow of information. Connectivity is then what provides security and vitality, but also danger and malignant growth at the same time. Networks are thus not inherently secure or insecure, but both; security and insecurity are fundamental parts of the Internet's make-up and their occurrence cannot necessarily be determined in advance. These are some of the reasons why it is considered challenging to develop policies and governmental programs for Internet security. Such programs need to speak to the distributed and asymmetric workings of the Internet. Internet security requires programs that suppress adverse and support favorable circulation. Such programs would have to exploit change (Galloway and Thacker 2007) in order to render emergence productive as opposed to destructive.

These rationalities and problematizations of insecurity are very much reflected in the program that the European Network and Information Security Agency (ENISA) suggests for Internet security: resilience. ENISA's recent Internet security policies make an insightful case study, because they not only incorporate a turn from program to programming, but they are also expressive of programs that seek to govern connectivity and interconnected societies at large. ENISA's policies articulate the rationalities, technologies and practices that seek to answer the challenges of governing complex systems and interconnected societies. In that context, it is significant what kind of language ENISA uses to speak about the security of the Internet, the epitome of complex spaces. The move from the singular concept of cyberspace, originally an offspring from popular culture (Gibson 1984), to the image of the "Interconnection Ecosystem" (ENISA 2011c) is here most indicative. It signifies that Internet security is increasingly conceptualized through the vocabulary of resilience and of re-establishing unsettled equilibria in complex systems. According to ENISA, network resilience refers to a steady state of the Internet, maintaining an acceptable level of service in the face of faults (ENISA 2009). While resilience is thought to be inherent in networks, the focus of ENISA's current governance efforts is to understand and strengthen this capacity (ENISA 2011c). Taking this shift in EU Internet politics as a vantage point, this chapter focuses on the following questions: How does the Internet ecosystem affect the understanding of the Internet as space? How does it legitimize resilience as a form of organizing this space? What notion of security does this approach imply?

The reconceptualization of the Internet as interconnection ecosystem is a highly political move. With the interconnection ecosystem, ENISA promotes an understanding of the Internet as a heterogeneous space that needs to be governed through resilience. This entails concrete consequences for the politics and practices of Internet security. The Internet ecosystem not only enables ENISA to enact particular resilience policies and suggests the EU as the central facilitator of these, but the ecosystem also implicates the specific understanding of security described above. Internet security is no longer the protection of a singular cyberspace, but in complex, uncertain, and ever-changing environments like the Internet ecosystem, security is ever-emerging: "[t]he equilibrium (if we can call it that) arises from the behavior of tens of thousands of independent networks, each seeking to maximize its own profits" (ENISA 2011c: 36). The program that stands behind the Internet ecosystem links security to insecurity and unpredictability. This does not only limit abilities to evaluate problems and prevent failure (Dunn Cavelty 2007), but the ecosystem's conceptual link to complexity promotes the idea of insecurity and vulnerability as system-inherent (ibid.; ENISA 2011c; Duffield 2012). Insecurity becomes a structural part of the interconnected world and security is an active process of dealing with disruption on the lowest level possible.

In developing this argument about resilience and spatiality, this chapter pays specific attention to the centrality of language in the analysis of governmental programs. It follows an understanding of space, discourse and governance as mutually constitutive: they bring each other into being (Foucault 1986). Foucault's theorization of discourse, matter, space and governance as fundamentally entangled has inspired two theoretical arguments that this chapter draws upon. First, performativity theories highlight the special role that language takes within governmental programs. Butler argues that language produces performative effects, meaning that the reiterative framing of the Internet as a particular form of space has the power to "produce the phenomena that it regulates and constrains" (Butler 1993: 2). A second argument building on Foucault and other poststructuralists is the idea that space is not to be understood in Euclidian terms or singular ontologies, but that space is perceived, understood and created by different groups. It is relational. Discourse is expressive of the imaginations and conceptualizations of spatiality, which again influence the way in which space is organized and governed. Space and discourse are thus closely interlinked with questions of power, which are also explored vis-à-vis the EU's reconceptualization of the Internet as ecosystem.

In order to explore its performative effect, this chapter follows the reiterated expressions of the Internet ecosystem and examines a range of documents that are central within the EU approach to network resilience. Documents on the technical specifications of infrastructures are consulted to study infrastructural and material approaches to Internet resilience. Policy documents provide insights into the governmental logics that shape such spaces. Both types of documents are understood to form a larger discourse on the Internet ecosystem, which portrays the Internet as a complex space of heterogeneity and in/security. The selected material includes different data sources, such as the European Commission's Digital Agenda for Europe, studies, technical reports, public interviews, policy papers, resolutions and communications by the Council of the European Union, the European Parliament, the European Commission, but first and foremost by ENISA.

The following section briefly traces the trajectory of different discursive framings of the Internet as space. Furthermore, it introduces the main theoretical premises of performativity and relational space, which provides the analytical basis for exploring the various dimensions of the Internet ecosystem, its actors and forms of governance. The subsequent section deploys this framework to conduct a critical spatial analysis of the Internet ecosystem and its correlated forms of resilience governance. The Internet ecosystem is first described in terms of its material dimensions. The way in which the Internet's material arrangements give rise to political dimensions of space forms the second part of the analysis. It describes how the Internet ecosystem becomes a site of political struggle between heterogeneous actors, who seek to engender approaches of resilience governance. These analyses lead to the argument that network resilience and the Internet ecosystem imply a re-organization of power over connectivity and a specific understanding of in/security. Instead of stability and absence of disruption, insecurity in the dynamic Internet ecosystem is a permanent condition and resilience is a modus of emergent, self-organized security. As such, the argument developed here ties in with existing critical discussions of resilience (Zebrowski 2009; Joseph 2013; Kaufmann 2013; Chandler 2014; Evans and Reid 2014). However, it shifts the focus from the resilient subject (Joseph 2013; Reid 2012; Dunn Cavelty *et al.* 2015) to spatial arrangements and the resilience politics they constitute. It foregrounds the way in which digital technologies such as protocol and *self x* become expressive of resilience as a governmental program.

The Internet: from cyberspace to the ecosystem

Arguments about the spatiality of the Internet vary vastly and they are more often than not expressed by a specific terminology. To begin with, one could argue that the Internet is simply perceived as space, because it is reflected in our language. Online, spatiality is experienced in the form of landmarks, such as websites. The distances between these landmarks are experienced through retrieval times and clicks. These perceptions are relative, but once they are hard-wired, the perceived spatiality is inscribed into our language (Lakoff and Johnson 1980, 1999). We can find examples of spatial vocabulary in our everyday expressions, such as up- and download, and navigation. Users of the Internet do not only go back and forth in order to visit platforms, the spatial perception of the Internet is also anchored in political language. According to the European Commission, traffic within cyberspace is in need of direction (Commission of the European Communities 2009), and data is moved to clouds (European Commission 2010c).

Discourse theory further explores how the language of such programs, its conceptualizations and terminologies, not only reflect a certain style of governing, but also how it effects the perception and organization of the Internet as space. A vast variety of discourse theories go back to the work of Foucault, who found that discursive practices "form the objects of which they speak" (Foucault 1972: 49). As a branch of discourse theory, performativity theory focuses specifically on the "reiterative and citational practice by which discourse produces the effects that it names" (Butler 1993: 2). This does not mean that a single time pronunciation of a concept creates an object, but the repeated use of a concept over time, so Butler argues, influences contents, representations, identities and political practices related to that concept (cf. Bialasiewicz et al. 2007). Performativity is, however, to be distinguished from those constructivist approaches that place agency exclusively within language, arguing that discourse alone acts over the subject. Such constructivist theories would position the subject itself outside of the domain of construction (ibid.). According to performativity, discourse and subject are mutually constitutive, reducing neither the agency to the subject, nor to language alone. Performativity theory is also used to explore how discourse influences both ideal and material conceptions of space (cf. Nash 2000; Bialasiewicz et al. 2007).

To what extent a concept, spatiality and related practices are co-constitutive can also be traced by looking at the terms that have been chosen to describe the Internet. The topology of the Internet is as contested as its terminology. Early online activists relied heavily on the term *cyberspace*, arguing that it is "a world that is both everywhere and nowhere, but it is not where bodies live" (Barlow 1996). In a similar way, some of the first legal scholars to work on Internet law claimed that, in cyberspace, territorial borders and sovereignty are absent (Johnson and Post 1996), which disconnects it from real-world orderings. While current image searches of cyberspace seem to reflect this understanding of a space without place, conveying the image of infinite connections that form an ever-changing cloud, some scholars have focused on mapping and outlining the material and social infrastructure of cyberspace. Through that, they introduced a shift from the everywhere-and-nowhere connotation of cyberspace to its infrastructural spatiality. Kitchin, for example, traced the cultural, political and economic dimensions of cyberspace in *Cyberspace: The World in the Wires* (1998), Dodge and Kitchin mapped wires, fibre-optic cables, satellites, website evolution, emails and domain names in the *Atlas of Cyberspace* (Dodge and Kitchin 2001).

The increasing focus on the Internet's physical reality also led to a critique of the term *cyberspace*, which was considered too ethereal by some scholars. As a response to the early debates on Internet regulation, legal scholar Goldsmith argued that the Internet is *just a network* (coined by Cohen 2007), in which transactions are no different from real-space transactions, since they are connected to real-space territories and jurisdictions, which permit regulatory control (Goldsmith 1998). Using the term *Internet* rather than cyberspace, other geographers further fostered the infrastructural, material facet of spatiality by analyzing private and public provider networks in the US (Gorman and Malecki 2000) or the spatial patterns that emerged from the investments in fibre-optic lines and upgrades (Malecki 2002). One of the more recent popular examples tracing the physical geography of the Internet is Blum's *Tubes* (2012) – a term which equally foregrounds the material and physical aspect of the Internet. His book is an elaborate and dedicated description of the various infrastructures and technologies that seem to make the Internet into what it is.

Poststructuralist geographers argue, however, that neither cyberspace, nor just-a-network conceptualizations of the Internet are exhaustive. The just-a-network position fails to address the way in which the Internet is created by each user, neither is the Internet as abstract, singular and ethereal as the word cyberspace suggests. They generally refer to and understand the Internet as characterized by multiple spatialities.

A broad scholarship following Foucault, Latour, Law, and Deleuze understands space not as static, but as relational and processual. Spaces are what they are because of their participation in relationships (Massey 2011; Malpas 2012):

> Instead, then, of thinking of places with boundaries around, they can be imagined as articulated moments in networks of social relations and understandings, but where a larger proportion of these relations, experiences and understandings are constructed on a far larger scale than what we happen to define for that moment as the place itself.
>
> (Massey 1994: 154)

This allows for an understanding of space as in flux, heterogeneous and placed in diverse networks on the one hand, as well as territorially institutionalized, standardized and characterized by a stable set of relations on the other (Murdoch 2006). Even though poststructural approaches to space have emerged from research on urban geographies (cf. Hart 2002; Ward and McCann 2011; Wise

2005), they are now applied to the conceptualization of the Internet as a heterogeneous space. This enables a study of the various elements that make up the spatiality of the Internet, including the human, non-human, organic, inorganic, technical, natural, online, offline and all the stages in between (Murdoch 2006; Wakeford 1999). Most important is relational space as an expression of critique. By understanding the Internet not as a single ontic space, but a network with highly selective connections (Graham 2013), it becomes possible to point to the broad variety of digital divides and the uneven topologies, which are dependent on the positionalities of each potential user. These unequal network geographies are tied to and reinforce "existing social, economic and political power structures" (Graham 2011: 223; cf. Brunn and Dodge 2001; Zook 2005, 2006).

Graham's investigation of Internet access shows that a critical analysis of space is also a critical analysis of power (Graham 2011, 2013). Space and power, Foucault argues, are mutually constitutive, because power is tied to knowledge that specifies how particular sites should be organized (Foucault 1979). Power is thus as heterogeneous as space itself. Various kinds of power can coexist; they are neither centrally governed, nor equally distributed (Anderson and McFarlane 2011; cf. Doel 1996; Deleuze 1988; Foucault 1988). In acknowledging that "space is fundamental in any exercise of power" (Foucault 1986: 252; Murdoch 2006), relationality allows for a study of the variety of power relations that appear in heterogeneous spaces. It enables a critical assessment of the various governmental rationales and techniques that seek to regulate a space. Finally, relationality also ties spatiality back to discourse: space is an instantiation of power, knowledge and discourse (cf. Foucault 1979, 1986) that is relative and influenced by the different concepts that seek to describe and organize it.

Understanding space as relational, heterogeneous and intimately tied to discourses that describe and organize it, the following paragraphs will examine what an articulation of the Internet as "Internet Interconnection Ecosystem" (ENISA 2011c) implies. Relationality and performativity are used as methodological tools that enable the critical assessment of conceptualizations of space and how they are tied to power structures. They draw attention to the kind of knowledge and the rationalities that specific conceptualizations imply and to the particular strategies deployed to organize this space. Precisely because the Internet ecosystem is a political attempt to capture the heterogeneity and topological complexity of the Internet itself, it invites us to study the different kinds of power at play and the variety of rationales that are combined in the organization of this space. The following part will take a snapshot of the various materialities, actors, processes, knowledge productions and power structures that determine the Internet ecosystem and critically discuss resilience as its correlated technique of governance. What becomes visible from this analysis is also how resilience is turning from a program to programming as it incorporates rationalities of network thinking, such as protocological control and self x, into its governmental technologies.

A spatial analysis of the Internet ecosystem

In 2010, the Digital Agenda for Europe identified the Internet as a global critical information infrastructure that "must be resilient against all sorts of threat" (European Commission 2010a). In response, the idea of fostering resilience became the main focus of ENISA's 2011 report, *Inter-X: Resilience of the Internet Interconnection Ecosystem* (ENISA 2011c). The various documents that embrace and forward the Internet ecosystem and resilience as a political strategy include a number of reports, directives, and agreements, but also interviews and media reports. The choice to redefine the Internet as an ecosystem is not only an attempt to capture and describe the heterogeneity of the Internet. It becomes expressive of a specific form of space that necessitates resilience as an approach to Internet security governance. As such, the term is not only descriptive and expressive of a specific form of rule, but performative. It is serves as a political leitmotif that is productive of a particular form of Internet governance. The subsequent analysis explores how ENISA's resilient ecosystem describes the Internet as a specific space with interrelated infrastructural and political dimensions. It illustrates what kind of performative effects the conceptualization of the Internet as ecosystem entails.

The section is subdivided in two parts. It first discusses the material and infrastructural aspects of ecosystemic space that is constructed, created and designed by a multitude of engineers, technology providers and political actors. This material dimension of the ecosystem follows concrete design elements such as multiplicity and diversity, which not only create a heterogeneous whole, but also ambiguities. Since the organization of a space is always related to power, the resilient ecosystem also creates a political dimension that is constantly in the making. As such, the material and political dimension of the ecosystem give rise to each other. Emphasizing the power-related aspects that are interwoven with ecosystemic space, the second half of this section describes this political dimension as heteroscapes of power. It explores the techniques of resilience governance that are being negotiated and practiced, touching upon issues of regulation and the interplay of local responsibility and global standardization.

A space of heterogeneous structures

ENISA's redefinition of the Internet as ecosystem seeks to take account of the continuous modifications that take place here. It describes the Internet as an assemblage of ever-changing and diverse infrastructures that are designed, physically built, programmed and constructed by designers, engineers and diverse end users. The infrastructural dimension of the Internet ecosystem refers not only to wires, cables and servers, the geographic properties of which are mapped in physical network topologies. It also includes the communication architectures – logical topologies – that direct the way in which the different physical devices communicate with each other through protocols. This interplay of physical and logical layers is changing constantly. The Internet Mapping Project by William

Cheswick and Hal Burch, for example, illustrates in a gallery of maps the way in which the Internet's infrastructure is continually expanded and how paths of data flow change steadily (Cheswick and Burch (n.d.). Even though maps seem to stabilize the Internet as something concrete and manifest, infrastructural spaces are not a fixed, univalent reality (Graham 2011), but continuously constructed by those who trace, engineer and define them. The term *Internet ecosystem* seeks to reflect exactly this fluidity of the heterogeneous whole: "Its shape changes all the time, as new connections are made, or existing connections fail or are removed" (ENISA 2011c: 8).

The term does, however, not only express that the Internet is an ever-transforming, heterogeneous space; it also underlines the complexity that this setup entails. This emphasis on material complexity implies concrete rationales about the security of the system. According to ENISA, the major security challenge in the ecosystem is the "large number of separate, but interconnected local issues" (ENISA 2011c: 8). Due to this interconnectedness, the Internet is prone to cascading disruption (ibid.). This suggests the concept of a tightly woven, dynamic net, in which boundaries between intended and unintended effects are blurred and where disruption may lead to far-reaching and cascading emergencies. Complexity further complicates the detection of risks (ENISA n.d.a), which renders the Internet prone to faults and challenges. Its increasing number of components, its openness and flexibility renders the Internet inherently insecure (cf. Dunn Cavelty 2007) and vulnerable (ENISA 2011c).

For ENISA, resilience is thus the most evident modus of dealing with this complexity, because it refers to "the ability to adapt [itself] to recover from a serious failure, or more generally to its ability to survive in the face of threats" (ENISA 2011c: 10). Resilience is profiled as the answer to uncertainty-inducing complexity. The concept of resilience seeks to embrace uncertainty about future disruptions and responds to threats that cannot be averted in time. The language of ecosystemic resilience implies that the Internet's equilibrium is re-established as quickly as possible after disruption occurs. The equilibrium is then an expression of security in a system that is always in flux. The term ecosystem conceptualizes the Internet as a dynamic, heavily interdependent and constantly evolving space (ibid.), but – as opposed to single ontic spaces – it comprehends insecurity and disruption as its permanent condition. The exposure to uncertainty is part of the Internet ecosystem's ontology, as it evolves through the constant interplay of disruption and equilibrium, which is enhanced by resilience. As such, security is more an activity instead of a state. It is something that constantly needs to be established in relation to ontological insecurity.

ENISA's framing of the Internet as ecosystem thus not only emphasizes heterogeneity and complexity and ties it to rationales of uncertainty, it also suggests concrete strategies to strengthen the resilience of the Internet's material dimension. Resilience is advanced through ecosystemic infrastructures that can accommodate for disruption and establish the equilibrium after insecurities have materialized. ENISA's main approach to build and engineer this infrastructural resilience follows principles of flexibility and redundancy (ENISA 2009). Flexibility is

Resilience and spatiality 87

enhanced by building "headroom" (ENISA 2011b: 16) or multiple and diverse redundancies for each component. Redundancies are extra spaces and interconnections, which are included in the individual component parts of the infrastructure. Such buffers are used for so-called "load-sharing" or "failover" (ibid.), through backups that allow for the circumvention of disrupted nodes. Engineering resilience is thus a technical solution of preparedness, which snaps into action as soon as disruption hits. Building additional interconnections, so ENISA argues, allows for the local storage of information and the switching between alternative media of data transmission, which enables the continued operation in the event of failure (ENISA 2011c: 17). Redundancy and flexibility-by-design thus requires multiple components and forms of operations which are characteristically diverse to promote self-repair and adaptation. This illustrates that insecurity, disruption and flexibility are anchored in the material spatiality of the Internet's technical design, since alternative interconnections are engineered on the presumption that disruption will occur. As opposed to protection, which seeks to avert disruption, resilient systems seek to enhance multiplicity and diversity, in order to absorb and respond to disruption after it appears and before it can cascade.

Multiple and diverse infrastructures, however, not only support a network's resilience, they also enhance complexity. This means that dealing with complexity also adds to complexity, especially when different devices and services are owned by a variety of providers. By March 2011, the Internet accommodated 37,000 autonomous systems, such as internet service providers (ENISA 2011c). The multiplicity of local resilience approaches and autonomous systems can, ironically, reinforce the potential for disruption. In 2013, for example, the technology magazine *Wired* published the results of a worldwide survey on IT complexity. More than half of the respondents from mid-sized enterprises and organizations stated that "complex policies ultimately led to a security breach, system outage or both" (Baron 2013; cf. Algosec 2012). The approach to enhance resilience through diversity, multiplicity and redundancy thus adds to the complexity and the potentiality for insecurity that the concept of the Internet ecosystem accentuates.

This problem of adding complexity entails furthermore practical challenges. ENISA analyzed that

> most of the things that service providers can do to make the internet more resilient, benefit other providers much more than the firm that pays for them. This leads to a potential tragedy of the commons. Resilience mechanisms are not implemented because no-one has found a way to roll them out that gives sufficiently local benefit.
>
> (ENISA 2011c: 4)

Originally discussed in the contexts of resource management and global warming (Hardin 1968), the tragedy of the commons is yet another ecological concept that is applied to Internet security, and which implies its own rationality about the impossibility of the organization of a complex space. It foregrounds the missing local benefits for security providers as a problem that necessarily arises from the complexity of the Internet and the attempt to enhance resilience. Complexity then becomes a practical problem for providers, not only as a source of disruption, but as a problem that resilience is not a cost-effective solution for. The impacts of resilience engineering may benefit others more than the party that invests into it, they may create no effect if implemented on too small a scale, or – in the worst case – they create detrimental effects if they enhance the complexity of Internet policies, all of which translates into practical apathy and the impossibility of organizing a complex space.

The way in which ENISA's reconceptualization of the Internet as ecosystemic space embraces complexity then becomes a problem that is potentially detrimental to ENISA's own cause. The discussion has, furthermore, indicated that the Internet ecosystem not only refers to material solutions, but also includes political dimensions and rationalities that seek to organize this space. The Internet ecosystem becomes a site for the production and extension of power, which we will turn to now.

A space of heterogeneous power: protocols and self x as new modes of governing

The term ecosystem not only reconceptualizes the Internet as a space of heterogeneous infrastructures, but it is also interpreted and filled with different contents by its diverse stakeholders. Analyst Demchak summarizes that each element of networked space is established, maintained or disposed of by someone, may it be "designers, abusers, social controllers, trend watchers and users" (Demchak 2012: 261; cf. Goldsmith and Wu 2006), all of which may have their own conception of Internet resilience. The concept of "ecosystem" describes complexity. It combines various political actors, rationales and multiple approaches to resilience, which form the political dimension of ecosystemic space. The ecosystem is thus a heteroscape of power, a heterogeneous site of political approaches and power negotiations. Here, power not only lies in the ability of being connected, which is already unevenly distributed, but also in the control over connectivity and the standards according to which this connectivity is governed. Processes of negotiating control over such standards involve actors from at least three administrative domains: national and sub-national institutions, referred to as the local actors; the EU as a superordinate body; and the private actors. According to ENISA's documents, all of these actors play different roles in making the ecosystem resilient. Some of the prominent rationales and approaches to Internet resilience are explored below, also to shed light on the tensions that arise from them.

The concept of resilience itself places emphasis on local approaches to deal with disruption, which is why resilience policies often entail a redistribution of responsibilities from centralized to local actors (cf. Kaufmann 2013; UK Cabinet Office 2013; IFRC 2012). A similar redistribution is also a principle for network security, since rapid collaborative action and sense-making from fragmented information is difficult to achieve over long distances (Demchak 2012). The local approach is also in line with EU Internet resilience programs (ENISA n.d.b). Politically, the local emerges as a new domain for response and responsibility. According to the European Commission's communication on critical information infrastructure protection, the EU member states remain ultimately responsible for defining critical information infrastructure-related policies (Commission of the European Communities 2009). Decisions are handled at the least centralized authority capable of addressing the problem effectively. In fact, even sub-national organizations and institutions, such as NGOs, citizens and individuals, are being asked to define and register elements of offenses and issues in order to enforce accountability (Bendiek 2012). Internet resilience is thus a collective effort, with an emphasis on local response.

The documents and studies accompanying the Commission's communication 149 on Internet security and resilience identify, however, that the major part of work to implement this form of distributed response yet remains to be done (Commission of the European Communities 2009). Because local strategies have grown organically, the EU member states have unequal approaches to Internet resilience, reflecting varying levels of expertise and preparedness (Council of the European Union 2009), which again gives rise to the other side of the EU's approach to Internet resilience. Since "no member state is an island" (Council of the European Union 2009: 15), European Union policies repeatedly stress the limited realm of action for single member states when it comes to managing and securing global connectivity. Unequal standards, ENISA argues similarly, make local policies at times ineffective or even counter-productive (ENISA 2011c).

According to ENISA and the Council of the European Union, the global nature of the Internet requires a holistic and systemic approach to network and cross-border information security and resilience (Council of the European Union 2009; ENISA 2011a). This means that distributed responsibilities are only politically desired and considered effective as long as they share certain universal standards. Because differences in national approaches reduce the effectiveness of Internet security measures (European Commission 2010b), global codes of conduct and systematic cross-border cooperation become a necessity. The Commission's communication 149 thus promotes the effort to harmonize the diverse approaches to Internet resilience, while keeping responsibilities at the local level (Commission of the European Communities 2009) – an approach that summarizes ENISA's resilience politics in the Internet ecosystem.

Several activities have been undertaken to accomplish exactly this harmonization, such as conducting exercises, devising a global code of conduct, supporting strategic cooperation, establishing a common language and standardizing the definition of gaps. So far, two pan-European exercises have been conducted in 2010 and 2012 under the name *Cyber Europe*. Member states are furthermore invited to conduct regular exercises on a national level (Commission of the European Communities 2009; European Commission 2010b). The workings of such exercises for instilling resilience are discussed in more depth in Chapter 6. Another EU approach to harmonize the constantly evolving and uneven policies of cyber-resilience is to define a common language. ENISA has set up agreements about shared resilience conceptualizations and vocabulary that can be used by people and systems, so-called ontologies and taxonomies of resilience (ENISA 2011e). Harmonization is also suggested in terms of the identification of technological gaps in standardization related to Internet resilience, reaching from protocols and domain name systems to file formats – some of these concepts are explored in more detail below. Yet, ENISA requires the commitment of many other institutions to implement these standardization efforts, such as the European Committee for Standardization (CEN), the International Organization for Standardization (ISO) and the nonprofit organization Internet Corporation for Assigned Names and Numbers, who coordinate, for example, the addresses of domains (ENISA 2009).

According to ENISA, a common language and definition of standards, however, are only some aspects to foster the cross-border policies that are needed for a transboundary infrastructure such as the Internet ecosystem. Some documents identify the need for a minimum of cooperation agreements and information exchange mechanisms inside the EU (ENISA 2011a). The harmonization of Internet resilience approaches is thus advanced through best practice guides and cooperation contracts between member states, an example of which are Mutual Aid Agreements. Such agreements are made between two or more parties concerning provisions "for lending assistance across normal boundaries during an emergency situation" (ENISA 2011d: 3). These formalized agreements are supposed to have important "benefits over ad hoc approaches, since they enhance contacts that extend beyond a few personal relationships" (ibid.: 1), which may not be sufficient in a crisis. Since these agreements seek to overcome "regulatory, legal and competitive barriers – both real and perceived," they emerge as central means to emergency preparedness and Internet resilience (ibid.: 1f.).

While distributed localism and global standardization may seem like contradicting logics at first, they are captured by the ecosystemic rationale that combines local actors into one overarching, complex system that follows a set of harmonized rules. This combination of localism and standardization, furthermore, features similarities of technical coordination and control within networks. In networks, shared values and goals are controlled through common protocol. Protocol defines what it means to be included in the network. At the same time, the focus of protocol is to optimize the joint operation of two layers within a complex whole. This stresses the role of local self-organization, as the functioning of higher layers is dependent on the self-sufficiency of lower layers (Galloway and Thacker 2007). The governmental technology of protocol speaks not only to network governance, but to that of heterogeneous and interconnected environments at large. It speaks to the governance of spaces that are not only inherently insecure, but also decentrally organized. Thus, the logic of protocol does not have to be reduced to the digital world. The coexistence of heterogeneous topologies, which sometimes collide, but are mainly meant to communicate with each other, could also pertain to the climate, to traffic or the economy, which are all complex environments exposed to their respective

Resilience and spatiality 91

contingencies. In such different heteroscapes of power, protocol would represent a governmental logic that regulates the efficient collaboration between the systems' different parts. It disperses tasks across the different layers of such systems, meaning that it regulates the cooperation between heterogeneous parts by orchestrating self-organization. The political imaginary of protocol is not discipline, but the creation of opportunities through stimulation and control via modulation, distribution and flexibility (Deleuze 1995; Galloway 2004). The security strategy inherent in protocol is to let local change happen, but to manage it in order to make it productive for the whole system. At the least, protocol identifies alternative routes for information flow when emergencies occur. As such, the aim of protocol is not to protect singular nodes or parts of complex systems, but to control the connectivity and flow between their different parts and to exploit changes by learning from them.

Protocol's main aim is to guide self-organization that is also visible in ENISA's promotion of the logic of *self x* that regulates the Internet ecosystem:

> To deal with the increasing complexity of systems and uncertainty of their environments, networking has turned to self x concept that can be read as self-reconfiguration, self-optimising, self-diagnosing, self-healing, self-protecting, self-organization, self-forming, self-adaptivity or self-management. Self x leverages wireline and wireless systems and provides transmission resiliency resulting in an autonomous behaviour. The self x features and facilities relate to both hardware and software. All such solutions work with feedback loops that probe the whole infrastructure.
> (ENISA 2011b: 31)

ENISA's *self x* thus expresses that every part of the ecosystem is increasingly included into resilience efforts. It emphasizes that the Internet ecosystem is not flexible enough if it has resilient endpoints only, but each component of the system plays a part in avoiding cascade or failure (ENISA 2011b). *Self x* is here that which enables protocol to be efficient. Protocol functions on the basis that every part answers local challenges in a self-reliant way. As such, *self x* is in fact very similar to Foucault's technologies of the self that describe the making of the entrepreneurial subject not through discipline, but through stimulation. In a similar manner, *self x* self-management follows given principles that guide the way in which the respective part is developing itself. These principles, however, are not forced by some central instance, but they arise from negotiation. Furthermore, *self x* stands for a subject or a single part of a system that internalizes insecurity in order to render it productive to the complete network that it is part of. It utilizes insecurities to learn from them, to adapt to them and to reflect about them. Through that, *self x* becomes a key to life in interconnected spaces, a means to sustain the network as a whole and to make it vital.

This form of guided self-management is also reflected in ENISA's resilience policies of global standardization described above. According to ENISA, distributed decision-making, local responsibilities and coordination between two member-states are key instruments to Internet resilience, but in order to work in a heterogeneous whole, they also need shared values, goals and global standards. Thus, through the term ecosystem, ENISA not only chooses to express already existing heterogeneity and the combination of localism and standardization, but the concept also enables ENISA to enact the associated practices.

This ecosystemic approach to Internet security, however, entails aspects that are in need of evaluation. As much as harmonization efforts and global standards enable distributed localism, they also constrain it by limiting variety and locally grown approaches:

> [e]fforts to build new forms of distributed localism are both enabled and constrained by the form and content of technical standards, and the politics of distributed localism in turn enable and constrain the technical evolution of network standards.
>
> (Cohen 2007: 254)

The approach of combining standardization with the distribution of responsibilities eventually leads from diversification to homogenization. Should global standards not be fulfilled, the self-responsible local institution suffers harmful consequences in case of emergency and also penalization for not conforming to common regulative standards. If the local is responsible for its own connectivity, it is also responsible for its own exclusion from a network should it not be able to conform. If non-functioning or infected nodes fail to self-repair, they are actively blocked, circumvented or excluded from the overarching network (He et al. 2011). If the same exclusive form of protocological control applies to political institutions, digital divides are broadened should institutions not be able to comply with standards. The idea of a global Internet would be undermined. It may also be worth considering to what extent excessive homogenization can also threaten the stability of the ecosystem, which – as discussed above – relies on diversity to a certain extent. For now, the EU does not discuss the potential negative effects of homogenization, but rather points to the benefits of global standards.

According to ENISA, the combination of local responsibility with centralized standardization entails a concrete political consequence: a supranational leader is needed to facilitate negotiation and implement global standardization. This also means that considerable power lies with those who define what the global standards are; it is "the power of the standards of the network over its components" (Castells 2009: 43). By conceptualizing the Internet as ecosystem that is in need of a coordinating, harmonizing body, the very act of reconceptualization has the performative efficacy to emphasize the EU's role as the facilitator for cooperation and developer of global standards. While acknowledging the difficulty to uptake Europe-wide governance models, diverse EU documents identify a course of action for the EU with opportunities for collecting and integrating information of national weaknesses, vulnerabilities and gaps as well as the definition of governance roles and responsibilities, which could create a direct positive impact (Council of the European Union 2009; ENISA 2011d; Bendiek 2012). This central coordination and facilitation would add value to the national programs for Internet security, which are already in place in the Member States (Council of the European Union 2009). These documents and formulations are clear attempts to stabilize the EU's position within the Internet ecosystem, suggesting one of the most powerful roles as the central coordinator and facilitator of its overall resilience activities.

Taking on the role of the facilitator can, however, not simply be declared. Whereas prevalent approaches to disaster resilience tend to emanate from a central political organ, which redistributes responsibilities and knowledge to smaller and more local units, knowledge and authority within the Internet is distributed already and held by a multitude of stakeholders. Because this distribution grew organically, it is now challenging to determine the central organ that defines and manages shared values and goals.

Furthermore, there is not only a lag between rhetorical commitments to expanding the EU's role and the actual transfer of authority to Brussels (Boin and Rhinard 2008), but the expertise for defining and implementing shared standards also lies within the private sector. Bendiek stresses that knowledge is a weak resource within governments, and EU bodies alone do not have the competence to determine agendas and shape processes (Bendiek 2012). It is the expert knowledge of the private sector that is decisive for consensus-building within a multi-level, multi-stakeholder structure. As a result, the desired shift of power toward the EU as a facilitating and coordinating actor is not a self-evident one. Furthermore, given the current movement toward a multi-stakeholder convergence of the public and the private, a public steering body such as the EU would have to harmonize diverse national approaches to Internet resilience with those of private actors. However, neither market forces nor standardization efforts by public bodies have provided sufficient incentives to the private sector for investing into the resilience of critical information infrastructure (Council of the European Union 2009). An additional question is whether public–private partnerships, even though they become evident as an important mode of sharing responsibilities, may lead to politically precarious dependencies, precisely because public authorities would rely on information from and implementation of standards within the private sector and security would become the matter of private initiatives. The collection of network vulnerabilities and the implementation of standards by the private sector may not only help enhance resilience, but it may also be used for other purposes than security, for example, to nurture commercial interests. There is thus a need to discuss whether the private sector should have an influence on public security policies. As a result, the Internet ecosystem becomes a site of political struggle over responsibilities between national, supranational and transnational actors.

This discussion has shown that the EU shares the struggle over power in their self-constituted Internet ecosystem with other actors, such as the private sector and national actors. The Internet is thus not only a heterogeneous, but a highly contested space. It is a space that does not necessarily translate into a coherent

94 *Part II: Governing the Internet*

whole. It gives rise to various technologies, actors and techniques of governance that do not always work according to the desired global standards. Together, they form a heteroscape that is currently characterized by rationales of diversity, distribution and localism, on the one hand, and standardization and centralized facilitation, on the other. Power here lies in the control over cooperation and connectivity in a heterogeneous whole. This notion of power over standards corresponds much to Castells' idea of networked power (1996, 2009). Based on the empirical analysis and the observations concerning the heteroscape of power, however, this chapter draws a conclusion about the enactment of power that expands Castells'. Power in complex systems and networks is not only enacted by the systemic inclusion and exclusion of passive nodes (Luhmann 1984; Castells 1996, 2009; cf. Stalder 2006) – or, in this case, actors, which either conform to a specific policy or not. The determination of standards provokes an active struggle over power. The discussion has illustrated that various actors enter into this struggle about power and interfere with the EU's foreseen trajectory to enact resilience and become the central coordinator of distributed activity.

To govern complex spaces is to embrace insecurity

This chapter analyzed the theoretical, political and practical effects that ENISA's reconceptualization of the Internet as interconnection ecosystem entails. As expressed in performativity and relational space theory, the chapter followed the idea that the understanding of space is closely linked to the discourses that describe it and the way in which actors relate to space through experience, practices and concepts (Butler 1993; Massey 1994; Murdoch 2006; Bialasiewicz *et al.* 2007). Reconceptualizing the Internet as ecosystem is thus an act that influences and expresses the way in which different actors relate to and actively construct this space.

For ENISA, the strategic value of using the term "Internet Interconnection Ecosystem" (ENISA 2011c) is that it embraces heterogeneity and seeks to provide for the governance of a space that is not only complex and distributed, but in flux. This means that the very ontology of the Internet ecosystem incorporates characteristics of diversity and flexibility, but also insecurity, since sources of disruption are difficult to know. This ontological insecurity constitutes reason and reasoning for ENISA's Internet security politics, and resilience arises as the answer to govern the Internet ecosystem. ENISA's act to reconceptualize the Internet as ecosystem and introduce resilience as a mode of governance thus legitimizes a range of concrete security practices; it introduces new security actors and security rationales. As such, this reconceptualization is a highly political move.

A significant structural effect of recasting the Internet as ecosystem is that security actors are less concerned with the immediate protection of *cyberspace*, but with procedures that regulate the efficient cooperation of the system's heterogeneous and resilient parts. Within the diverse and ever-changing stakeholder-setup of the Internet ecosystem, the EU seeks to stabilize their position as a central actor that fosters the responsibilization of the local on the one hand, and manages collective interests on the other (cf. ENISA 2011c). The role of this central security actor becomes that of a facilitator who administers standards, while the active responsibility to establish resilience lies with the local actors, such as national governments or infrastructure owners, who act in accordance with overarching principles. Not only does the ecosystemic logic influence the political praxis of Internet security, but this shift in roles and procedures of security governance encounters practical challenges; it involves a change in the political reasoning about security and transforms the understanding of security as such.

First, it is questionable whether the suggested form of standardization, of creating harmonized principles for Internet security, is really practicable. If the Internet ecosystem grew organically in the first place, the heterogeneity and diversity of its components can challenge the applicability of universal standards. The power to decide these standards is not a concern of public actors alone, but also involves private parties. This multi-stakeholder setup turns the question of centralized facilitation and standardization into a struggle over power, on the one hand, and a fight against the tragedy of the Internet commons, on the other.

Second, the formulation of security standards is a political decision with the power to normalize what it means to be secure. Whatever part of the system does not live up to these standards is then per regulation useless, weak or threatening and needs to be blocked, circumvented or excluded. In combination with the *self* x-logic, the idea of local self-organization, Internet resilience then involves a particular political rationale about security. The combination is expressive of a larger trend toward advanced liberalism in security politics that prioritizes the evolution of the system as a whole by means of its competing, self-governed single parts (cf. Joseph 2013; Kaufmann 2013; Reid 2012; Zebrowski 2009), which are excluded or blocked if they don't follow pre-given standards.

Third, by embracing the concept of the ecosystem fluidity and insecurity are accepted as the predominant state of existence, which grants resilience a reason to exist in its own right. Resilience, in turn, is characterized by the constant interplay of disruption and response, which is fundamentally different from security as the protection of singular ontologies associated with cyberspace. Security understood through resilience is thus not a passive state of being protected from harm, but it becomes an active mode of dealing with harm. As opposed to Reid, who argues that resilience governance abandons the idea of security completely (2012), this chapter traced how security is redefined as a process instead of a state. Due to the idea of continuous and active adaptation, resilience is productive of a self-made, emergent and strictly temporary notion of security.

Vis-à-vis the recent increase in the application of ecosystemic concepts and resilience approaches to any kind of complex security contexts and spatialities, the chapter provides an evaluation of these moves. The program of resilience has come to signify not only techniques of governing the Internet, but the governance of complex and networked spaces at large. Or, vice versa, what this chapter shows us is that the politics around a space such as the Internet give us insights about the program of resilience. Since narratives of rising complexity will continue to shape future governance, it is insightful to conclude this chapter with a few observations about how resilience and networked or complex structures speak to each other.

Networked space is conceptually tied to a form of governing that exhibits several features of resilience. On a material level, networks exhibit vulnerability, because they are prone to emergences and domino effects at the same time they feature security, since blocked or disrupted spaces can be bypassed as well as extra margins and headrooms lead to redundancies. On a theoretical level, networks need to continuously renew themselves in order to exist, since weak or unused links are likely to disappear. Networks prevail in a constant tension between disintegration and renewal, which is fundamentally different from a form of security that is tied to the protection of singular ontic spaces. As much as this aspect is true on a theoretical level, in practice, these renewals are not always a given, especially where hardware is concerned. Concerning the level of internal organization, networks are amenable to protocols as a technology of governance. It is a technology that works through the negotiation of governmental standards that any local parts utilize as guidance for their self-organization. Those parts that do not work according to protocol are likely to be excluded from the network – unless they manage to influence protocol at large through processes of negotiation. These three aspects of governing have also become visible in resilience programs in general. It goes to show that the invocation of networks, interconnections and complexity in discourses of government are linked to the resilience discourse. Together, they represent a specific rationalization, a program of government that is central in the security politics of today.

An aspect that is not yet widely studied is how networks react when they reach the limits of their internal self-organization, redundancy or headroom. Ecological theory suggests that ecosystems collapse, deform, disappear or migrate to a different area when they reach their resilient limits (Handmer and Dovers 1996; Smithers and Smit 1997; Walker *et al.* 2002; Roylance 2001). Vis-à-vis the governmental program of resilience, the implication of limits could take various forms. One of them is discussed in the next chapter and in Chapter 9. While Chapters 7 and 8 of this book will expand on what the digital and the network contribute to the creation of the resilient subject and self-organization on a practical level, the next chapter will take a closer look at how *self x*, or rather self-organization, can be further conceptualized through affect.

References

Algosec (2012) *Examining the Dangers of Complexity in Network Security Environments. AlgoSec Survey Insights.* Boston, MA. Available at: http://wp.eurosecglobal.de/wp-content/uploads/2013/04/www.algosec.com_resources_files_Specials_Survey%20files_12_10_11_security_complexity.pdf (accessed 11 August 2016).

Anderson B, McFarlane C (2011) Assemblage and Geography. *Area* 43(2): 124–127.
Barlow JP (1996) *A Declaration of the Independence of Cyberspace*. Available at: projects.eff.org/~barlow/Declaration-Final.html (accessed 15 July 2016).
Baron Y (2013) *Uncovering the Dangers of Network Security Complexity. 1 February.* Available at: www.wired.com/insights/2013/01/uncovering-the-dangers-of-network-security-complexity (accessed 15 July 2016).
Bendiek A (2012) *Die Mehrebenen- und Multistakeholder-Struktur der Cybersicherheitspolitik. Europäische Cybersicherheitspolitik.* Berlin: SWP Studie.
Bialasiewicz L, Campbell D, Elden S, Graham S, Jeffrey A and AJ Williams (2007) Performing Security: The Imaginative Geographies of Current US Strategy. *Political Geography* 26(4): 405–422.
Blum A (2012) *Tubes. Journey to the Center of the Internet.* New York: Ecco and Harper Collins Publishers.
Boin A, Rhinard M (2008) Managing Transboundary Crises: What Role for the European Union? *International Studies Review* 10(1): 1–26.
Brunn S, Dodge M (2001) Mapping the "Worlds" of the World Wide Web. *American Behavioral Scientist* 44(10): 1717–1739.
Butler J (1993) *Bodies that Matter. On the Discursive Limits of Sex.* London and New York: Routledge.
Castells M (1996) *The Rise of the Network Society.* Oxford: Blackwell.
Castells M (2009) *Communication Power.* Oxford: Oxford University Press.
Chandler D (2014) *Resilience. The Governance of Complexity.* London: Routledge.
Cheswick W, Burch, H (n.d.) Internet Mapping Project. Available at: www.cheswick.com/ches/index.html (accessed 15 July 2016).
Cohen JE (2007) Cyberspace as/and Space. *Columbia Law Review* 107(201): 210–256.
Commission of the European Communities (2009) *COM(2009) 149 Final. Communication from the Commission to the European Parliament, the Council, the European Economic and Social Committee and the Committee of the Regions on Critical Information Infrastructure Protection. "Protecting Europe from Large Scale Cyber Attacks and Disruptions: Enhancing Preparedness, Security and Resilience." Brussels.* Available at: http://eur-lex.europa.eu/LexUriServ/LexUriServ.do?uri=COM:2009:0149:FIN:EN:PDF (accessed 15 July 2016).
Council of the European Union (2009) *Protecting Europe from Large Scale Cyber-Attacks and Disruptions: Enhancing Preparedness, Security and Resilience. 8375/09, ADD1 and ADD 4. Brussels.* Available at: http://test.webactiv.ro/seci/doc/EC.%20Commission%20staff%20working%20doc.%20Cyber%20Crimes.Impact%20assesment.part%201.02.04.2009.pdf and www.secicenter.org/doc/EC.%20Summary%20of%20the%20Impact%20assessment%2002.04.2009.pdf (accessed 15 July 2016).
Deleuze G (1988) *Foucault.* Minneapolis, MN: University of Minnesota Press.
Deleuze G (1995) *Negotiations 1972–1990.* New York: Columbia University Press.
Demchak CC (2012) Resilience and Cyberspace: Recognizing the Challenges of the Global Socio-Cyber-Infrastructure (GSCI). *Journal of Comparative Policy Analysis: Research and Practice* 14(3): 254–269.
Dodge M, Kitchin R (2001) *Atlas of Cyberspace.* London: Pearson Education Limited.
Doel MA (1996) A Hundred Thousand Lines of Flight: A Machinic Introduction to The Nomad Thought and Scrumpled Geography of Gilles Deleuze and Félix Guattari. *Environment and Planning D: Society and Space* 14(4): 421–439.
Duffield M (2012) Challenging Environments: Danger, Resilience and the Aid Industry. *Security Dialogue* 43(5): 475–492.

Part II: Governing the Internet

Dunn Cavelty M (2007) *Cyber-Security and Threat Politics. US efforts to Secure the Information Age.* Abingdon, Oxon and New York: Routledge.

Dunn Cavelty M, Kaufmann M, Søby Kristiansen K (2015) Resilience and (In)security: Practices, Subjects, Temporalities. *Security Dialogue* 46(1): 1–12.

ENISA (n.d.a) *Interview – ENISA Report on Resilience of Communication Networks – Pascal Manzano.* Available at: www.enisa.europa.eu/media/news-items/interviews/interviews/InterviewResilience-1.pdf (accessed 15 July 2016).

ENISA (n.d.b) Resilience and CIIP. Available at: www.enisa.europa.eu/activities/Resilience-and-CIIP (accessed 15 July 2016).

ENISA (2009) *Gaps in Standardization related to resilience of communication networks. Heraklios.* Available at: www.enisa.europa.eu/publications/archive/gapsstd (accessed 15 July 2016).

ENISA (2011a) *Analysis of Cyber Security Aspects in the Maritime Sector. Heraklios.* Available at: www.enisa.europa.eu/activities/Resilience-and-CIIP/critical-infrastructure-and-services/dependencies-of-maritime-transport-to-icts/cyber-security-aspects-in-the-maritime-sector-1 (accessed 15 July 2016).

ENISA (2011b) *Enabling and Managing End-to-end Resilience.* Available at: www.enisa.europa.eu/activities/identity-and-trust/library/deliverables/e2eres (accessed 15 July 2016).

ENISA (2011c) *Inter-X: Resilience of the Internet Interconnection Ecosystem.* Full report. Available at: www.enisa.europa.eu/publications/interx-report/at_download/fullReport (accessed 11 August 2016).

ENISA (2011d) *Mutual Aid for Electronic Infrastructure in Europe. Key Observations Report.* Heraklios. Available at: www.enisa.europa.eu/activities/Resilience-and-CIIP/critical-infrastructure-and-services/mutual-aid-assistance/mutual-aid-agreements/at_download/fullReport (accessed 15 July 2016).

ENISA (2011e) *Ontology and Taxonomies of Resilience. Version 1.0. Heraklios.* Available at: www.enisa.europa.eu/activities/Resilience-and-CIIP/Incidents-reporting/metrics/ontology/resontax-draft/at_download/file (accessed 15 July 2016).

European Commission (2010a) *Digital Agenda for Europe, Action 28: Reinforced Network and Information Security Policy. Brussels.* Available at: ec.europa.eu/digital-agenda/en/pillar-iii-trust-security/action-28-reinforced-network-and-information-security-policy (accessed 15 July 2016).

European Commission (2010b) *Digital Agenda for Europe, Action 39: Member States to Carry Our Cyber Attack Simulations. Brussels.* Available at: ec.europa.eu/digital-agenda/en/pillar-iii-trust-security/action-39-member-states-carry-out-cyber-attack-simulations (accessed 15 July 2016).

European Commission (2010c) *Digital Agenda for Europe, Cloud computing.* Brussels. Available at: ec.europa.eu/digital-agenda/en/cloud-computing (15 July 2016).

Evans B, Reid J (2014) *Resilient Life: The Art of Living Dangerously.* New York: Polity Press.

Foucault M (1972) *The Archaeology of Knowledge.* Trans. Smith AS. New York: Pantheon Books.

Foucault M (1979) *Discipline and Punish: The Birth of the Prison.* Harmondsworth: Penguin.

Foucault M (1986) Space, Knowledge and Power. In: Rabinow P (ed.) *The Foucault Reader.* London: Penguin. 239–254.

Foucault M (1988) *History of Sexuality. Vol. 2, The Use of Pleasure.* London: Penguin.

Galloway A (2004) *Protocol: How Control Exists After Decentralization.* Cambridge, MA: MIT Press.

Galloway AR, Thacker E (2007) *Exploit: A Theory of Networks*. Minneapolis, MN: University of Minnesota Press.
Gibson W (1984) *Neuromancer*. New York: Ace Books.
Goldsmith JL (1998) Against Cyberanarchy. *The University of Chicago Law Review* 65: 1199–1250.
Goldsmith JL, Wu T (2006) *Who Controls the Internet? Illusions of a Borderless World*. New York: Oxford University Press.
Gorman SP, Malecki EJ (2000) The Networks of the Internet: An Analysis of Provider Networks in the USA. *Telecommunications Policy* 24: 113–134.
Graham M (2011) Time Machines and Virtual Portals: The Spatialities of the Digital Divide. *Progress in Development Studies* 11(3): 211–227.
Graham M (2013) Geography/Internet: Ethereal Alternate Dimensions of Cyberspace or Grounded Augmented Realities? *The Geographical Journal* 179(2): 177–182.
Handmer JW, Dovers SR (1996) A Typology of Resilience: Rethinking Institutions for Sustainable Development. *Industrial and Environmental Crisis Quarterly* 9(4): 482–511.
Hardin G (1968) The Tragedy of the Commons. *Science* 162: 1243–1248.
Hart G (2002) *Disabling Globalization: Places of Power in Postapartheid South Africa*. Berkeley, CA: University of California Press.
He J, Liang H, Yuan H (2011) Controlling Infection by Blocking Nodes and Links Simultaneously. *Internet and Network Economics* 7090: 206–217.
IFRC (2012) *The Road to Resilience Bridging Relief and Development for a More Sustainable Future*. International Federation of the Red Cross and Red Crescent Societies. Available at: www.ifrc.org/PageFiles/96178/1224500-Road%20to%20resilience-EN-LowRes%20(2).pdf (accessed 11 August 2016).
Johnson DR, Post DG (1996) Law and Borders: The Rise of Law in Cyberspace. *Stanford Law Review* 48: 1367–1374.
Joseph J (2013) Resilience as Embedded Neoliberalism: A Governmentality Approach. *Resilience. International Policies, Practices and Discourses* 1(1): 38–52.
Kaufmann M (2013) Emergent Self-Organisation in Emergencies: Resilience Rationales in Interconnected Societies. *Resilience: International Policies, Practices and Discourses* 1(1): 53–68.
Kitchin R (1998) *Cyberspace. The World in the Wires*. Chichester, Sussex: Wiley.
Lakoff G, Johnson M (1980) *Metaphors We Live By*. Chicago: University of Chicago Press.
Lakoff G, Johnson M (1999) *Philosophy in the Flesh: The Embodied Mind and Its Challenge to Western Thought*. New York: Basic Books.
Luhmann N (1984) *Soziale Systeme. Grundriss einer allgemeinen Theorie*. Frankfurt am Main: Suhrkamp.
Malecki EJ (2002) The Economic Geography of the Internet's Infrastructure. *Economic Geography* 78(4): 399–424.
Malpas J (2012) Putting Space in Place: Philosophical Topography and Relational Geography. *Environment and Planning D: Society and Space* 30(2): 226–242.
Massey D (1994) *A Global Sense of Place*. In: Massey D (ed.) *Space, Place and Gender*. Minneapolis, MN: University of Minnesota Press. 146–156.
Massey D (2011) A Counterhegemonic Relationality of Place. In: Ward K, McCann E (eds) *Globalization and Community. Mobile Urbanism: Cities and Policymaking in the Global Age*. Minneapolis, MN: University of Minnesota Press. 1–14.
Murdoch J (2006) *Post-structuralist Geography – A Guide to Relational Space*. London: Sage Publications.

Nash C (2000) Performativity in Practice: Some Recent Work in Cultural Geography. *Progress in Human Geography* 24(4): 653–664.

Reid J (2012) The Disastrous and Politically Debased Subject of Resilience. *Development Dialogue* 58: 67–79.

Roylance D (2001) *Stress-Strain Curves*. Available at: http://ocw.mit.edu/courses/materials-science-and-engineering/3-11-mechanics-of-materials-fall-1999/modules/ss.pdf (accessed 15 July 2016).

Smithers J, Smit B (1997) Human Adaptation to Climatic Variability and Change. *Global Environmental Change* 7(2): 129–146.

Stalder F (2006) *Manuel Castells and the Theory of the Network Society*. Cambridge: Polity Press.

UK Cabinet Office (2013) *Improving the UK's Ability to Absorb, Respond to and Recover from Emergencies*. London. Available at: www.gov.uk/government/policies/improving-the-uks-ability-to-absorb-respond-to-and-recover-from-emergencies (accessed 15 July 2016).

Walker B, Carpenter S, Anderies J, Abel N, Cumming G, Janssen MA, Lebel L, Norberg J, Peterson GD, Pritchard R (2002) Resilience Management in Social-Ecological Systems: A Working Hypothesis for a Participatory Approach. *Conservation Ecology* 6(1): Article 14. Available at: ecologyandsociety.org/vol. 6/iss1/art14/print.pdf (accessed 15 July 2016).

Wakeford N (1999) Gender and the Landscapes of Computing in an Internet Café. In: Crang M, Crang, P, May J (eds) *Virtual Geographies: Bodies, Spaces and Relations*. London: Routledge.

Ward K, McCann E (2011) Conclusion: Cities Assembled. Space, Neoliberalization, (Re)erritorialization, and Comparison. In: Ward K, McCann E (eds) *Globalization and Community. Mobile Urbanism: Cities and Policymaking in the Global Age*. Minneapolis, MN: University of Minnesota Press. 167–184.

Wise JM (2005) Assemblage. In: Stivale CJ (ed.) *Gilles Deleuze: Key Concepts*. Durham, UK: Acumen Publishing. 77–87.

Zebrowski C (2009) Governing the Network Society: A Biopolitical Critique of Resilience. *Political Perspectives* 3(1): 1–44.

Zook MA (2005) *The Geography of the Internet Industry: Venture Capital, Dot-coms, and Local Knowledge*. Hoboken, NJ: Blackwell.

Zook MA (2006) The Geographies of the Internet. *Annual Review of Information Science and Technology* 40: 53–78.

6 Resilience and affect

The idea of resilience changes the very core of security: security no longer means being protected, but with resilience it becomes an activity of dealing with harm. This responsibility of dealing with harm lies within the self-organized subject. This is not only visible in the way in which Internet security policies, such as those of ENISA discussed in Chapter 5, are redefining the very core of security through *self x* and protocol. But on a more overarching level, the self-organization of populations that are affected by emergencies is integral to resilience programs at large, which has a strong conceptual influence on security governance. This is why the idea of self-organization deserves a closer look. The security exercise is a site where self-organization is trained and where any action and reaction takes place in the name of creating security. As a key practice of building resilient subjects, the exercise is an ideal example to study how security is acted out. The cyber-exercise, in particular, is a rich and characteristic site because its scenario is based on the archetypical imaginary of the complex emergency. The cyber-attack inspires abundant fictions of domino effects and infrastructure breakdown that need to be addressed through new emergency management strategies (Exercise field notes 2011). In this chapter, which explores another dimension of resilience as a form of governing the Internet, a German cyber-exercise case study will provide insights into the imaginaries of insecurity in an interconnected world and make observable the dynamics of acting-out security. The case study will be reflected upon using Spinozist affect theory – which understands affect as the onset for action – to further conceptualize self-organization and the different forms of action that come about in emergency response.

Security as an activity

Emergencies happen anywhere, anytime, across different sectors and domains – at least that is one conclusion that Adey *et al.* draw from the proliferation of the term and its "excessive exactness" (2015: 6). This excess does not necessarily signify a broadening of a "state of exception," as works building on Agamben have suggested (cf. Agamben 2005; Fassin and Pandolfi 2010). Rather, it entails that emergencies have become distributed, integrated into the mundane, bureaucratic and quotidian (Adey *et al.* 2015: 8ff.). The inseparability of emergencies from the "promise that some form of action can make a difference to the emerging event" (ibid.: 5), and the affect of emergency – urgency – determine the response to emergencies. This combination of *urgency* and *faith in action* also makes the emergency a site of power, where a dynamic interplay of affect and action unfolds. This is why Adey *et al.* suggest that researchers further investigate: "What alternatives to forms of power open up in emergency, how are forms of power contested, negotiated and reworked and how do new ways of being and living happen in emergency settings?" (ibid.: 15).

This chapter takes this question as a vantage point to explore how resilience – the capacity to self-organize, to act out security and adapt to disruption – gained prominence as a technique of governing emergencies. Adey *et al.*'s appeal pushes us to investigate how resilience reworks power, how it recasts security and life itself as a form of living through emergencies and of being in-formation. In a complex and uncertain world, where life-threatening events are no longer considered preventable, resilience is adopted into security governance. It provides for a reaction to emergencies. The epistemology of resilience thus reflects a shift in security practices, which changes the focus from security-as-protection toward an active form of security, which is established as a response to harm and insecurity (Kaufmann 2013). As a new strategy for security governance, resilience places both the structural insecurity and the responsibility to react and act out security within the resilient subject. In view of that, the chapter develops the argument that resilience instills specific power dynamics that are closely linked to the affectivity of the emergency: resilience relies upon the subject's capacity to be affected by insecurity and its power to respond to this urgency with action.

The involvement of citizens in security practices is nothing new. However, while risk practices see the role of the citizen to perform "generalized borderwalks" (Vaughan-Williams 2008: 64) and to report suspicious behavior for the sake of prevention, resilience practices involve the citizen as a key actor in emergency response (Dunn Cavelty *et al.* 2015). This trend has harvested both praise and criticism. Supporters emphasize the way in which resilience speaks to the empowerment of subjects and helps them to "bounce back better" (e.g., UNISDR 2010). Critics refer to the way in which the outsourcing of security tasks and the responsibilization of the threatened subject becomes an expression of neoliberal governance (Reid 2012; Joseph 2013). According to the latter, the subject itself is programmed to react in a fashion that internalizes such neoliberal values (Grove 2014): the subject is trained through specific resilience practices, such as exercises, which seek to conduct the conduct of emergency populations (Zebrowski 2009; cf. Duffield 2012). This eventually instantiates active subjects, which do, however, act in an automated fashion (Aradau 2010) and are robbed of their agency because they are merely subjects molded by resilience programs (Grove 2014; Howell 2014; Oels and Methmann 2015).

As significant as these insights are, there have been calls to investigate the pluralities of resilience (Brassett *et al.* 2013; Dunn Cavelty *et al.* 2015). Asking whether the resilient subject is only ever programmed or an instance of dominating and depoliticizing power, this chapter offers a closer, empirical look at how the supposed self-organization occurs. Even though resilience locates the responsibility to act out security within the subject, thus invoking specific bodily states to secure life, the focus on the physical and affect have only lately entered the critical discussions on resilience (Adey and Anderson 2012; Grove 2014). In addition to that, only few authors challenge the criticism that resilience creates only trained forms of self-organization (with exception cf. Adey and Anderson 2012; Schmidt 2014). This chapter suggests that an empirical examination of the way in which resilience is acted out, in combination with affect theory, provides valuable insights into how resilient action can be conceptualized.

This chapter draws upon the case study of a German cyber-security exercise to develop this argument. The cyber-attack is easily framed as the archetype of the complex emergency, because disruption tends to cascade in an unpredictable fashion (BBK Exercise PowerPoint, slide 8). The status of the cyber-attack as the prototype of the complex emergency is even more emphasized by the gravity of dis-connectivity: modern life, so Simon and de Goede argue, "is considered to be impossible or valueless if disconnected" (2015: 80). The fact that connectivity is indispensable for society, however, meets the challenge of cyber-security, which "directs itself at a milieu considered unmappable in its entirety and unknowable in its essence" (ibid.: 89). As a result of limited options for prevention, so the narrative goes, effort needs to be spent on strengthening response. Exercising represents here one of the main instruments to train resilience. While Simon and de Goede study the cyber-security exercise as an instance of "bureaucratic vitalism" (2015), where the entrainment of open-ended responsiveness as an instance of "becoming ... movement ... action" (Lash 2006: 323; Simon and de Goede 2015: 82) is locked to the bureaucratic creation of rather banal practices, this chapter uses the same setting to take a closer look at the affective making of the active, resilient subject. It examines the way in which emergency exercises produce different powers of acting. The chapter explores in what way affective life is part of dealing with emergencies and how resilience relates to the subject's capacity to act (McCormack 2015; Adey *et al.* 2015). It unveils resilience as an affective technique of governing emergencies that imbues life with a sense of "urgency that demands response" (McCormack 2015: 143). But how did resilience as an active form of establishing security gain prominence in the first place? The answer, again, lies in the rise of the emergency paradigm, the way in which the powerful imaginary of radical uncertainty has gained influence in security governance.

The narrative of the complex emergency features heavily in today's security and safety politics (O'Malley 2009; Duffield 2012; Simon and de Goede 2015). With the shift from modernism to postmodernism, the emergency is no longer considered external to the societal system – an event to be stopped through prediction and planning, but it has been reconceptualized as endemic to society (Duffield 2012). By now, the emergency is understood to be a part of the interwoven society: it rises from connectedness and grows in urgency through the idea of nonlinear cascade. This language is well reflected in, but not reduced to the cyber-discourse (cf. ENISA 2011b). Under conditions of complexity, insecurity can only be minimized, but it is never removed (Reid 2012; Chandler 2014).

This persistence of insecurity and the failure to secure in postmodern societies has inspired research on the conceptualization of security failure. Failure can be understood as an opening for resistance, as suggested by Stern (2006). She argues that the failure of narrating insecuring identities can be used as space for contestation (201f.):

> a subject is too large, excessive, messy, fluid, changing, contradictory and unbounded to be adequately or fully represented or therewith secured. It is always "becoming," and therefore cannot be pinned down in a single representation.

Failure, here, gives space for rethinking identities. In a similar vein, Howell sees that the failure of one security technique can evoke new strategies of governing issues at stake – in her case, this concerns the mental health of Iraqis in the context of war and liberation (2010). Anderson also conceptualizes failure as something that "makes move" and inspires a "politics of becoming" (Anderson 2006: 740). Parallel to the emergence of critical research on the generative nature of failure, that same insight on the productivity of failure is also being fashioned into concrete practices of governing emergencies. In fact, the concept of resilience strategically foresees the productive engagement of failure, where "failure becomes part of the story about security learning and improvements in capability" (Heath-Kelly 2015: 69). Conceptually, resilience claims that "security can be furthered through the failure to secure" (ibid.: 75), as emergencies "are turned into productive positives" (ibid.: 74). A number of scholars see this productivity of failure claimed by resilience as embedded in neoliberal government that has the circulatory functions of the polity as its aim (Walker and Cooper 2011; Joseph 2013; Oels and Methmann 2015). Within a politics of resilience, the emergency is thus not only accepted as inevitable, but it is framed as opportunity to develop foresight, enterprise, self-management and responsibility (O'Malley 2009). As a result, security is now an act of dealing with security failure, which necessitates an increased involvement of engaged and active citizens (cf. Brasset *et al.* 2013; Kaufmann 2013).

In fact, the mobilization of the active subject within security governance has been discussed on a general level, for example in terms of techniques of voice and consultation (Dean 2010). In particular, the active subject has been deployed as a key strategy for the prevention of emergencies, for example, in the shape of the citizen-detective, the "vigilant subject constantly on the look-out for suspicious behaviour" (Vaughan-Williams 2008: 77). However, within the context of unpredictable disruption, the active citizen is recast through the lens of resilience, the adaptation to disruption and the attempt to render security failure productive. Within the past decade, the concept of resilience has become central to emergency management in the UK (e.g., Challen *et al.* 2010), Australia (e.g., Australian Government 2011), the US (e.g., US Department of Homeland Security 2013), but also in the European Union (e.g., European Commission 2010), where it takes a prominent position in the management of cyber-emergencies (ENISA 2011a,b). Even though definitions of resilience vary across domains, all of them emphasize the capacity of an individual or system to deal with the experience of emergency in a self-organized fashion.

While Bourbeau's review of resilience literature finds that most contributions identify and promote resilience as a positive characteristic (Bourbeau 2013), the critical discourse perceives of resilience as the state's withdrawal from the difficult task of protection (Duffield 2012; Evans and Reid 2014; Bourbeau 2015), which would require the management and prevention of the causes of insecurity (cf. Agamben 2014). With resilience, the responsibility to re-establish security after disaster struck is now outsourced to the citizen and this responsibility is framed as an opportunity to develop into a strong, resilient subject (Reid 2012; Kaufmann 2013). Within this setup, however, the state never withdraws completely. Claiming that self-organization is not necessarily an organic development, but the result of strategic institutionalization, Malcolm discusses how the citizen is encouraged by the state to play an active role in emergency management (2013). In fact, he points to a "bargain" that is struck between the citizen, who acquires extra knowledge and learns to use local resources, and the state, that can count on the citizens' engagement (Malcolm 2013: 319). Rogers, however, distinguishes between positive engagement tactics of empowerment and participatory decision-making, and negative tactics of responsibilization without granting the citizen access to decision-making (2013). In that vein, the state is also found to exercise distributed forms of power over the subject (Lentzos and Rose 2009). These distributed forms of power are less visible precisely because they appear in the shape of training modules (Grove 2014) or psychological instructions (Howell 2014).

Grove summarizes the entirety of these governmental practices as part of a *resilience program*: resilience is being mediated through affective policies and immunizes the subject in a way that does not pose threats to hierarchy and neoliberal order (2014). While he suggests to increase the focus on those techniques that "manipulate affective relations in ways that produce agential subjects" (ibid.: 245), he also asks whether resilience actually is "something to be technocratically managed, an object of disaster management's liberal will to truth [...] or can it be allowed to flourish in whatever direction it may take?" (ibid.: 253). Schmidt takes this latter impulse further by emphasizing the positive and pragmatist agenda of resilience through self-referential learning processes – a self-governance that exceeds neoliberal logics (2014: 15f.) and recasts resilience as a resource for democratic empowerment (ibid.: 6). Learning would then be a "'routine of spontaneity'. That is, contingency and resilience can unblock institutional stalemates and unleash unknown human potentialities" (ibid.: 7). That being said, however, resilience still remains the central aim of governmental security practices that render failure productive.

One prominent practice of training citizens is the security exercise. As a governmental tool, it seeks to create active citizens by affectively modulating their relationship to emergency (Aradau 2010; Anderson and Adey 2011; Aradau and van Munster 2012). In studying exercises Anderson and Adey find it is through affect that threats impress upon bodies, whether that is in a vague atmosphere of unease or in a punctual moment of heightened apprehension – threat being the future quasicause for an affective change in the present that is use to legitimise action.

(2011: 1096)

Exercises do not just legitimize action, they are also said to break down "the potentially catastrophic event into manageable segments" (Aradau and van Munster 2012: 236). The guiding motivation for exercising is that complex situations can only be understood when acted out and by juxtaposing data, technologies, objects and people in such an enactment (Collier 2008). Within this setup, matter, for example, also inspires affective relations and becomes part of the making of active subjects (Adey and Anderson 2012; Dewsbury *et al.* 2002). It is through this carefully organized rehearsal that specific behaviors are imprinted upon the body (Aradau and van Munster 2012).

Much in line with the critical assessments of resilience, exercises have been discussed as a governmental technique that affectively molds the subject to respond in a specific way – to the extent that the subject "takes on automaton-like qualities" (Aradau 2010: 5). While this entrainment of disciplinary power through ritual play constitutes one criticism, Adey and Anderson draw our attention, again, to failure and the way in which the exercise collects more than the singular logic of successful training. Focusing on affective instances of doubt, uncertainty, the excessive, and the contingent, they ask: "What's more, where is exercise play as creative and surprising or unpredictable and contingent?" (2012: 103). In confronting the idea of routine with the excess material of the exercise, they "complicate the overdetermining assumptions that power and technique are successful, and remind ourselves, as Foucault (1977) did, that practices of power are commonly frustrated, escaped and clearly uncertain" (Adey and Anderson 2012: 104).

If we understand resilience as a governmental technique that affectively forges active and self-organized citizens, and if one instance of training citizens is the exercise, some questions follow from the positions presented above: Do governments succeed in programming and "immunizing the subject" (Grove 2014), making it act in an automated fashion (Aradau 2010)? Can these practices unblock unexpected agency or be paralleled by creativity and spontaneity, all of which eventually escape such programs (Anderson and Adey 2011; Rogers 2013; Schmidt 2014)? And can such programs produce unintended effects and frustrations that do not speak to resilience altogether (Foucault 1977)?

The concept of affect can help to understand and theorize the different dynamics that are at play during exercises. As we have seen, affect plays a role in resilience studies, but mainly as an instrument of power over the resilient subject (Grove 2014). Yet, affect, so this chapter argues, provides a more fine-grained conceptualization of the power dynamics that take part in the making of the active, resilient subject.

From affect to action

Resilience is a governmental program that affectively modulates populations' relationship to emergencies. The aim of such programs is to open up populations to the unexpected, envisaging that affects of urgency and emergency eventually translate into action. At the same time, does affect provide a framework through which self-organization and the interplay of action and re-action can be theorized?

Affect itself is a contested term and notoriously difficult to define. It is deployed "in divergent ways across different literatures" (Anderson 2006: 734), where it is often used interchangeably with concepts such as mood, the intense, feelings, or emotion (ibid.). Massumi, one of the most prominent figures in the affect discourse, states that "Affect is the whole world" (2002b: 43) and Deleuze, who provided an early reading of Spinoza's writings on affect, resists a clear conceptualization, using affect instead to proliferate theory (cf. Cole 2009). Yet there are recurring elements in the different writings on affect, which allow us to theorize body knowledge, the logics of becoming, as well as the relationship between action and re-action, all of which take a central role in the politics and governmental practices of resilience. In particular, this chapter follows Spinozist writings on affect, drawing largely on Massumi's work (1995, 2002a, 2002b) in describing how affect comes into being, what it is and what it sets into motion. Broadly speaking, affect is understood as the capacity of the body to effectuate change: it is a pre-personal and pre-conscious incitement, a capacity of being stimulated to act; it is emergent and constitutive of the body. In order to appreciate this coarse definition in full, some of affect's core characteristics need to be presented in more detail.

Affect emerges at the moment of the encounter (Deleuze and Deleuze 1978). It may be the encounter between different individuals, as well as between individuals and a situation or material environment (Seyfert 2012). Massumi characterizes this encounter as "a state of suspense, potentially of disruption. It's like a temporal sink, a hole in time [...] it is filled with motion, vibratory motion, resonation" (1995: 86). At this moment of the encounter subjects are in a receiving state. They receive new information. At the same time, they are in motion, but they have not yet begun to re-act. For now, they are affected. But what is affect exactly? And how do affect and action relate to each other?

Affect is a capacity, not property of the body. It is what a body may be able to do (Massumi 1995; Deleuze 1988), and describes a potentiality for "self-organization in being in-formational" (Clough 2008: 1). As such, affect is the pre-text for action and autonomous bodily response (ibid.). Clough continues to describe affect as anticipation and disposition (2008: 5) that propels and compels activation (2009: 49). Baruch Spinoza, whose writings on human and non-human bodies are invoked as the origins of affect studies, relates this affective capability directly to the power of acting, which also sits at the core of resilience: "By affect [affectum] I understand affections [affectiones] of the body by which the body's power [potentia] of acting is increased or diminished, aided or restrained" (Spinoza 2002: 278, E3 def. 3).

As such, affect is constitutive of the body (Geroult 1968; Ruddick 2010; Seyfert 2012), but is not a property of the individual. In fact, it is a pre-personal (Clough 2008: 1, 2009: 48) and inter-corporeal (Seyfert 2012: 36) capacity that oscillates between "two sides of the same dynamic shift" (Massumi 2002a: 212): it describes not only the capacity of being affected, but also of affecting (Clough 2009: 48; Seyfert 2012: 34), which is why affect is radically relational and never fully self-contained or self-present. It can apply to myriad subjects, human and non-human, all of which have the ability to affect and be affected – and transformed in their capacity to act. The empirical example below will trace exactly this dynamic back-and-forth of affecting and being affected during an emergency exercise situation. Affect here appears as urgency and as a sense of emergency that mediates the participant's relationship to insecurity: it activates the physical state of suspense and the onset for re-/action.

Affect as the capacity to act is furthermore emergent in nature (cf. Clough 2008: 3; Guyau 1887, in Seyfert 2012) and it inspires continuous variation (Deleuze 1988: 49), while it can vary according to cultural and historical difference (Seyfert 2012: 31). It describes the "opening of the body to its indeterminacy" (Clough 2008: 3) and its implicit potential (2008, 2009: 48). The body has "not yet become," which is why the study of affect is concerned with a politics of becoming (Anderson 2006). Affect is not yet a coherent, linear, narrated set of emotions.

In fact, a variety of authors distinguish between affect, feeling and emotion. While feelings act as the assessment of affect (Anderson 2006), emotions are always already a qualified affect, linear, personal, cognitivized: "the qualification of an emotion is quite often, in other contexts, itself a narrative element that moves the action ahead" (Massumi 1995: 86). As opposed to affect emotions are "semantically and semiotically formed progressions" (Massumi 2002b: 28). Affect thus mobilizes emotion, but it is not emotion (Ruddick 2010: 22). Clough describes how affect moves through feeling and eventually ends up with "subjectively felt states of emotion" (Clough 2008: 1; cf. Anderson 2006: 737). This understanding of affect as pre-emotion is different from scholars who study affect as emotions located in the individual body (as argued by Ahmed 2004 and other scholars of the Sociology of Emotions). Spinozist scholars instead argue that affect is pre-cognitive (Clough 2008: 3), challenging "notions of will, causality and possibility" (MacCormack 2004: 182). It is what Massumi would call the autonomy of affect: it works without being consciously invoked and it is unclear in which direction it will lead (1995). Ruddick argues that – while affect itself is the capacity of the body to act – it is the interplay of affect and reason that determines the actual acting (2010: 38, quoting Deleuze 1988: 90).

This emergence of action expresses the specific temporality of affect, especially when looked at in the context of resilience and emergency exercises. Here, "affect draws the future into the present as indeterminate state of activation, what can become constant alertness" (Clough 2009: 49). Affects of alertness and fear, as extensively studied by Massumi (1993, 2005), or, respectively, hope (Anderson 2006), tie the future to the present. In the same way, urgency and a sense of emergency invoked at resilience exercises appeal to both the uncertain future and potentially even disruptive past, through which they affectively form self-organized, alert subjects in the present. While writing about related security practices of pre-emption Clough (2009) and Ong (2006) find that affect induces "self-animation" and "self-government" so that populations can "optimize choices efficiency and competitiveness in turbulent (...) conditions" (Ong 2006: 6). Ruddick also finds that affect describes a tendency to self-preserve (2010: 35). This chapter argues that it is precisely because affect is about the instigation of action and acting that it serves as a theoretical framework to understand the activist politics of becoming and self-government that resilience inspires. Affect is the continual flux and the continuous constitution and reconstitution of the active subject (Seyfert 2012: 30ff.), which describes the power dynamics at play in the formation of active, resilient subjects, as happens, for example, at the exercise.

Studying affect, studying action

The analysis of affect and action at the cyber-exercise required some preparation with regards to both methodology and content. A few illustrative facts can provide an insight into the scene of the exercise, its participants and the physical setting. The exercise was conducted by the German Federal Office of Civil Protection and Disaster Assistance (German acronym: BBK). The BBK was established in 2004 and is a central organ in Germany's Ministry of the Interior. Its mandate is to "ensure the safety of the population" (BBK Homepage). It combines different functions of civil protection, emergency planning and critical infrastructure protection, amongst which one task is to enhance the "citizens' ability to help themselves" (BBK Homepage). As part of their mandate, the BBK runs nationwide exercises, which take place in a two-year cycle, as they need extensive preparation. In general, several federal states exercise simultaneously and the whole exercise is documented in a nationwide computer-based system, a program into which the participants enter any exercise moves. These specific exercises are enshrined in §14 of the German Civil Protection and Disaster Assistance law (BBK LÜKEX Leaflet). They include participants ranging from decision-makers in central governmental institutions to private business owners, members of the emergency services, psychologists and the average citizen.

Following the cyber-exercise in its entirety consisted of participatory observation at the three-day exercise and attendance of preparatory meetings. It also included the study of: leaflets, brochures and other supplementary documents as well as several hundred pages of the exercise plan, which set out all concrete steps of the exercising procedure. The contents of the exercise as such were confidential, which is why the amount of sources quoted in this chapter is small. At the three-day exercise, access to the site was closed to the public. As part of this study I did, however, obtain permission to attend all meetings and to conduct interviews within the different exercise groups. There were groups representing the general population, the finance and insurance sector, the institutions of the different federal states, the political administration, media institutions, and the overall steering committee. These groups met physically in dedicated locations, where they discussed their moves and where the interviews took place. All interviews were conducted in German and translated into English. In the translation, special attention was paid to diction, metaphors and expressions, in order to keep the translation as close to the original quote as possible. Even though I was one of a few researchers allowed at the site, my presence was not perceived as an interruption. While the interviewees were presented to me as experts, they were surprisingly open when they reflected about their experience of emergency, the different encounters at the site and their abilities and inabilities to react. What did determine the findings of the interviews, however, was the time and situational pressure under which the interviews had to be conducted.

Since the participants acted within a given scenario and registered their acts in a computer system, which is even removed from the physicality of acting, one could ask whether the exercise is only a lab in which situations, affects and actions are artificially produced. In many ways, exercises are not like real situations, but designed to test scenarios, as well as harvest and analyze reactions (BBK Leitfaden 2011: 12f.). First, however, the exercise situation is supposed to imitate reality, cause realistic problems and real reactions. In order to achieve that, exercise managers bring together stakeholders and participants whose actions would also be required in real emergency situations. Additionally, probabilities of past incidents (ibid.: 12) and data from real cases is integrated into the scenario to make it as realistic as possible (ibid.: 9). Assessing what kind of incident would create the biggest impact for a society is influential in the selection of a scenario (ibid.: 9). Yet it is constantly insured that the scenario does not get too apocalyptic and thus unrealistic (ibid.: 18; BBK Exercise PowerPoint, slide 6). Second, and more importantly, this chapter argues that despite the various degrees of removal from an actual emergency situation, the exercising subject is still affected by the exercise situation. This situation, even though bureaucratically managed (Simon and de Goede 2015), is real, to the extent that it is part of Germany's agenda setting for emergency management. The exercising subject acts and interacts with other individuals in the name of security. Here, pressures are taken seriously, not least because one of the intentions of conducting an exercise is to detect and prepare for potential problems in a real emergency situation.

In addition, the exercise did produce its own affectivity. During the cyber-exercise, participants could receive information at any time, experience pressure from a specific party of the exercise, they could be interrupted in their strategic move, insert several reactions at once, lose overview over the current developments or feel relief when a favorable development took place. Irregular interruptions were caused by media releases, which confronted the participants with a new situation. Affective encounters took place between the participants and the physicality of the setting. This included amongst other things fast-moving bodies, concentrated typing, intensive discussions, constant streams of information on TV screens and a clear presence of technical infrastructure. The exercise created not only technical and organizational knowledge, but also body knowledge through the experience of pre-individual affect and individual acting. Security exercises, in fact, intend to create body knowledge within the subject in the context of security politics. As such, the exercise is not limited to the artificiality of a lab situation, but it is a situation with its own affective setup. Anderson and Adey even argue that these affects in fact exceed the exercise situation (2011).

A more challenging aspect of studying affect is that its emergent character makes it difficult to pinpoint the appearance of affect empirically. It is admittedly difficult to uphold the theoretical distinction between emotions and affect in practice. Where does affect begin and at what point may it become emotion? And how to investigate something that is pre-conscious? This challenge explains why many contributions in affect studies are theoretical. Others are based on interviews (cf. Anderson 2006; Anderson and Adey 2011), despite the fact that affect first and foremost concerns bodily, pre-narrativizable experience. Precisely because affect exceeds cognitive closure, it is hard to study. Narration is only a substraction, mediated, smooth and linear, it is already analyzed and reduced in complexity (Clough 2008: 3). The scholarly community, however, produces narrated outputs of empirical studies of affect, whether in test results or field notes that describe atmospheres and physical reactions, or academic papers. Meaning that, if narration were to eradicate affect completely, one would also have to ask how it is possible to write about affect. Written scholarly outputs on empirical affect studies include, for example, Hansen, who explored how digital information connects to the affective register (2003). Stäheli has conducted studies of affect at the stock market (2004), Grusin explored the relationship between affect, security and news media (2004) and Adey researched the affectivity of aerial life (2010) – to name just a few. Interviews are one particular way of trying to transfer the study of affect from the programmatic to the empirical realm. This is why this case study is based on both participant observation and interviews for the study of affect. Why and how, then, can interviews contribute to the study of affect?

Even though affect is always more than what can be gained from narration, affect can still be appropriated through language. Some scholars talk about the affect of language (Cole 2009) and language as one of many affective interaction modi (Seyfert 2012: 35). As a modus of interaction, affect can be understood as that which connects the world with a body and vice versa, which is maybe also why Deleuze invites us to use affect to proliferate theory (1988). Discourse, as something that can form subjects and that subjects are part of, must be taken seriously as one of many affective interaction modi. This means that narration may provide a starting point for an investigation of affect, but it can never fully represent the totality of affect. Since affect is always "something to come" (Massumi 2002a: 215; cf. Anderson 2006), analysts need to find the moments where affect "leaks into the actual" (Massumi 2002b: 43; cf. Anderson 2006). Narrations of affective encounters and the experience of pressure, anger, helplessness, fear and relief can thus be used as a starting point for a reverse analysis:

what do these linearized narratives about emotions tell us about affective encounters? If language is that which connects desire with reason (Cole 2009: 2), then the cognitive closure of affect is not only happening through narration, but narrations reveal qualified affects, which can be used as the onset for further investigation (Massumi 2002b; Anderson 2006; Clough 2008). Furthermore, affects may be talked about without being made explicit, sometimes even without the interviewee noticing, for example, by using symbols, by narrating affective experiences or performing non-intentional communication. All of these components of an interview can give insights into the states and capacities of interviewees' bodies and that which incited individuals to perform specific acts (Clough 2009: 49). A careful analysis needs to reflect on such narratives and interview components vis-à-vis the cognitive urge to create linearity and claim intentionality (cf. Athanasiou *et al*. 2008: 10–11). Affect scholars need to account for the tension between narration and affect, both when it comes to methodological choice and when eventually writing about affect. For a more holistic methodology, the study of affect also needs to take account of non-verbal reactions, physical states, enactments and the unsaid through participant observation.

Within the context of the cyber-exercise, it was possible to observe moments of the encounter and the effects they produced. Exercise participants would be exposed to new pieces of information in dedicated meetings at particular times during the day, but also throughout the whole exercise on a smaller scale. At these points, participants would literally be in a receiving state, and experience, if not emergency, then at least urgency and the need to react. It was these moments of encountering new information, people, material, circumstances, in which affect appeared and their power of re-acting and acting was constituted. Part of this affectivity are also pictures and sounds: videos, moving images of emergency, and the sound of alarms that typically signify and generate an urge to react but the body has not begun to act. From observation alone, however, it was not always possible to tell the difference between affect and emotion. This is why it was necessary to add interviews with group leaders to the design, which gave the participants the possibility to reflect and talk about their moments of encounter with emergency. The following part will now turn to affect in action.

Affect in action: insights from a cyber-security exercise

Any exercise begins with the process of setting the stage, one part of which is the exercising rationale. The BBK's rationale for exercising is the complex emergency (BBK Leitfaden 2011: 3), the archetype of which is the scenario of the cyber-attack. Cyber-scenarios combine infrastructure breakdown with cascading failure, which again create affiliated problems, such as societal unrest. Cyber-attacks also lend themselves to a particular framing of terrorism. While the terrorist here is a fusion of the angry, disillusioned (non-)citizen and the remotely operating computer expert, presented as enigmatical and unknown, the use of terms such as cyberspace and virtuality equally signify obscurity, all of which points to the limited knowledge available to prevent such emergencies. Already the rhetoric of the scenario creates affects of urgency. The language of fire emergencies, for example, which employs metaphors such as vertical growth, accumulation and exhaustion (Serres 2000: 64), is well reflected in the diction of the cyber-emergencies that refer to interconnectivity, unidentified vulnerabilities and cascade. These characteristics in fact constitute the BBK's main justification for a cyber-security exercise: they refer amongst other things to the problem of "target-oriented attacks on vulnerabilities" and related "domino-effects" (BBK Exercise PowerPoint, slides 5 and 8). Since the writing of the scenario is itself a linear technique that synchronizes moves, the exercise needed careful planning to insure capture of the nonlinear character of such an incident without being overwhelming. Similar to what Simon and de Goede observe, this interplay is reached through diverse techniques of "disciplining imagination" (2015: 98), by means of not quite realistic newsflashes or particularly designed exercise templates (ibid.: 97f.). The following paragraphs draw attention to the way in which affect works in such a bureaucratic-vitalist setting and how the dynamic powers of acting come into play.

During the acting-out of the scenario, the overall atmosphere developed from a professional relaxedness and excitement toward moments of pressure, which were at times filled with pounding concentration and discussion, but also involved anger, exhaustion or phases of boredom. The atmosphere finally reached a form of dissatisfied catharsis, when the source of the cyber-attack was presented in the form of a joke – and not as a realistic plot. While this describes a typical trajectory of physical states during exercises (cf. Anderson and Adey 2011), this particular exercise also featured a central and equally typical affect that could be best described as urgency (cf. Massumi 1995; Seyfert 2012). In most cases, it was the onset for action and response. Like any affect, urgency emerges at the moment of the encounter. Three kinds of encounter were particularly prominent sources of this affect: the encounter with new information in media releases; the encounter with technical failure; and the encounter between people. The analytical value of these three encounters is high, since they seem to stand out as sources of affect in many exercise situations. Let's take a brief look at these sources of affect.

According to the exercise leadership, some of which also participated in the exercise (i1),[1] media are an important source of affect. They shape the emergency situation. Not only was a TV report the starting point for the whole exercise, but the various fictitious reports and newspaper articles constantly confronted the participants with new information that affected their exercise situation directly. While most media reports featured visuals of disruption, it was the language that was also an important source of creating pressure. The first media report already deployed vocabulary such as "helpless," "fatal," "massive," "overburdened," "previously unknown intensity" and "highest alert" (BBK LÜKEX Exercise TV). Later reports heightened the level of intensity by choosing expressions such as "parents are rioting," "nothing works," "civilians feel deceived," "attack on vitally important infrastructures," "impossible to capture in its entirety" (BBK LÜKEX Exercise Press; BBK LÜKEX Exercise Social Media; BBK LÜKEX Exercise TV). This choice of language signifies that while the media were, in fact, intended to create affect, they were designed to evoke reactions. Throughout the exercise, the media created a sense of emergency for all participants, simply by listing all the vital functions that seemed to be disrupted, and by expressing collective moments of helplessness and anger. More could be said about the mechanisms with which media create affect and the way in which they mediate emergency (cf. Grusin 2004). For this analysis, it is important to point out that their main role was to distribute new information and to create urgency with the objective to evoke reactions by both participants and organizers.

Another related source of affect was the encounter with the idea of technical failure that would cascade through an entire society. In order to evoke this affect, the exercise didn't even need to produce an actual encounter with technical failure. The mere imagination and the process of envisioning technical failure already produced a sense of emergency. A vast number of narratives contributed to this imagination. Almost all interviewed participants referred to the elusive nature of the disruptive domino effect within infrastructures, which would, however, create concrete and tangible situations. Most participants focused on the concrete impacts in their everyday life, concerning public transport, banking systems, flight traffic, food chains, water and energy flows, communication channels. Other impacts were described more concretely: students who could not register for their exams, welfare recipients without welfare, pensioners without a pension, shoppers without the possibility to pay. One participant said: "then you suddenly have a totally different problem, which has nothing to do with bits and bytes, but with people" (i1). It would not be the disastrous event, but the plurality of small crises that would lead to an emergency within society. These narratives of technological failure had concrete effects on the participants, which is why the information received through the exercising software or through exercising media created an atmosphere of urgency.

Affect also arose from the encounter between people. While discussing newly received information, the different groups would experience the need to respond. Potential reactions would range from individual responses to something social and more complex, such as consensus-building and the process of developing the next collective move. All of these reactions were preceded by a complex interplay of affecting and being affected. Similar moments occurred on the administrative level, where members of the steering committee would also be confronted with new developments. The regular briefing and review meetings were the main moment of the encounter between the steering committee members. They were marked by a high intensity and urgency. These encounters were imbued by the need to act and decide upon the development of the exercise, which was then translated into concrete actions and cause-and-effect narratives.

These three moments of encounter – defined by urgency – spurred the dynamic interplay of affect and acting at the emergency exercise. In sum, the exercise itself evoked manifold instances of affecting and being affected, of acting and reacting. This interplay was well captured in the words of a media group member, who used the image of "pingpong" (i3). According to him, any exercise situation would be characterized by overarching patterns of affecting and being affected, of acting and causing reaction. Each party in the exercise would receive information and would be affected, but they also would influence this situation by reacting, by applying pressure and by affecting others. This interplay, this constant back and forth, he said, would mainly take place between the steering group and the participants. Within this situation of pingpong or "seesaw," as another participant called it (i4), time pressure and the complexity of the emergency situation itself were frequently mentioned as sources of urgency for everyone. Since the idea of pingpong offers a simplified, yet comprehensible structure to disentangle the complex interplay of affects and actions at work during the exercise, the following paragraphs deploy this image to describe some of the most prominent dynamics.

Ping

To begin with, let's consider the way in which the steering committee of the exercise created a situation that affected the participants. Evoking and managing urgency and a sense of emergency is part of the scenario's overall script. Interviewee 1, who was a participant and part of the steering committee at the same time, talked about the "fictitious real side" of the situation:

> Here, we obviously create pressure [...]. We make sure that the population uses the media to put pressure on those who are supposed to manage the situation. It's supposed to be an enormous pressure to take decisions. And managers really get affected [...] all of these managers do engage in the exercise. That's important and surprising, because from my experience I would say that they would play along somehow, but they are very emotional. It's great that they really allow this pressure to happen.
>
> (i1)

The members of the steering committee described their task mainly as managing pressure and producing activity (i3), which they did themselves under considerable time constraints. During the exercise briefings, some of the steering managers described their power to shape the course of the exercise and the interplay of all its parts as a form of "orchestrating" that builds up to a "final concert" (Exercise field notes 2011). It was a challenge to synchronize different strands of the exercise and to make sure that responses are being elicited and noticed (i1): "We haven't reached a crisis situation yet. The population is not challenged enough by this scenario – they need to be actors, not just emotional mass and recipients" (Exercise field notes 2011).

Throughout the exercise, however, the participants clearly became increasingly affected. One member of the population group described how affect did not only elicit actions, but also more concrete emotions:

> At first, there was insecurity. Insecurity and ambiguity. What's happening? How does this work? Am I getting my money paid out or not? [...] Then there was frustration, because things didn't function as expected. And there was distrust towards those who were supposed to govern the situation. Is it true what they say? From my social networks I heard otherwise. There is something wrong here. Distrust. And from fear and frustration easily arises anger, right?
>
> (i4)

This excerpt from the interview captures how the pressure produced by the steering committee created affect. It generated an atmosphere of urgency, which was either turned into concrete actions in order to make a difference to the event that was emerging, but also caused reactions of confusion, insecurity and frustrations. Other participants were affected, because they were confronted with situations that "shook the citizen's very foundations" (i1). It was noticed that during these moments, the traditional emergency services could not help and the population had to self-organize, which points clearly to the logic of resilience. The idea to make the population become part of the exercise as one that needed to help itself (i2) was formulated in the exercise's compendium. The citizen's "potential" to help out (i5) was at the core of the exercise. After being affected by these various encounters with the emergency situation, the population indeed started to react– and with that to act as a source of affect themselves.

Pong

The experience of urgency and the translation of this affect into action took many shapes. The media group, for example, not only spread information, but also created excitement. Students and welfare recipients expressed their anger on social media (i3) or through complaints (i4) when infrastructure broke down. Other representatives of the population group spontaneously devised solutions for their problems and founded self-help initiatives. A group called "Cyber Vigilantes"[2] attempted to deal with the situation in a self-organized fashion. The finance group, who had to turn off some of their web services due to a virus, would find ways to substitute these functions (i2). All of these groups did receive some instructions in the exercise compendium, but they acted mainly "autarkic" (i4). The participants organized their re-/actions, some of which were based on experiences from former emergencies.

These moves increased the exercise's level of complexity rapidly, which again created a sense of urgency for the steering committee and those who performed the government. The steering committee was challenged to insure that the same information reached all participants at the same time. The government

Resilience and affect 117

group, in turn, had to take complex decisions under immense time constraints. One of the members of the IT governance group described the intensity and the time-criticality of the situation using the image of fire:

> When it burns you need to get the main section under control. Applying this image to the IT landscape is a little bit more difficult. Things become more complex. It would mean to identify a network or a software that is infected with a virus [...]. The classic measure is here to isolate the problem. However in IT, the [measures] are different from simply isolating a burning house so that the neighbourhood would not catch fire. The problem is that not only my neighbour's house may burn and I can watch the fire flaring, but it may actually already burn at my place, too, but I simply don't know about it. IT is everywhere [...]. You do experience helplessness when you see that it can be anywhere and how vast parts of society are dependent on [a functioning network] and suddenly they are affected by the virus, too.
>
> (i5)

While the fire metaphor described a high level of urgency for the steering committee, others emphasized their professionalism in dealing with such affects: "The steering won't be unsettled. Here you notice that professionals are at work" (i1). Other participants confirmed that the steering committee would experience urgency, but this wouldn't translate into reactions of panic or emotions of fear. Interviewee 3 likened the steering committee to soldiers who learned to stay stable under stress. The exercise would be an important instrument, which allows its participants to learn how it is to be affected (i3) in a specific way and how to respond to the experience of urgency by developing creative solutions.

Ping

During the exercise, the participants were supposed to experience the translation of affect into action, which introduced a new round of affecting and being affected. While some of these reactions were part of the exercise compendium – they were foreseen or foreseeable, others were answering unpredictable developments or were developed off-script. The exercise compendium frames such off-script reactions as one of the values-added that exercising would yield, namely the "closing of gaps" (Exercise field notes 2011; BBK Leitfaden 2011). Creativity that follows from a sense of emergency is an integral component of the exercising rationale.

> During exercises you can practice a confrontation with new aspects and new damages, which you have not prepared for. And that's the aim of the exercise: to complete networks and structures, but also to detect and define gaps – not with the intent to blame anyone for it, but to signal where more work needs to be done.
>
> (i2)

118 *Part II: Governing the Internet*

This relationship between the programmed and off-script responses brings us back to the opening questions of this chapter.

Understanding resilience through affect

The affect relationships that unfolded during the exercise were messier than the pingpong metaphor suggests. However, the simplified description helped to unpack the dynamic interplay of affect and action that took place at the site. If one understands the exercise as a governmental program that affectively forges resilient subjects and their capacity to act, the following questions arise: Would such an exercise succeed in programming resilient subjects that now act in an automated fashion? Would participants afford unexpected agency that escapes the original intentions of this program? Or would the exercise produce unintended effects and frustrations that do not speak to resilience altogether?

The brief portrayal of the dynamics at the site illustrate that all three instances took place. In order to substantiate this conclusion, it is important to expand on the understanding of affect as the body's capacity to act (Spinoza 2002) – as that, which brings about different forms of power. Building on Spinoza, Negri discussed how the power of acting that follows from affect can be understood. He distinguishes between two kinds of power: a constitutive and a dominating form of power. He argues that the "capacity to act" implies the potential for an "expansive power" of "ontological opening" that is a "power of freedom" (Negri 1999: 9). This is not the power that seeks to dominate life, but it is a "constituent power" (Negri and Casarino 2008: 167). This constituent power, *potentia*, is distinct from the other side of power that dominates, invalidates and subtracts: *potestas*. Power understood as potestas, "denotes the centralised, mediating, transcendental force of command," whereas power understood as potentia "is the local, immediate, actual force of constitution" (Hardt 1991, xiii). Literature on active citizenship makes a similar distinction of different aspects of acting. Isin, for example, distinguishes between the act as a constitutive form of power, which is different from routinized action. Acts performed by citizens "create a scene" and "call into question the script itself" (Isin 2009: 379). They introduce a break: "To act is to actualize a rupture in the given, to act always means to enact the unexpected and the unpredictable" (ibid.: 380). The opposite of acts are "disciplined social [re-]actions" (ibid.: 379), routines.

Distinguishing between different kinds of power is helpful to better understand the different dynamics at play during the exercise. Even though the exercise is first and foremost a disciplinary instrument, disciplinary power does neither always work in a straightforward manner, nor do exercises necessarily succeed in disciplining subjects (Adey and Anderson 2012; Adey *et al.* 2015). As a result, different forms of power and of acting emerge in the context of the exercise. It is difficult to empirically grasp how the power of acting is being determined, but it is possible to analyze the instances of action that followed from the affective encounters at the site. Here, we can distinguish between those actions that were foreseen in the script and those moments that created a scene (cf. Isin 2009). Potestas was expressed in the steering committee's orchestration of the exercise. The way in which participants acted in accordance with the script, in a routinized and disciplined fashion, revealed moments of successful programming. Moments of potentia, however, were those that called the exercise script into question. These were actions that the steering group had not foreseen, such as uprising students or the spontaneous formation of cyber-vigilantes. And yet, these moments are, one could argue, instances of resilience: affect translated into action that seeks to re-establish a form of security without being part of the provided disciplinary program. In fact, such unforeseen reactions are also harvested for future crisis management (BBK Leitfaden 2011), and thus eventually tied back into disciplinary formats of resilience practices, which would correspond to Simon and de Goede's notion of bureaucratic vitalism (2015).

If resilience is a form of governing that is based on the acting-out of security, affect and the way in which it incites physical action plays an important role in understanding how resilience can be further conceptualized. Affect determines the course of the encounter between the subject and emergency. It pushes the subject to act (McCormack 2015) and introduces a dynamic interplay of affect and acting. The affectivity of the subject, which includes both the capability of affecting and being affected (Stäheli 2004), relates at first to the receiving state of the subject: it receives information and experiences urgency, but has not yet begun to translate this tension into action. At this stage, affect may be contagious and produce endless deferrals of value (Massumi 2002b). The subject is modulated and stimulated by affect (Massumi 1995, 2002b), or, as Clough describes it: affect creates moments of disposition and activation (Clough 2008, 2009). In the context of resilience, this means that the affect of the emergency, urgency, transforms the subject's capacity to react. It is that which precedes the action and the self-organization that resilience is based upon. Affect is here the body in-formation, it relates to a moment of becoming. Just like the emergency, affect itself is also emergent. With that, it forecloses a prior knowledge about the future and excludes strategic action. Thus, affect may not explain the resultant action as such, but it is still paramount to resilience. Resilience programs harness the affectivity of the subject. Resilience is an affective form of governance, because it seeks to create subjects that are *activated* and *at disposition* (Clough 2008, 2009) to react to emergency. The emergency here creates urgency, but whether and how this affect is translated into action remains open. During the exercise, urgency was observable in the form of physical composure and subsequent reaction.

As such, the emergency opens up for different forms of power, just like Adey *et al.* suggest (2015). More specifically, through affect, the emergency generates different forms of power. While affect itself is non-intentional, the forms of power that may follow from affect can be theorized through potentia, the constitutive form of the power to act, which can also challenge given power structures and norms, or potestas, the dominating and depoliticizing form of power, the result or the expression of a normalizing and administrative form of resilience governance. For example, the "exhausted self" (Ehrenberg 2004; Han 2010;

Bröckling 2012), is symptomatic of the resilient subject that acts according to given norms. Both kinds of powers meet in the resilient subject and are a result of the subjects affectivity and urgency, the need to react to the emergency.

If we thus understand resilience through affect, resilience is the acting-out of security that can be both an expression of potestas or potentia. The active citizen can be an instance of dominating power that programs, normalizes and administers self-organization. At the same time can the active citizen also be an instance of power that exceeds and subverts discipline, generating an act of creative response. Potentia and potestas are inextricably linked to each other (Anderson 2012). Potestas seeks to administer life and make it productive of a specific kind of security, at the same time as potentia exceeds norms that seek to make it productive by creating its own (cf. Foucault 1978). How both aspects are intertwined becomes clearly visible during the emergency exercise. While exercising instruments, such as scenarios, compendiums, and performance indicators, seek to forge resilient automats, creative and unforeseen reactions to affect may exceed these standards.

Finally, there was an instance that escaped the logic of resilience altogether: the moment of powerlessness. A few participants mentioned that some pressures were experienced in a way that resulted in the incapacity to act or to react at all. Interviewee 5 described this moment with the German word *Ohnmacht*, which refers to the moment of fainting, but also to a state of being without power. The word is generally used in a moment of being overwhelmed. Exercising instruments thus generated moments of powerlessness, where neither the effective immunization, nor the constitutive powers of *creating a scene* got to work. These moments neither express a dominating, nor a constituent form of power, but they annul the power to act altogether. As such, they can neither be captured by potestas/potentia, nor by resilience as the productive engagement of failure and its activist politics of becoming. They stand in tension with the political strategy of exercising and resilience, since they contradict the creative engagement of emergency and the evasion of standstill. During the exercise, *Ohnmacht* referred to that moment in which the participants were overwhelmed by the urgency of the situation: affect simply did not translate into action. The body experienced urgency, but could not effectuate change – it could not be productive, creative or active. Affect, here, ended up in a vacuum. Massumi describes these moments as "self-abstracted affect" (2005; cf. Clough 2009). Here, the activating potential of affect is not translated into action, into something productive, but it is mere abstract affect, an example of which is self-abstracted fear (Massumi 2005). Resilience cannot capture this moment, because *Ohnmacht* contradicts the logic of becoming and of making-productive that resilience is based upon. *Ohnmacht* or powerlessness is, then, a moment that is radically non-relational (Dillon 2000; cf. discussion in Chapter 3 on the radically non-relational, that which cannot be drawn into the logic of relation).

In sum, through affect, the resilient subject can be conceptualized as one who is either indirectly being dominated by scripts and training, or as one who has the capacity to act off-script. However, in both instances, the subject has no choice but to act, which describes the governmental logic of resilience. What disrupts the activist politics of resilience is *Ohnmacht* – the self-abstracted urgency and the state of being without the power to act. Similar to Heath-Kelly's argument that empty bombsites stand "in excess of all efforts to resignify security failure as something productive," which reveals "a lacuna within the performance of resilience" (2015: 73), this book suggests that a conceptualization of resilience through affect offers valuable insights into the different forms of power at play when emergency is experienced and acted upon. However, in the form of self-abstracted urgency, affect also points to a void in resilience, namely that resilience cannot account for powerlessness, even though it is an expectable phenomenon during emergencies. This moment of powerlessness demonstrates the limits of resilience – that is: the limits of the productivity of failure. It makes us ask whether resilience as a form of security governance can account for powerlessness, and whether powerlessness has space in a (body)politics geared toward productivity at all.

Notes

1 (i1), (i2), (i3), etc. denotes interview material from the case study.
2 German term: "Cyber Bürgerwehr."

References

Adey P (2010) *Aerial Life: Spaces, Mobilities, Affects.* Oxford: Wiley-Blackwell.
Adey P, Anderson, B (2012) Anticipating Emergencies: Technologies of Preparedness and Matter of Security. *Security Dialogue* 43(2): 99–117.
Adey P, Anderson B, Graham S (2015) Introduction: Governing Emergencies: Beyond Exceptionality. *Theory, Culture & Society* 32(2): 3–17
Agamben G (2005) *State of Exception.* Trans. Attell K. Chicago: Chicago University Press.
Agamben G (2014), quoted in Morozov E, The Rise of Data and the Death of Politics. *Observer*, 20 July: 1–14. Available at: www.theguardian.com/technology/2014/jul/20/rise-of-data-death-of-politics-evgeny-morozov-algorithmic-regulation (accessed 22 February 2016).
Ahmed S (2004) Collective Feelings: or, The Impressions Left by Others. *Theory, Culture & Society* 21(2): 25–42.
Anderson B (2006) Becoming and Being Hopeful: Towards a Theory of Affect. *Environment and Planning D: Society and Space* 24(5): 733–752.
Anderson B (2012) Affect and Biopower: Towards a Politics of Life. *Transactions of the Institute of British Geographers* 37: 28–43.
Anderson B, Adey P (2011) Affect and Security: Exercising Emergency in "UK Civil Contingencies." *Environment and Planning D: Society and Space* (29): 1092–1109.
Aradau C (2010) The Myth of Preparedness. *Radical Philosophy* 161: 2–7.
Aradau C, van Munster R (2012) The Securitization of Catastrophic Events: Trauma, Enactment, and Preparedness Exercises. *Alternatives: Global, Local, Political* 37(3): 227–239.

Athanasiou A, Hantzaroula P, Yannakopoulos K (2008) Towards a New Epistemology: The "Affective Turn." *Historein* 8: 5–16.
Australian Government (2011) *National Strategy for Disaster Resilience*. Available at: www.coag.gov.au/node/81 (accessed 11 August 2016).
Bourbeau P (2013) Resiliencism: Premises and Promises in Securitization Research. *Resilience: International Policies, Practices and Discourses* 1(1): 3–17.
Bourbeau P (2015) Migration, Resilience, and Security: Responses to New Inflows of Asylum Seekers and Migrants. *Journal of Ethnic and Migration Studies* 41(12): 1958–77.
Brassett J, Croft S, Vaughan-Williams N (2013) Introduction: An Agenda for Resilience Research in Politics and International Relations. *Politics* 33(4): 221–228.
Bröckling U (2012) Dispositive der Vorbeugung: Gefahrenabwehr, Resilienz, Precaution. In: Daase C, Offermann P, Rauer, V (eds) *Sicherheitskultur. Soziale und politische Praktiken der Gefahrenabwehr*. Frankfurt am Main and New York: Campus Verlag. 93–108
Challen A, Noden P, West A, Machin S (2010) UK Resilience Programme Evaluation: Final Report. Available at: www.gov.uk/government/uploads/system/uploads/attachment_data/file/182419/DFE-RR097.pdf (accessed 11 August 2016).
Chandler D (2014) *Resilience: The Governance of Complexity. Critical Issues in Global Politics*. New York: Routledge.
Clough PT (2008) The Affective Turn: Political Economy, Biomedia and Bodies. *Theory, Culture & Society* 25(1): 1–22.
Clough PT (2009) The New Empiricism: Affect and Sociological Method. *European Journal of Social Theory* 12(1): 43–61.
Cole D (2009) The Actions of Affect in Deleuze: Others Using Language and the Language That We Make ... *Educational Philosophy and Theory* 43(6): 549–561.
Collier S (2008) Enacting Catastrophy: Preparedness, Insurance, Budgetary Rationalization. *Economy and Society* 37(2): 224–250.
Dean M (2010) *Governmentality. Power and Rule in Modern Society*. 2nd edn. London: Sage.
Deleuze G (1988) *Spinoza: Practical Philosophy*. San Francisco: City Lights Books.
Deleuze E, Deleuze J (1978) *Gilles Deleuze, Lecture, Transcripts on Spinoza's Concept of Affect*. Available at: www.webdeleuze.com/php/sommaire.html (accessed 11 August 2016).
Dewsbury JD, Harrison P, Rose M, Wylie J (2002) Enacting Geographies: Editorial Introduction. *Geoforum* 33(4): 437–440.
Dillon M (2000) Poststructuralism, Complexity and Poetics. *Theory, Culture & Society* 17(5): 1–26.
Duffield M (2012) Challenging Environments: Danger, Resilience and the Aid Industry. *Security Dialogue* 43(5): 475–492.
Dunn Cavelty D, Kaufmann M, Søby Kristensen K (2015) Resilience and (In)security: Practices, Subjects and Temporalities. *Security Dialogue* 46(1): 1–12.
Ehrenberg A (2004) *Das erschöpfte Selbst. Depression und Gesellschaft in der Gegenwart*. Frankfurt am Main: Campus Verlag.
ENISA (2011a) *Inter-X: Resilience of the Internet Interconnection Ecosystem*. Full report. Available at: www.enisa.europa.eu/publications/interx-report/at_download/fullReport (accessed 11 August 2016).
ENISA (2011b) *Enabling and Managing End-to-end Resilience*. Available at: www.enisa.europa.eu/activities/identity-and-trust/library/deliverables/e2eres (accessed 11 August 2016).

European Commission (2010) *The EU Internal Security Strategy in Action: Five Steps Towards a More Secure Europe.* Available at: http://ec.europa.eu/commission_2010-2014/malmstrom/pdf/news/internal_security_strategy_in_action_en.pdf (accessed 11 August 2016).

Evans B, Reid J (2014) *Resilient Life. The Art of Living Dangerously.* Cambridge: Polity Press.

Exercise field notes (2011) Field notes taken by the author at the German LÜKEX cyber security exercise 2011.

Fassin D, Pandolfi M (2010) Introduction: Military and Humanitarian Government in the Age of Intervention. In: Fassin D, Pandolfi M (eds) *Contemporary States of Emergency: The Politics of Military and Humanitarian Interventions.* New York: Zone Books. 9–25.

Foucault M (1977) *Discipline and Punish.* New York: Random House.

Foucault M (1978) *The History of Sexuality: An Introduction. Vol 1.* London. Penguin.

Geroult M (1968) *Spinoza 1: Dieu.* Hildesheim, Germany: Georg Olms Verlag.

Grove K (2014) Agency, Affect, and the Immunological Politics of Disaster Resilience. *Environment and Planning D: Society and Space* 32(2): 240–256.

Grusin R (2004) Premediation. *Criticism* 46(1): 17–39.

Guyau JM (1887) *L'Art au point de vue sociologique.* Paris: Félix Alcan.

Han, Byul-Chung (2010) *Müdigkeitsgesellschaft.* Berlin: Matthes & Seitz.

Hansen M (2003) Affect as Medium, or the "Digital-Facial-Image." *Journal of Visual Culture* 2(2) 205–228.

Hardt M (1991) Translator's foreword in: *Negri, Antonio The Savage Anomaly.* Minneapolis, MN: University of Minnesota Press. xi–xvii.

Heath-Kelly C (2015) Securing through the Failure to Secure? The Ambiguity of Resilience at the Bombsite. *Security Dialogue* 46(1): 69–85.

Howell A (2010) Sovereignty, Security, Psychiatry: Liberation and the Failure of Mental Health Governance in Iraq. *Security Dialogue* 41(4): 347–367.

Howell A (2014) Resilience, War, and Austerity: The Ethics of Military Human Enhancement and the Politics of Data. *Security Dialogue* 46(1): 15–31.

Isin EF (2009) Citizenship in Flux: The Figure of the Activist Citizen. *Subjectivity* 29: 367–388.

Joseph J (2013) Resilience as Embedded Neoliberalism: A Governmentality Approach. *Resilience: International Policies, Practices and Discourses* 1 (1) 38–52.

Kaufmann M (2013) Emergent Self-Organisation in Emergencies: Resilience Rationales in Interconnected Societies. *Resilience: International Policies, Practices and Discourses* 1(1): 53–68.

Lash S (2006) Life (Vitalism). *Theory, Culture & Society* 23(2–3): 323–349.

Lentzos F, Rose N (2009) Governing Insecurity: Contingency Planning, Protection, Resilience. *Economy and Society* 38(2): 230–254.

Malcolm JA (2013) Project Argus and the Resilient Citizen. *Politics* 33(4): 311–321.

Massumi B (1993) *Politics of Everyday Fear.* Minneapolis, MN: University of Minnesota Press.

Massumi B (1995) The Autonomy of Affect. *Cultural Critique* 31(2): 83–109.

Massumi B (2002a) Navigating Movements. In: Zournazi M (ed.) *Hope: New Philosophies for Change.* Annandale, New South Wales: Pluto Press. 210–244.

Massumi B (2002b) *Parables for the Virtual: Movement, Affect, Sensation.* Durham, NC and London: Duke University Press.

Massumi B (2005) Fear (The Spectrum Said). *Positions* 13: 31–48.

MacCormack P (2004) Parabolic Philosophies. Analogue and Affect. *Theory, Culture & Society* 21(6): 179–187.

McCormack D (2015) Governing Inflation: Price and Atmospheres of Emergency. *Theory, Culture & Society* 32(2): 131–154.

Negri A (1999) Value and Affect. *Boundary* 2: 26–86.

Negri A, Casarino C (2008) *In Praise of the Common.* Minnesota, MN: University of Minnesota Press.

Oels A, Methmann C (2015) From "Fearing" to "Empowering" Climate Refugees: Governing Climate-induced Migration in the Name of Resilience. *Security Dialogue* 46(1): 51–68.

O'Malley P (2009) "Uncertainty makes us free": Liberalism, Risk and Individual Security. *Behemoth: A Journal on Civilisation* 2(3): 24–38.

Ong A (2006) *Neoliberalism as Exception.* Durham, NC: Duke University Press.

Reid J (2012) The Disastrous and Politically Debased Subject of Resilience. *Development Dialogue* 58: 67–79.

Rogers P (2013) Rethinking Resilience: Articulating Community and the UK Riots. *Politics* 33(4): 322–333.

Ruddick S (2010) The Politics of Affect: Spinoza in the Work of Negri and Deleuze. *Theory Culture & Society* 27 (4) 21–45.

Schmidt J (2014) Intuitively Neoliberal? Towards a Critical Understanding of Resilience Governance. *European Journal of International Relations* 21(2): 402–426.

Serres M (2000) *The Birth of Physics.* Manchester: Clinamen Press Ltd.

Seyfert R (2012) Beyond Personal Feelings and Collective Emotions: Toward a Theory of Social Affect. *Theory, Culture & Society* 29 (6) 27–46.

Simon S, de Goede M (2015) Cybersecurity, Bureaucratic Vitalism and European Emergency. *Theory, Culture & Society* 32(2) 79–106.

Spinoza B (2002) *Spinoza – Complete Works.* Trans. Shirley S. Indianapolis, IN: Hackett Publishing Co.

Stäheli U (2004) Der Takt der Börse. Inklusionseffekte von Verbreitungsmedien am Beispiel des Börsen-Tickers. *Zeitschrift für Soziologie* 33(3): 245–63.

Stern M (2006) "We" the Subject: The Power and Failure of (In)Security. *Security Dialogue* 37(2): 187–205.

UNISDR (2010) *Building Back Better for Next Time. Experiences and Lessons Learnt from the Project "Building Resilience to Tsunamis in the Indian Ocean."* Available at: www.unisdr.org/files/14499_buildingbackbetterforthenexttime.pdf (accessed 11 August 2016).

US Department of Homeland Security (2013) *National Infrastructure Protection Plan.* Available at: www.dhs.gov/national-infrastructure-protection-plan (accessed 11 August 2016).

Vaughan-Williams N (2008) Borderwork beyond the Inside/Outside? Frontex, the Citizen-Detective and the War on Terror. *Space and Polity* 12(1): 63–79.

Walker J, Cooper M (2011) Genealogies of Resilience. From Systems Ecology to Political Economy of Crisis Adaptation. *Security Dialogue* 42 (2) 143–160.

Zebrowksi C (2009) Governing the Network Society: A Biopolitical Critique of Resilience. *Political Perspectives* 3(1) 1–44.

BBK material

BBK Exercise PowerPoint. Grundlagen, Übungsrahmen, Übungsszenario. *BBK IV.6/PG LÜKEX Bund*.

BBK Homepage. Available at: www.bbk.bund.de/EN/Home/home_node.html (accessed 11 August 2016).

BBK Leitfaden (2011) *Leitfaden für strategische Krisenmanagement-Übungen*. Bonn: Bevölkerungsschutz.

BBK LÜKEX Exercise Press. Press material edited specifically for the LÜKEX cyber security exercise 2011. The material was produced and used during and exclusively for the exercise.

BBK LÜKEX Exercise Social Media. Social medial material edited specifically for the LÜKEX cyber security exercise 2011. The material was produced and used during and exclusively for the exercise.

BBK LÜKEX Exercise TV. Television program edited specifically for the LÜKEX cyber security exercise 2011. The program was used during and exclusively for the exercise.

BBK LÜKEX Leaflet. Available at: www.bbk.bund.de/DE/AufgabenundAusstattung/Krisenmanagement/Luekex/Luekex_node.html (accessed 11 August 2016).

Part III
Resilience as a way of governing through the Internet

7 Resilience and the digital

Resilience means to act out of security, but the emergency exercise is surely not the only site where resilience operates. Exercises may be the most emblematic form of acting-out security, but resilience takes a vast variety of shapes. In fact, resilience seems to have gained relevance as a response to any situation of complexity and uncertainty. The Internet can easily be understood as the perfect example of complexity; it is a space where a lot of resilience programs are realized. Yet, cyber-security is not only a domain where the politics of resilience have become very popular, but the Internet also changes how resilience is governed. While it is still far from being fundamental to society, the Internet's increasing presence in everyday activities impacts the way in which resilience takes shape in emergency situations. The Internet has become a tool to re-establish security after crises.

This part of the book directs attention from the Internet as a site where resilience programs are implemented to the way in which digital interconnectedness itself influences responses to insecurity. It changes the focus from *resilience as a way of governing the Internet* to *resilience as a way of governing through the Internet*. The next two chapters explore what it means to act out security in the informationalized society and how the Internet influences resilience as the idea of constant adaptation, of being in-formation. This chapter investigates how the digital – (big) data and algorithms – encourages the programming of resilience, and how subjects act out security according to such programs. The following chapter, in turn, will discuss the way in which the networked character of the Internet also gives room to self-determined forms of acting-out security, for example, through the use of social media. The active, resilient subject that utilizes the Internet as a means for self-organization remains at the center of both discussions.

The dawn of new emergency management?

The integration of portable and wearable technologies into our everyday lives has made computing so ubiquitous that it has begun to transform resilience management. Already during the 2010 Haiti earthquake large amounts of digital data were circulated via social media, a process that was later termed "knowledge sharing" (Yates and Paquette 2011: 7). This information was harvested and translated into "knowledge applications" (ibid.: 10), such as the identification of urgent cases, the coordination of resource distribution or fundraising for disaster relief (cf. Gao *et al.* 2011). Since the upsurge of smart phones in early 2010, apps and every-ware, as well as social media and digital mapping tools, have been identified as a "tremendous opportunity" (Crowe 2011: 418) for emergency response and resilience planning. Technologies that can remotely understand and visualize "social behaviour in conditions of shock and rapid change have emerged" (Duffield 2016: 7; cf. UNGP 2013), which researchers and institutions largely identify as a promise "to positively empower and create new forms of self-realisation" (cf. Duffield 2016: 1). European Commission investments into the "next generation emergency services" (European Commission 2014) endorse this trend. Dedicated social movements such as *Effective Altruism* even seek to maximize the positive effects of crisis response by using, amongst other things, digitally available, crowd-sourced information to perform cost-effectiveness calculations on resilience measures (Herzog 2016; Nygren 2015). Internet entrepreneurs such as Facebook's co-founder Dustin Moskovitz and Utilitarian philosopher Peter Singer are some of their most prominent promoters. In light of these developments and the ongoing informationalization of society this chapter asks: What are the specific properties of digital information and how do they influence resilience governance?

It suggests that the rapid transferability of digital information not only inspires new forms of emergency communication for affected populations and crisis managers. The fact that digital information is traceable, storable and computable also allows for new resilience analytics, méaning the identification of correlations and patterns based on big data. The analytical procedures that the digital enables affect resilience epistemologies and the contents of resilience as such. This means that the digital affects how knowledge about insecurity is produced and how security is acted out in response to emergencies. The chapter will first outline the properties of digital information and the activities they afford (Gibson 1986), in order to establish a theoretical base, which makes it possible to investigate how the increased circulation of digital information influences resilience practices and epistemologies. Based on a review of academic literature and policy papers about resilience as well as online emergency management tools, it identifies and discusses three aspects of resilience management that are influenced by the rise of the digital. First, practices of mapping, visualizing and assessing emergencies; second, approaches that actively manage and direct emergencies; and third, post-emergency activities such as analyzing response, learning and designing future resilience. All three aspects feed into a discussion about the digitization of resilience, pointing to the way in which the digital fosters the focus on the crowd as the main performer of resilience activities, and the pattern as a new epistemological rationale for "resilience programming" (Grove 2014) in an interconnected society.

Understanding digital information

Digital information has become a key asset for emergency management and resilience practice. The digital format of information, in fact, makes a difference in the way that resilience is being thought about and enacted. Both communication and analytical practices have experienced remarkable transformations with the rise of the digital. In order to trace this influence of the digital on resilience programming, it is essential to first understand what the properties of digital information are and how they render specific activities possible. Gibson argues that it is the composition of an object, a landscape or a substance that constitutes what kind of action it permits and enables (Gibson 1986). His argument goes back to Gestalt psychology and the term "Aufforderungscharakter" (Lewin 1969), meaning that something literally invites for a specific usage. It has "affordances" (Gibson 1986). The way in which an object is constituted thus makes a difference in action. Affordances do not necessarily turn an object into a political subject, but it is also not just neutral object, since it can "authorize, allow, afford, encourage, permit, suggest, influence, block, render possible, forbid, and so on" (Latour 2005: 72). Its oriented form of existence, or – to put it in Galloway's words – that bodies must not only always speak, but "must always speak as" (Galloway 2012: 137), facilitates some activities over others. Following this premise, the paragraphs below describe the interrelation between the affordances of the digital and actors that utilize, harness and design these affordances. The digital, then, cannot be divorced from the social: digital data is not a naked piece of information or a "pure information object" (Paul 2009: 19) – self-evident, neutral and transparent in its existence, but it is always shaped and generated by their users (Gitelman and Jackson 2013). At the same time, one could say that the digital has characteristics, which prioritize specific uses over others. These properties also enable or constrain the digital as an artifact (cf. Blanchette 2011: 1045–1046; cf. Leonardi 2010). The next paragraphs will investigate what these properties are,[1] what actions they permit and how specific contexts fill these actions with meaning. Only in describing them is it possible to point to the powerful influence digital information unfolds in the production of resilience knowledge and practices.

Hardware has a fundamental influence in constituting digital information. The way in which information is manipulated, stored and exchanged not only mediates material properties of digital data and establishes it as an artifact (Blanchette 2011), but hardware also encodes information as electronic. Information is codified in discrete digits, which are transformed into electronic impulses that can travel through the network – simultaneously, over long distances and at a considerable speed. The properties of electronic data are further determined by computing languages. With their own grammar and linguistic varieties, they constitute the way in which digital data travel. File formats, such as JPEG and TIF, not only constrain the mutability of bits (Blanchette 2011), but also make digital information storable. Due to their numeric properties, digital data can furthermore be copied and reproduced, counted and computed. As basic as these affordances may seem, they are currently important influence factors in emergency communication, where fast-traveling information (Meier 2013) and the collection and storage of data are key assets for situational analysis. While digital data can generally be subdivided in content data and metadata, metadata here plays a particularly important role. Through tracking logins, for example, metadata makes it possible for contents to be related across different websites as well as devices. This means that information can be traced back to specific users or GPS positions. Metadata is thus the origin of many analytical practices, because it makes digital information traceable and searchable. Geospatial information mapping, for example, is increasingly used in emergency management and resilience programming (Committee on Planning for Catastrophe 2007).

The existence of digital information in distributed networks; their rapid exchangeability, their storability, traceability and computability are key to analytical processes. These characteristics make it possible to gather and reassemble digital information in different contexts – online and offline, in an emergency situation and for a long time thereafter. These processes of data collection and analysis is what inspired Andrejevic and Gates to argue that digital data "gathers beyond its design": all data is "collected and stored for its future use-value [...] even if there are no envisioned uses for it at present" (2014: 187). They come to conclude that the function of digital data *is* the creep (ibid.). The fact that digital data is storable in large amounts, that it is traceable, numeric and computable is what enables the continuous repurposing of information through ever new forms of association and correlation. One could say that the digital format of information *affords* analysis through forms and patterns. Precisely because digital data affords or favors computation over other forms of analysis, the way in which digital data are used for computational analysis, how digital data are searched and scanned for results, come to matter. Here, the relevant information for political practices, so Amoore argues, doesn't sit in the data nodes as such, but in the way they are being associated with each other (2013). Associating data with each other is a way of assigning meaning and value to it. A prime example of such an associative, correlative and pattern-oriented tool of analysis is the algorithm. Algorithmic analysis is characterized by mobile lines and loose associations, allowing for the disaggregation of data and for limitless amounts of re-combinations to make visible whatever resilience management practices seek to target (cf. Amoore 2013). As a result, the detection of phenomena "takes place within form itself, in the links and patterns that materialize and take shape" (ibid.: 133). Thus, algorithmic form works with digital information through de- and recontextualization. It takes data out of contexts and places them in new contexts. Even the very translation of information into digital code already disconnects information from its contexts and reconnects it in the form of lists; the digitization of information means to list information. Thus, in *Listing the Global*, Stäheli describes how the digital not only establishes connectivity, but also disconnectivity: it dissolves originally connected elements into lists and digital units in order to reconnect them anew (2012b). The digital dis-embeds objects from their environments in order to render them differentiable, to classify them, and to recombine them in new contexts. This process of listing is deeply embedded in the character of digital interconnectedness. Listing establishes new forms of closeness, proximity and connectivity at the same time as it creates distance, displacement and decontextualization.

Digital information then affords associative practices of connecting the dots, of de- and recontextualization. It allows for an analytic of form and pattern that assigns meaning to and "imagines" digital information (Gitelman and Jackson 2013). As a consequence, digital information also lends itself to a specific form of decision-making during emergency management, because conclusions and concrete actions are based on such analytic practices. This ability of the digital to install new forms of sense-making about complexity by unearthing emerging and supposedly indiscernible patterns (Andrejevic and Gates 2014) has been identified as a big promise – especially in contexts that are equally characterized by indiscernible and emergent dynamics, such as disasters and emergencies (cf. Stauffacher *et al.* 2012; Meier 2013; Ikanow.com n.d.a). Digital analytics is thus presented as a white hope to deal with shocks, it is seen as a rational solution for resilience management, whether that concerns situational analysis, the identification of self-organizing patterns in communities, or lessons learned activities.

This promise, however, has encountered diverse concerns and criticisms. A prominent concern is that about privacy and data protection (Crawford *et al.* 2013). This concern is not easy to address, since the question about protection is related to the very design of digital infrastructures, which often foresees for infrastructure providers to access the data. The encryption of data is not necessarily in the interest of commercial players, who structure Internet access in the first place, since to them the information is their currency. The process of what Andrejevic calls "digital enclosure" (2009) describes here how the material existence of data in and through infrastructures is closely entwined with the commercial capturing of information about populations. The default surveillance of our actions online remains the condition under which we can be part of the Internet. This is a fact that changes social relations. Since existing relationships are reproduced through privately owned platforms, any digital activity becomes an important asset to the platform owners and also a resource to socio-economic life at large. We see that most clearly in the workings of Google and the fact that online rankings and networks are not always separable from offline existences. Andrejevic argues that the users of such platforms perform "digital labor" (2009). Using digital infrastructure is then no longer mere exchange, but it produces value. Online, digital information is turned into capital and maintaining social relationships is instrumentalized for the data mine. As a result, Andrejevic argues, the digital enclosure strips citizens of their freedom to make their digital activities an object of consciousness and will (2009). In addition, anyone who wants to pull information from the Internet is in need of processing power, hardware, digital and non-digital infrastructures, which are used to collect, store and analyze the available information. This brings us back to the more fundamental criticisms of digital analytics. Working with large amounts of digital information is a method that is only available to those with processing power, who are few, vis-à-vis those who produce the data. Large amounts of data need new scales and knowledge of analytics as well as processing infrastructure (Andrejevic and Gates 2014). Such large infrastructures are generally owned by corporate entities that then structure, not only the access to information, but also the character of the knowledge that is drawn from it.

Here, the systematic non-transparency of digital information described above is that which adds speculative elements to analysis and challenges objectivity. Or, as Gitelman and Jackson would say, analysis is always driven by the imagination of those who work with the data (2013). As discussed above, datasets do not just exist, ready for objective or neutral measure (Amoore 2013). Data has to be defined by their analysts and generated in the first place: "Data creators have to collect data and organize it, or create it from scratch" (Manovich 2002b: 224). This is already an act of creativity that influences the results that digital analytics can generate. Boyd and Crawford argue similarly that decisions have to be taken about which variables to count and which ones to ignore. The process of imagining datasets according to one's own norms and values, as well as data errors and other limitations challenge the objectivity of the calculated result (Boyd and Crawford 2012). There is power in creating and imagining data.

Challenges to objectivity do not only occur in the production of digital datasets, but also while reading and interpreting them. In the context of the mining of legal texts Hildebrandt points to the difficulty of digital hermeneutics and semiotics vis-à-vis their analogue counterparts. She asks whether new and different forms of reading are needed to analyze and interpret digital data (Hildebrandt 2012). The digital presupposes a semiotics that does not necessarily equate a sign with a letter or other literal metaphors, but it may include symbolisms, metaphors and analogies that can be an instance of form in the mathematical or aesthetic sense. In order to insure a meaningful reading of data, such semiotics have to be identified and implemented before reading and interpretation take place (ibid.). This fundamentally influences the production of knowledge. The digital changes the way in which we engage with information and create knowledge altogether – it foregrounds epistemologies of the countable. Digital data is mainly deployed to reason numerically. Here, Boyd and Crawford emphasize the general, but importantly point out that numbers don't necessarily speak for themselves (Boyd and Crawford 2012) – which is, however, often taken for granted. Knowledge created through numeric models simply lacks the insights of other approaches to find out why and how people do, write and make things.

Understanding the digital through its properties and affordances of transferability, traceability, storability and computability does not lead to a critique of the digital altogether, neither does it encourage the adoption of the attitude that the digital is a technology that merely needs better design to avoid causing unintended side effects. At least, none of these challenges are solved by augmenting the amount of digital data one uses for analysis, because the challenges lie within the characteristics and affordances of data itself: "Bigger data is not always better data" (Boyd and Crawford 2012: 6), precisely because it removes context and depends on specific tools to harvest and interpret data. It is thus important to disclose and discuss the specific affordances of digital data, as well as to keep these challenges in mind while analyzing the influence of digital information. In paying attention to these affordances, we take digital data out of the realm of inconspicuousness within our everyday practices (Manovich 2002a), where it is concealed from critical study. It also helps us to rethink our ways of working with and representing large volumes of digital data. In the context of this chapter, paying attention to the affordances of the digital makes it possible to study how digital data changes resilience epistemologies and practices. Digital information on emergencies has become interesting to private and public actors, because it seems to answer the urge to access and share actionable information during emergencies. It enables crowdsourcing, associative knowledge production and bears the potential for rapid intervention. As such, digital modes of communication and analytics enable new resilience practices. As we shall see, however, they also make, transform and reconfigure resilience itself (cf. Derosières 2014).

When resilience goes digital

As the everyday usage of digital technology increases, the role that digital information plays for resilience management grows, too (cf. IFRC 2013). Key sources of digital information during emergencies are social media and apps. While data on platforms such as Twitter, Instagram and Tumblr are available to the public, data on platforms with restricted access can, in many cases, be collected as well, since terms and conditions create loopholes for governments to access data, especially if related to security situations (cf. Rushe 2013). Some social media providers have established their own crisis management tools through which they can crowd-task and collect information. Facebook, for example, decided to add the Safety Check function to their services in 2014, which users in a disaster-affected area can activate to indicate whether they are "safe" and that any user can generally consult to "check on others" (Gleit *et al.* 2014). The company, however, first needs to activate the function for each specific situation, which gives them not only access to the data, but also the power to decide in which kind of disaster situation such a function should be used. A similar function is Google's open-source project "Person Finder," which provides for information about people's wellbeing and whereabouts in disaster-affected areas (Google Person Finder n.d.). Google's crisis-response page, which was created as a response to the Haiti Earthquake in 2010, also features tools to collect and provide satellite photographs, information about shelter locations, road conditions and power outages. This goes to show that the digital information collected during disasters not only refers to written content data, which is increasingly abbreviated and summarized in one-click functions, but also audio and visual data, like photos and satellite imagery, and, as discussed above, metadata, for example, geolocation or IP addresses. This increased circulation of digital information fosters new forms of crisis communication, as well as new analytic practices that generate resilience knowledge.

While the scholarly discourse predominantly points to the benefits of digital information for resilience practices (Meier 2011, 2013; Yates and Paquette 2011; Keim and Noji 2011; Stauffacher *et al.* 2012;), critical scholarship questions whether a state of exception (Schmitt 1921; Agamben 2005) legally and morally justifies the collection of potentially personal data – especially when this data is not shared knowingly (Buchanan and Ess 2008; Boyd and Crawford 2012; Crawford *et al.* 2013). Digital data analytics for crisis management, even if conducted for benevolent purposes, has raised a range of concerns. It brings about issues of ownership of personal data, questions of accountabilities for conclusions drawn from collective data, the potential for rising technology dependency and the creation of new vulnerabilities, in terms of hackable, but sensitive information. Furthermore, it is unclear who profits from this move toward the digital, and whether a digitization of resilience practices inspires a privatization and commercialization of emergency management in the form of different web-based services – especially when reflected upon in terms of the *digital enclosure* (Andrejevic 2009). Vis-à-vis these concerns, Crawford *et al.* point to the need for good governance principles in data-driven projects, the informed use of technology for data collection, as well as the importance of local data and sociocultural contexts in interpreting data (2013). These critical questions and guidelines, however, largely refer to the way in which digital practices are being executed. They seem to substantiate the argument that technology development and analytical practice simply need to get better at addressing these issues. As such, these discourses do not reflect upon the way in which the specific affordances of digital information influence resilience programming altogether, creating new practices, forms of knowledge and understandings of resilience itself. The remainder of this chapter describes and discusses these transformations in relation to three broad developments: mapping emergencies; directing emergencies; and learning for future emergencies.

Mapping emergencies

Due to its traceability and transferability, digital information about emergencies can be gathered from and sent to isolated locations within affected areas. Duffield summarizes that

> Computer and mobile phone users self-broadcast both directly – through Internet searches, mobile phone calls, text messaging or social media like Twitter, Facebook, YouTube or hundreds of other apps – and indirectly, in terms of the geo-temporal electronic traces, or metadata, that such usage leaves behind and which the corporations harvest and store as "data exhaust."
>
> (Duffield 2016: 6)

Accordingly, new resilience strategies foresee the inclusion of citizens as "active collection nodes" for relevant information (Ikanow.com n.d.b). Such strategies utilize the familiarity of users with social media and the low degrees of separation between each user (Meier 2011) to push information to the public in emergency situations or to pull information from bystanders. This allows resilience managers, on the one hand, to provide guidance or raise awareness by communicating through these networks. Here, smart-phone apps are currently being discussed as specified services, through which guidance can be received (Meier 2013). Social media can, on the other hand, be used for collecting information, for example, about damages and losses. In accessing this information, resilience managers can visualize emergency impacts, as well as resilience and response mechanisms (Meier 2013).

Since all this information travels in the form of electronic pulses, this gathering process can be conducted at a considerable speed. The circulation of digital information is considered to be "real time" (Emergency Journalism 2012), which means that it is possible to receive new information without perceivable delay. Programmers consider a system to be real-time if it "controls an environment by receiving data, processing them, and returning the results sufficiently quickly to affect the environment at that time" (Martin 1965: 4). Following the argument above, the relevance of the notion of *real-time* can be debated as the digital influences its environments at any point in time, constantly, with and without delay, fast and slowly. The digital can be considered a mode of being in-formation. More on the temporality of digital interconnectedness will be explored in the subsequent chapters. Yet, this specific understanding of real-time information monitoring created optimism about the possibilities to program and accelerate emergency response (Puhorit *et al.* 2014). In fact, the optimism grew so strong that real-time computing systems are already understood to be mission-critical (Crowe 2011).

Since digital information is traceable, searchable and storable, it also affords new modes of situational analysis. Summarized under the term "neogeography" (Turner 2006), initiatives such as the *International Network of Crisis Mappers*, *Open Street Maps* and *Random Hacks of Kindness* leverage mobile platforms, geospatial technologies and visual analytics to map emergent challenges and resilience initiatives in order to accelerate response. Since one of the main challenges is in fact to handle the vast amount of circulated information, some services, as, for example, the *Internet Response League*, suggest embedding visual Twitter and Instagram data into online games, where players get game rewards in return for the analysis of the material (Internet Response League 2013). The verified and categorized information can then be fed into an emerging crisis map. Through such practices, not only would the shared information be crowdsourced, but the cleaning of data would also become a task to be performed by the crowd.

As these trends in emergency management show, digital data inspire new resilience practices. Here, the digital reinforces a characteristic that is already present in resilience practices: the focus in the citizen. Through crowd-sourcing and crowd-tasking, the public becomes part of the response network. The act of soliciting information about emergencies from large groups of people, rather than traditional emergency responders, speaks to the idea of self-organization. Even traditional key players, such as the US Federal Emergency Management Agency find that through digital communication modes, individuals become less dependent on the government since they "turn to their virtual communities for information and assistance" (FEMA 2011: 4). Crowds and public communities begin to self-organize emergency knowledge through the digital. Emergency managers seize their role, not only in pulling information from social networks that users have already circulated, but also by creating incentives to mobilize help, for example, by distributing rewards for sharing helpful information (Economist 2012). Initiatives such as *idisaster* and *MicroMappers* actively encourage the public to volunteer. MicroMappers' approach of "micro-tasking" very much reflects the idea of resilient self-organization, as it asks people to "spend a little bit of time performing a small task. Anyone can become a MicroMapper – there are no special skills or exceptional time commitments required" (Gilbert-Knight 2013). With the rise of digital information, knowledge about emergencies is neither exclusively produced, nor solely accessed by traditional emergency management authorities. By giving rise to the affected crowd as a new epistemic community, the digital is indicative of a shift in the status of expertise. It creates the expert status of the affected citizen who shares information, as well as that of the analyst and engineer, who cleans the data, subjects it to algorithms and seeks to make this knowledge work in the emergency management apparatus. While the role of the data provider and the analyst can converge in the crowd, the role of the analyst no longer necessarily overlaps with that of traditional emergency management institutions.

The latter is a result of another development that the digital affords, namely new forms of analysis, which not all emergency organizations are prepared and equipped to use. Not only does the analysis of digital information require infrastructure, but also computational expertise. Even though MicroMappers promise that "no special skills" are required to provide information (Gilbert-Knight 2013) and many databases are built using information that simply is at hand – so-called "convenience sampling" (Meier 2011: 6), those who search the data still need algorithmic expertise. By employing different modes of association and correlation, patterns arise as the main kind of knowledge about emergencies. They are key to generate dynamic maps and visual reports about behavior (FEMA 2011), hubs of action, processes over time, movements of people and goods, access to safe and dangerous areas, as well as to forecast hazards arising from the evolving situation. Patterns, then, represent a new form of mapped and configured knowledge about disasters, as well as a specific mode of viewing emergencies, because the disaster is perceived and observed through hot spots, clusters and repetitions. Here, the associative techniques and the analysts that shape these patterns and render the emergency observable also determine what of the emergency becomes visible and what remains invisible and unaccounted for.

Patterns and their visualizations in maps are thus not only enabled, but also restrained by digital properties. Morozov, for example, criticizes the use of digitally determined patterns and correlative knowledge as un-political, because they leave no room for political deliberation (2014). Some algorithms even find patterns where none exist. Patterns, as discussed above, are also limited in the kind of knowledge they provide. Yet, challenges arise long before the algorithmic work begins: the digital data that is collected in databases and subjected to algorithmic practices is always selective, and at times even deceptive. The circulation of misleading or wrongful information – trolling – is a prominent challenge for digital data analysis, especially during emergencies, since time to scrutinize the veracity and validity of the data is scarce. The creation of knowledge from digital information during emergencies has thus given rise to a specific approach to truth: Building on the insight that "(f)alse rumors tend to be questioned much more than confirmed truths" (Mendoza *et al.* 2010: 8) and that wrong messages "are often corrected by other users" (Merchant *et al.* 2011: 2), veracity seems to arise from a large number of people validating reports (Gao *et al.* 2011). This means that truth is established via consensus. This consensus can be provided by the "actively listening community" (Emergency Journalism 2012). The actively listening community is not only another instance of self-organization, but it represents also an approach to truth that is based on a peculiar mix of surveillance and quantity: finding a "statistical consensus between the crowd's contributions" (ibid.) is, amongst other things, exercised via credibility scores. Tools such as the *Seriously Rapid Source Review* feature predefined indicators for veracity, checking where the submitting user is located, whether the user was an eyewitness and what the top five entities of the user's tweet history are (Meier 2012a). This approach to truth fundamentally builds upon the assumption that veracity can be traced and quantified: the more people in the affected area confirm a piece of information, the more it becomes true. A similar form of judgment, so it is suggested, could be done by volunteer task forces, who establish the veracity and credibility of contents by checking inconsistencies in the user's tweeting habits, by reviewing the tweeter's followers and by triangulating the user's identity via mainstream media (Meier 2011: 15). As promising as such approaches to veracity are, they are not only time-consuming, but they inherently build upon digital surveillance. The traceability, networkability and computability of user data combined with an *actively listening community* that establishes truth by confirming or disproving a piece of information form this specific approach to truth. It is an approach to truth that is based on surveillance, quantified consensus, but also statistical likelihood. Truthfulness of digital information is scalable as it can vary from completely true to completely false; it is established via likelihood metrics (Merchant *et al.* 2011; Meier 2012a). While disaster maps and similar visual products are often perceived as a reproduction or a copy of reality, the probabilistic, speculative and surveillance-based approaches to truth that are entangled with the creation of such maps are not reflected in such images.

The veracity of digital information, however, is not the only challenge digital analytics face here, but most digital data is selective in the first place. The uneven distribution of digital technologies (Graham 2011), gendered and culturally diverse usage, as well as the specifics of defining, cleaning and imagining the datasets (Boyd and Crawford 2012) produces structural invisibilities within the creation of overviews and emergency maps. Information that is not digitized, not sent in a specific format or not covered by the algorithmic program will not be mapped and is thus rendered invisible.

Directing emergencies

What follows from the mapping of the emergency is the possibility to respond to and intervene in the emergent situation (Crowe 2011; FEMA 2011). Information about hubs of action, casualties or dangerous zones is translated into concrete advice to control the emergency's trajectory and instigate disaster response (cf. Stauffacher *et al.* 2012; Gao *et al.* 2011; Merchant *et al.* 2011; Yates and Paquette 2011; Keim and Noji 2011). Digital information can assist in making informed decisions and reduce emergency impacts by giving practical advice, such as pointing to road access and locations of infrastructures (Lindsay 2011). *Google Crisis Response*, for example, offers alert functions and person finders to locate lost individuals based on shared data. Social computing, artificial intelligence, machine learning and big data analysis are furthermore deployed to identify needs, allocate resources and match both with each other to install efficient resilience practices (Meier 2013). If the population's technical ability and expertise to access such information is guaranteed, it also enables populations to act upon this information. Offering a digital space for mutual assistance and neighborly help, Meier argues, aids the building of common norms and trust for faster recovery: "this bonding is not limited to offline dynamics but occurs also within and across online social networks" (ibid.). Digital "peer-to-peer feedback loops" (ibid.) are used to give advice for self-organization, but they also provide data that can be analyzed to predict evolving risks, which can be met before they create domino effects.

All of these initiatives describe the very idea of resilience: self-organized emergency response that is re-programmed through digital interconnectedness. Not only is the information about the emergency provided by the affected population, but the population can now draw upon available data to further organize itself. This self-organization includes practical aspects, but also the emotional facets of resilience:

> social media, specifically their core strengths of timely information exchange and promotion of connectedness, were able to act as sources of psychological first aid in the early stages of disaster and assist in supporting aspects of community resilience.
>
> (Taylor *et al.* 2012)

Since the digital emphasizes role and status of the self-organized individual in new ways, traditional emergency services are now in need of reinventing their roles and strategies. The analysis of digital data may provide new avenues for resilience programming, such as digital mapping and emergency communication

Resilience and the digital 141

networks to coordinate disaster response. Yet, if traditional emergency services choose to embrace these new opportunities and replace traditional emergency management approaches, the digital also increases the gap between the emergency setting and the emergency managers who analyze the given data. The digital may establish new connections and interrelations, but it also reinforces a spatiality of remote control that is characteristic of resilience. One dimension of this remoteness is an analytical one that is specific to the digital and its affordances of networkability, traceability and calculability. As information is increasingly crowd-sourced, meaning that it is collected from digital populations that are traced and identified to be in the affected areas, analyzers lack the experience of the context in which emergency data is produced (Boyd and Crawford 2012). This loss of context is intensified by the translation of offline information into digital, computable bits, which dis- and reconnect the data (cf. Stäheli 2012a). It is amplified by processes of cleaning and interpreting the data, as well as the workings of algorithms that constantly de- and recontextualize information.

A second dimension of this gap is the way in which digital communication replaces physical presence and face-to-face contact. The relationship between managers and the affected population is increasingly mediated. This lack of direct communication may not only influence the experience of emergency for the affected population, but it can also influence the relationship of professional responders toward emergencies. Screens become the interface through which resilience managers operate and their engagement is likely to become subject to gamification. Gamification refers here to the game-like experience of emergencies, where the application design triggers desires for mastery, competition and achievement and transforms the emergency context into a surreal or removed challenge that needs to be met (for an example of embedding emergency management tasks in games, cf. Internet Response League 2013). In the context of drone usage for emergency management, it has furthermore been discussed whether this mediated experience entails an emotional removal of the managers from the reality of the situation (Sandvik 2013). Digital interfaces not only mediate the emotional relationship of the user to the emergency situation by removing the emergency from or by bringing the emergency situation into a space that can be private or disconnected from the rest of the emergency setting (Kaufmann 2015; cf. Chapter 8). Digital interconnectedness also increases the physical distance between emergency populations and those authorities that analyze the emergency situation from the *control room* (Duffield 2011). As such, the digital enhances the idea of remote management, the exercise of emergency coordination and control from a distance (Collinson *et al*. 2013). Creating resilience would then be recast as a form of facilitating self-organization from a bunker (Duffield 2011), where analysts may veer away from the reality of the situation and toward a risk-aversion on the ground (Duffield 2016: 1). This physical remoteness is compensated by smart technology and the negative associations of remoteness are affirmatively redefined as "digital recapture" (ibid.: 3). At the same time, however, technologies provide a welcome means not to face ground friction, but to work around challenges (ibid.: 4). Even though it affords new ways of directing emergencies, the digital still instantiates its own spatiality (cf. Chapter 5), as Duffield describes: "It is a remoteness that, simultaneously, is a form of recapture and drawing near" (Duffield 2016: 3). It is a mediated interplay of proximity and distance that relates to both the analytic and the physical level. Some even claim this digital recapture abandons the need to acknowledge the motives and beliefs that shape actual human behavior (Duffield 2016: 1; Chandler 2015). The digital not only broadens the space for emergency intervention and brings responders closer to the emergency in some situations, but it also redefines physical proximity. It affords mediated closeness and physical remoteness.

Learning for future emergencies

Because digital information can be stored, it is not only used to organize acute emergency relief, but also to inform resilience programming in general: "Tweets and photographs linked to timelines and interactive maps can tell a cohesive story about a recovering community's capabilities und vulnerabilities" (Merchant *et al*. 2011: 2; Birkmann 2006). The idea here is to evaluate existing information for insights that can be harnessed for future resilience programs. Thus, a third development that the digitization of resilience inspires is the identification of patterns and resilience indicators to enhance a system's "capacity to learn from past incidences" (Holling 1973). Learning from past emergencies is an integral part of resilience programs already (Keck and Sakdapolrak 2013). The digital, once again, emphasizes this characteristic and transcribes it into resilience programming – not least because it affords storability.

In the same frame of reference, Merchant *et al*. suggest that "(n)ow is the time to begin deploying these technologies while developing meaningful metrics of their effectiveness and of the accuracy and usefulness of the information they provide" (2011: 2). The opportunities seem to be manifold: big data

> can also help when you want to go back and look at what happened during an emergency to see how an organization responded to data as it became available, or simply to look at how information flowed to try to optimize it for the next disaster.
>
> (Ikanow.com n.d.a)

Digital data thus allow to be repurposed and scanned for "socio-economic, ethnic, cultural, religious, partisan, political, tribal and other patterns that help [...] mitigation, response and recovery" (Stauffacher *et al*. 2012: 5). "A 'good' disaster," so Duffield comments critically, is believed to "disrupt and clear much social and institutional deadwood, making survivors receptive to new messages and inducements" (Duffield 2016: 7; cf. Klein 2007). And digital databases are here believed to assist in identifying new messages.

The idea to utilize digital information for designing future resilience practices was, for example, suggested in the report following the 22 July attacks in Norway,

Resilience and the digital 143

which recommended that information circulated on social media should be used for mastering situational analysis and information gathering in emergencies to come. Such analyses should, for example, examine data about efforts to contact potential victims and the experience of support (NOU 2012: 454–455). However, the collection of digital information about emergencies is surely not restricted to online sources. Many tabletop emergency exercises specifically produce offline digital data that allows for the assessment of resilience patterns and lessons to learn (BBK 2011).

Here, the traceability of digital information and its storage in databases provides for the identification of resilience indicators. It enables the analysis of relations between locations, events and people and the way in which they utilized available information and communication services. This search for patterns is not conducted to explore the causes of emergencies, but to optimize future interventions. In the same way in which resilience is inherently about the intervention after emergencies, the digital techniques employed to identify patterns are inherently an analytics of effects, of correlations and interventions. Both resilience and the knowledge produced by digital data analysis, focus on the ex post facto: they focus on that which follows after the emergency – even when analyzed for future response. As a result, the assessment of patterns for future resilience programs fosters the governance through effects and expectations of self-organization in its own way:

> With an additional click, perhaps off-duty nurses or paramedics who check in at a venue could also broadcast their professional background and willingness to help in the event of a nearby emergency.
> (Merchant *et al.* 2011: 1)

The computability, the traceability, storability and searchability, the networkability and interpretability of digital information afford the translation of resilience programs into resilience programming. It is through its digitization that emergency information can be analyzed and converted into new forms of resilience practices and curricula. These curricula focus on whichever lessons learned emergency managers prioritize. Resilience patterns, determined via association, correlation, averages and quantification, rise here as the dominant form of reasoning about emergency response and self-organization. It is through patterns that the digital assists in the strategic calibration of relations within communities and in instilling politically desired forms of adaptation (Grove 2014). The digitization of resilience thus combines the discretely countable with the accountable: while resilience promotes a subject that is accountable or held responsible for its own wellbeing, the analysis of resilience patterns within digital information tie this status to the logic of calculation, measurability and quantity. Resilience is, then, not only about individual response to emergency – personal and highly context-driven, but about dividuated, pattern-based response (Deleuze 1992).

144 *Part III: Governing through the Internet*

Crowds and effects take center stage

Resilience initiatives have become digitally mediated and will be even more so in the future (Fine Maron 2013). This increase in digital emergency information enables the collection and analysis of data for new forms of mapping and directing emergencies, as well as learning lessons for those to come. Digital information, then, allows for rewriting the program of resilience through the language of programming. It allows for the use of computation for emergency response, and the algorithmic analysis of efforts to deal with emergency situations. Due to that unique ability, digital technologies have already become key tools for crowd-oriented resilience activities.

This promise of the digital and its contribution to resilience programming, however, requires a careful investigation of the concepts, practices and knowledge regimes it inspires. Two overarching developments that are enabled by the digital shall be discussed here as emblematic: first, the way in which the digital gives new weight to the crowd as the main performer of resilience activities; and second, how the digital re-emphasizes the role of the effect and the ontology of intervention that is already present in the resilience concept. The way in which crowds and effects take center-stage summarizes the powerful impact of digital information and connectivity on resilience practices.

The notion of resilience, in theory and practice, already emphasizes the idea that emergency management is no longer a matter of traditional security institutions. By internalizing the emergency into society, all members of society are called upon to contribute to the re-establishing of security during times of crises (Joseph 2013; Kaufmann 2013). Self-organization is the key to resilience. Through the digital, this shift in focus from the protective work of institutions to the contribution of affected parties happens on yet a different dimension. While the crowd is traditionally the receiver of crisis-management help, the role of the affected is now to become an actor of digital self-organization. The digital facilitates the inclusion of the crowd into resilience activities. It is another entryway for the crowd to become an active participant of resilience management. Any member of the community that is affected by emergency is, as a matter of principle, expected to instantiate the security that they would like to experience. With respect to the digital this means that the crowd is, for example, commissioned to provide information via crowd-tasking. Such practices are symptomatic of much more fundamental expectations: digital crowds are expected to render emergency response more efficient through their function as an innovator and problem-solver (Wexler 2011). In fact, "living abandoned in the ruins," as Duffield calls it, "is portrayed as not only possible but somehow emancipatory" (Duffield 2016: 8; cf. Bittman 2015). Much in the spirit of resilient self-organization, the crowd is mobilized for the digital economies of emergency management. Because digital crowds are dispersed and subject to unlimited growth, their collective intelligence, their wisdom and their hidden knowledge seem to call for being harnessed (Aradau and Blanke 2014). The storability of digital information is here the key to scan and pattern the crowds' emerging knowledge in dealing with emergencies. Those pragmatic approaches that conceptualize and utilize the crowd as a problem-solver typically run into the challenges of reliable information and information management discussed above (cf. Meier 2012). These, however, are just the practical obstacles of digital analytics. Blanke, once again, draws attention to the deeper-seated challenge of the digital crowd as the exploited workforce (2014; Andrejevic 2009). As the "effective producers of digital value" (Aradau and Blanke 2014: 31), the crowd has become the main target of the information market and a "part of an emerging larger business infrastructure that supports new kinds of production and consumption of digital value" (ibid.: 33). Yet, their labor – utilized for ideological projects and businesses – remains unpaid (Blanke 2014).

Through the digital, in fact, the crowd experiences a new emphasis as an actor with specific tasks, but also specific opportunities. The sociology of crowds is a well-established topic, to which the digital only adds yet another dimension. Le Bon's conceptualization of the crowd as microbes that infect each other, as feminine and as destabilizing mob, different from the civilized society (1960 [1895]), has been contrasted with Canetti's (1973 [1960]) understanding of the crowd as political actor who negotiates and collectively advocates for rational-liberal interests (cf. Borch 2013). Negotiating interests and the establishing of a consensus, however, may be some forces that constitute the crowd. Yet, Mouffe emphasizes that crowds can just as well be mobilized through conflicts. Rather than being driven by rational purpose only, the crowd also expresses a need for collective identification (2005). In light of the increased digitization and its impact on resilience practices, one can see how social media, in particular, give room to the way in which challenges and conflicts that arise from emergencies are discussed online, giving rise to crowds that both negotiate interests, but are also shaped by a common need for identification. In that respect, the next chapter will more specifically focus on the way in which social media served as a digital space for shaping and making opinions, for digital mourning and virtual unity, but also unanswered ambiguities during the 2011 Norway attacks (cf. Kaufmann 2015). The formation of the crowd was here tied to a specific situation – the emergency. Situations that generate collective action can, according to Blumer (1951), reach from the disruption of a routine all the way to catastrophes. In the case of the 2011 Norway attacks, the digital crowd, affected and challenged by the emergency, assembled through social media, dispersed and yet connected.

A spontaneous digital assembly of people that collectively deal with emergencies – guided by "passions" (Mouffe 2005) rather than reason, moderation and consensus – is a very different crowd from the one that is *tasked* to contribute to emergency management. To put it differently, the emergent crowd guided by passions and driven by the urge to exchange views on the attacks via digital media is different from one that is summarized and generalized by the term and the appeal of having to be a self-organized *crowd*. This shows how the multiple affordances of the digital enable the emergence of different kinds of digital crowds. For example, the fact that the digital is traceable and storable enables the emergence of a crowd that is tasked with a specific duty and whose digital moves are surveilled and analyzed. The networkability of the digital, however, allows for a fine-grained split-up of communities of interests and identification; it provides a space where crowds can, dependent on motive and cause, arise and dissolve spontaneously, where they can express conflicts or common interests. The challenge here is that the digital is neither reduced to one affordance or the other, but it enables both kinds of crowds at the same time.

Any kind of digital crowd is only ever a mediated crowd. The idea of the digital crowd may still match Blumer's (1951) description of the crowd as a phenomenon of movement, dynamic and self-organized, to which the digital network, in fact, grants new spaces. However, it challenges Borch's understanding of the crowd as a body-to-body experience (2009). Borch describes a physical, anatomic, and affective dimension of the crowd, which foregrounds the human body and conceptualizes the crowd as that which grants physical affects a valve. The fact that the individual can overcome the fear of contact by merging with the unity of the crowd, he argues, contributes to a transformation that can only exist in the crowd (2009). While the Internet may not allow for an unmediated body-to-body experience, the digital does still instantiate its own materiality and its own spaces where affect, as a pre-individual experience, can take place, and the experience of community and unity, yet virtualized, takes effect (Kaufmann 2015; cf. Chapter 8).

If not a body-to-body experience, the digital crowd is still dependent on material-discursive arrangements (Aradau and Blanke 2014). Crowds, in general need an infrastructure to assemble, such as public places and means of transport, since the crowd is a process and not a simple aggregate (Stäheli 2012a). The Internet can be such an infrastructure. And it is exactly that – an infrastructure that also structures and mediates assembly. As an assemblage of hardware, software, of data, digital and non-digital places, it collects, orchestrates and structures different crowds. It provides the crowd with a specific form of material connectivity and experiential connectedness: the Internet allows for the establishing of ties of common experience for a specific time – albeit without a specific timing device, such as other infrastructures do (e.g., means of transport). The absence of such a timing device may even intensify the moment of assembly. In the analysis of social media use after the 2011 Norway attacks, which we will turn to in the next chapter, the Internet in fact stimulated a specific, digitally mediated experience of community and assembly. A shared digital experience can thus become constitutive of a digital crowd and it can entail its own affectivity (Kaufmann 2015; cf. Chapter 8).[2]

However, the same digital infrastructure that allows for shared digitally mediated experiences also makes collective experiences traceable, storable and renders them calculable. It is the same digital infrastructure that is used for the programming and the orchestration of resilience and self-organization. By translating the shared experience and the collective action of the crowd into digital bits, it splits the status of *the crowd* as a unity (Canetti 1973 [1960]; cf. Deleuze and Guattari 1987 [1980]) into the binary, the dual status of the digital. Digital infrastructures then connect and disconnect the members of the crowd. Digital infrastructures allow for specific crowds to become visible (mainly those that succeed in the politics of clicks), but they make invisible and depoliticize others. The digital renders the crowd calculable, which makes it possible to subject crowds to computational analysis, economic opportunity and resilience programming.

While Aradau and Blanke summarize the concern that "their emotions captured and 'free labour' extracted, [digital] crowds are separated from the political promise of collective power" (2014: 33; brackets added) they still see that "the production of temporal and spatial conditions of coming and being together in the digital world harbors the promise of a digital crowd event" (2014: 38). In light of the above, it can be argued that the spontaneous, user-driven collective activity, which followed the 2011 attacks in Norway – the creation of the Facebook event "I am in Oslo and I'm fine" (cf. Kaufmann 2015) – is an actual digital event. It was a spontaneous gathering of a crowd that was driven by the necessity to react to an emergency and appropriated the Internet as a platform to express a common concern. This very event, however, also reflects the duality of the digital crowd and the economic spirit it is subjected to, since the same idea was later harvested as an opportunity and turned into Facebook's Safety Check.

This leads us to the second emblematic development that the digital reinforces: the move from engagement with causes of emergencies to emergency governance led by patterns, correlations, effects and intervention. While the idea of the self-organized crowd was already existent in the resilience concept and recast through the digital, the way in which resilience conceptually focuses on intervention instead of prevention is once again emphasized by the digital. Digital crowds provide the data, the wisdom and the ideas needed for resilience management, which is only possible because their moves are inherently traceable. Their behavior has – within the given limits – become assessible through the correlative workings of algorithmic analysis that digital data affords. Repurposing existent digital information and unearthing patterns has become a key activity of digital resilience management and the pattern arises as the epistemological authority for resilience programming. Resilience programs, which suggest how affected populations should organize themselves, are thus increasingly based on the logic of association.

Resilience programs are based on those ideas and assumptions that drive the writing of algorithms and the creation of patterns. As such, the patterns that determine resilience programs are never as much a reflection of reality as they seem. The data that feeds into them is cleaned and does not (fully) capture the information of those who are on the disconnected side of the digital divide. Resilience patterns are furthermore based on the logic of mass, which is why they tend to neglect individual ways of coping. Morozov criticizes the use of such patterns as "unpolitical," because they leave no room for political deliberation. Or, to put it differently, the digital has its own politics, because it lends itself more easily to algorithmic regulation than to non-patterned deliberation processes (cf. Kaufmann and Jeandesboz 2016). Most importantly, the algorithms that analyze digital data cannot identify underlying explanations.

Algorithms don't have sorting power, but they "simply function" (Andrejevic and Gates 2014). In fact, most methods that work with digital data are not about providing explanations. The purpose of digital data analysis is neither to produce an accurate or complete view of the world nor to explain phenomena, but algorithmic and big data analysis is "about intervening in that world based on patterns available only to those with access to the data and the processing power" (Andrejevic and Gates 2014: 190). Agamben observes that this feeds into a form of politics "whereby the traditional hierarchical relation between causes and effects is inverted, so that, instead of governing the causes – a difficult and expensive undertaking – governments simply try to govern the effects" (cf. Morozov 2014). Digital technologies may offer new ways of optimizing adaptation and operationalizing resilience, but it has nothing to say about conditions or problems (cf. Duffield 2016). A politics that focuses on the causes of emergencies, explanations for the treatment of insecurity or a change of milieu is replaced by a politics of control, surveillance and administration.

> The aesthetic of smart is not to directly confront problems but, through immediate access to value-added information, to endlessly sidestep them [...]. Rather than progress, it's more a case of survivalism through encouraging improvisation, making do and inventive bricolage with existing communications' infrastructure, architecture and social capital.
>
> (Duffield 2016: 2)

The rise of the pattern as an epistemological authority entails here that causal knowledge, which leads to protection, is replaced by correlative knowledge that leads to effective intervention. Effective intervention, organized by the affected crowd themselves, is ultimately also the purpose of resilience management.

While the making of patterns – the de- and recontextualization of a phenomenon – can also be a creative and an inspiring process that allows for the discovery of new effects, the overarching implications of this analytics for security governance need to be reflected. This is why Manovich asks for new ways of working with and representing large volumes of digital data. He gives us a task: only when they are translated into meaningful experiences, patterns and algorithms are equipped "to show us other realities embedded in our own [...] or to show us what we normally don't notice or don't pay attention to" (Manovich 2002a).

When we explore where digital technologies introduce a shift from programs to programming in security governance, we need to question the self-evidence inherent in the arguments surrounding digital information and patterns. Only when we reflect on the emergence of the pattern as epistemological authority, and the way in which it moves away from causal explanations toward intervention, can we grasp the way it influences resilience. A critical analysis of the digital identifies how and by whom the value of information is created in the first place and uncovers what it means that the digital increases the focus on the self-organized and digitally mediated crowd. While acknowledging that digital infrastructures structure the crowd, we should not forget that they also allow for the rise of the digital event as a truly political instant (Aradau and Blanke 2014). The next chapter will focus on such an instant, where the Internet, more particularly social media, have been appropriated by a crowd that emerged spontaneously; a crowd that emerged as a reaction to the emergency of the 2011 terror attacks in Norway.

Notes

1 For an in-depth discussion, cf. Kaufmann and Jeandesboz (2016) Politics and the Digital in the *European Journal of Social Theory*, which also inspired some thoughts shared in the next paragraphs.
2 For a discussion of the digital and the body, cf. Hansen 2004.

References

Agamben G (2005) *State of Exception*. Chicago: University of Chicago Press.
Amoore L (2013) *The Politics of Possibility. Risk and Security Beyond Probability*. Durham, NC and London: Duke University Press.
Andrejevic M (2009) Privacy, Exploitation, and the Digital Enclosure. *Amsterdam Law Forum* 1(4). Available at: http://amsterdamlawforum.org/article/view/94/168 (accessed 25 February 2016).
Andrejevic M, Gates K (2014) Big Data Surveillance: Introduction. *Surveillance and Society* 12(2): 185–196.
Aradau C, Blanke T (2014) The Politics of Digital Crowds. *LosQuaderno* 33: 31–38.
BBK (2011) *Leitfaden für strategische Krisenmanagement-Übungen*. Bonn: Bevölkerungsschutz.
Birkmann J (2006) *Measuring Vulnerability to Natural Hazards: Toward Disaster Resilient Societies*. Tokyo: United Nations University Press.
Bittman M (2015) *A Walk on the Wild (Edibles) Side*. Available at: www.nytimes.com/2015/07/09/opinion/mark-bittman-a-walk-on-the-wild-edibles-side.html (accessed 19 July 2016).
Blanchette JF (2011) A Material History of Bits. *Journal of the American Society for Information Science and Technology* 62(6): 1042–1057.
Blanke T (2014) *Digital Asset Ecosystems: Rethinking Crowds and Clouds*. Oxford: Chandos/Elsevier.
Blumer H (1951) Collective Behavior. In: Lee AM (ed.) *New Outlines of the Principles of Sociology*. New York: Barnes & Noble. 170–222.
Borch (2009) Body to Body: On the Political Anatomy of Crowds. *Sociological Theory* 27(3): 271–290.
Borch (2013) *The Politics of Crowds. An Alternative History of Sociology*. Cambridge: Cambridge University Press.
Boyd D, Crawford K (2012) Critical Questions for Big Data. Provocations for a Cultural, Technological, and Scholarly Phenomenon. *Information, Communication and Society* 15(5): 662–679.
Buchanan EA, Ess C (2008) Internet Research Ethics: The Field and Its Critical Issues. In: Himma E, Tavani HT (eds) *The Handbook of Information and Computer Ethics*. Chichester, Sussex: Wiley.

Canetti E (1973 [1960]) *Crowds and Power*. Trans. Stewart C. London: Penguin.

Chandler D (2015) A World without Causation: Big Data and the Coming of Age of Posthumanism. *Millennium: Journal of International Studies* 43: 833–851.

Collinson S, Duffield M, Berger C, Felix da Costa D, Sandstrum K (2013) *Paradoxes of Presence. Risk Management and Aid Culture in Challenging Environments*. London: Humanitarian Policy Group.

Committee on Planning for Catastrophe (2007) *Successful Response Starts with a Map: Improving Geospatial Support for Disaster Management*. National Research Council. Washington, DC: National Academies Press.

Crawford K, Faleiros G, Luers A, Meier P, Perlich C, Thorp J (2013) Big Data, Communities and Ethical Resilience: A Framework for Action. *White Paper for PopTech and Rockefeller Foundation.* Available at: www.rockefellerfoundation.org/app/uploads/71b4c457-cdb7-47ec-81a9-a617c956e6af.pdf (accessed 11 August 2016).

Crowe A (2011) The Social Media Manifesto: A Comprehensive Review of the Impact of Social Media on Emergency Management. *Journal of Business Continuity and Emergency Planning* 5(1): 409–420.

Deleuze G (1992) Postscript on the Societies of Control. *October* 59: 3–7.

Deleuze G, Guattari F (1987 [1980]) *A Thousand Plateaus. Capitalism and Schizophrenia*. London: Athlone.

Derosières A (2014) *Prouver Et Gouverner. Une Analyse Politique Des Statistiques Publiques*. Paris: La Découverte.

Duffield M (2011) Environmental Terror: Uncertainty, Resilience and the Bunker. School of Sociology, Politics and International Studies. University of Bristol. *Working Paper No. 06–11*. Available at: www.bristol.ac.uk/spais/research/workingpapers/wpspaisfiles/duffield-0611.pdf (accessed 11 August 2016).

Duffield M (2016) The Resilience of the Ruins: Toward a Critique of Digital Humanitarianism. *Resilience – International Policies, Practices and Discourses.* 15 March: 1–19. Available at: http://dx.doi.org/10.1080/21693293.2016.1153772 (accessed 27 February 2017).

Economist (2012) *Six Degrees of Mobilization*. Available at: www.economist.com/node/21560977 (accessed 11 August 2016).

Emergency Journalism (2012) *Wildfires: Digital Age Tools for the Reporter*. Available at: http://emergencyjournalism.net/wildfires-digital-age-tools-for-the-reporter (accessed 29 July 2014).

European Commission (2014) *Disaster Resilience: Safeguarding and Securing Society, Including Adapting to Climate Change. Topic: Communication Technologies and Interoperability Topic 2: Next Generation Emergency Services. DRS-19–2014.* Available at: https://ec.europa.eu/research/participants/data/ref/h2020/wp/2014_2015/main/h2020-wp1415-security_en.pdf (accessed 11 August 2016).

FEMA (2011) *Universal Access to and Use of Information. Strategic Foresight Initiative.* Available at: www.fema.gov/pdf/about/programs/oppa/universal_access_paper_051011.pdf (accessed 11 August 2016).

Fine Maron D (2013) How Social Media is Changing Disaster Response. *Scientific American.* Available at: www.scientificamerican.com/article/how-social-media-is-changing-disaster-response (accessed 11 August 2016).

Galloway AR (2012) *The Interface Effect*. Cambridge: Polity Press.

Gao H, Barbier G, Goolsby R (2011) Harnessing the Crowdsourcing Power of Social Media for Disaster Relief. *Cyber-Physical-Social Systems* 26(3): 10–14.

Gibson JJ (1986) *The Ecological Approach to Visual Perception*. New York: Taylor & Francis.

Gilbert-Knight A (2013) Social Media, Crisis Mapping and the New Frontier in Disaster Response. *Guardian*, 8 October. Available at: www.theguardian.com/global-development-professionals-network/2013/oct/08/social-media-microtasking-disaster-response (accessed 11 August 2016).

Gitelman L, Jackson V (2013) Introduction. In: Gitelman L (ed.) *"Raw Data" Is an Oxymoron*. Cambridge, MA: MIT Press, pp. 1–14.

Gleit N, Zeng S, Cottle P (2014) Introducing Safety Check. Facebook Newsroom, 15 October. Available at: http://newsroom.fb.com/news/2014/10/introducing-safety-check (accessed 29 April 2016).

Google Person Finder (n.d.) Available at: http://google.org/personfinder/global/home.html (accessed 9 April 2016).

Graham M (2011) Time Machines and Virtual Portals: The Spatialities of the Digital Divide. *Progress in Development Studies* 11(3): 211–227.

Grove K (2014) Agency, Affect, and the Immunological Politics of Disaster Resilience. *Environment and Planning D: Society and Space* 32(2): 240–256.

Hansen MB (2004) *New Philosophy for New Media*. Cambridge, MA.: MIT Press.

Herzog L (2016) *Can "Effective Altruism" Really Change the World?* Available at: www.resilience.org/stories/2016-02-25/can-effective-altruism-really-change-the-world (accessed 4 May 2016).

Hildebrandt M (2012) The Meaning and the Mining of Legal Texts. In: Berry D (ed.) *Understanding Digitial Humanities*. Basingstoke: Palgrave Macmillan.

Holling CS (1973) Resilience and Stability of Ecological Systems. *Annual Review of Ecology and Systematics* 4: 1–23.

IFRC (2013) *World Disasters Report. Focus on Technology and the Future of Humanitarian Action*. International Federation of Red Cross and Red Crescent Societies, Geneva. Available at: http://worlddisastersreport.org/en (accessed 11 August 2016).

Ikanow.com (n.d.a) Crisis Management. Available at: https://ikanow.com/crisis-management (accessed 28 January 2014; no longer accessible).

Ikanow.com (n.d.b) Social Media. Available at: https://ikanow.com/five-tools-your-disaster-recovery-software-needs-to-have-when-using-social-media (accessed 28 January 2014; no longer accessible).

Internet Response League (2013) IRL Moving Forward. Available at: https://internet-response-league.com/2013/07/10/irl-moving-forward (accessed 20 April 2016).

Joseph J (2013) Resilience as Embedded in Neoliberalism: A Governmentality Approach. *Resilience: International Policies, Practices and Discourses* 1(1): 38–52.

Kaufmann M (2013) Emergent Self-Organisation in Emergencies: Resilience Rationales in Interconnected Societies. *Resilience: International Policies, Practices and Discourses* 1(1): 53–68.

Kaufmann M (2015) Resilience 2.0: Social Media and (Self-)care after 2011 Norway Attacks. *Media, Culture and Society* 37(7): 972–987.

Kaufmann M, Jeandesboz J (2016) Politics and the Digital. *European Journal of Social Theory*. DOI: 10.1177/1368431016677976: 1–20 (accessed 25 March 2017).

Keck M, Sakdapolrak P (2013) What is Social Resilience? Lessons Learned and Ways Forward. Erdkunde. *Archive for Scientific Geography* 67(1): 5–19.

Keim ME, Noji E (2011) Emergent Use of Social Media: A New Age of Opportunity for Disaster Resilience. *American Journal of Disaster Medicine* 6(1): 47–54.

Klein N (2007) *The Shock Doctrine: The Rise of Disaster Capitalism*. London: Penguin.

Latour B (2005) *Reassembling the Social. An Introduction to Actor-Network-Theory*. New York: Oxford University Press.

Le Bon G (1960 [1895]) *The Crowd: A Study of the Popular Mind.* Mineola, NY: Dover Publications.

Leonardi P (2010) Digital Materiality? How Artifacts Without Matter, Matter. *First Monday* 15 (6–7).

Lewin K (1969). *Grundzüge der topologischen Psychologie.* Posthume deutsche Ausgabe, ed. Falk R, Winnefeld F. Bern, Switzerland: Huber.

Lindsay BR (2011) Social Media and Disasters: Current Uses, Future Options, and Policy Considerations. *CRS Report for Congress. R 41987.*

Manovich L (2002a) *Data Visualisation as New Abstraction and Anti-Sublime.* Available at: www.zannahbot.com/data_art/DataVisAsNewAbstraction.pdf (accessed 11 August 2016).

Manovich L (2002b) *The Language of New Media.* Cambridge, MA: MIT Press.

Martin J (1965) *Programming Real-time Computer Systems.* Englewood Cliffs, NJ: Prentice-Hall Inc.

Meier P (2011) *Verifying Crowdsourced Social Media Reports for Live Crisis Mapping: An Introduction to Information Forensics.* Available at: http://irevolution.files.wordpress.com/2011/11/meier-verifying-crowdsourced-data-case-studies.pdf (accessed 11 August 2016).

Meier P (2012a) *Rapidly Verifying the Credibility of Information Sources on Twitter.* Available at: http://irevolution.net/2012/11/20/verifying-source-credibility (accessed 11 August 2016).

Meier P (2012b) *Truthiness and Probability: Moving Beyond the True or False Dichotomy When Verifying Social Media.* Available at: http://irevolution.net/2012/03/10/truthiness-as-probability (accessed 11 August 2016).

Meier P (2013) *Disaster Resilience 2.0.* Available at: http://irevolution.net/2013/01/11/disaster-resilience-2-0 (accessed 11 August 2016).

Mendoza M, Poblete B, Castillo C (2010) *Twitter Under Crisis: Can We Trust What We RT? 1–9.* Available at: http://snap.stanford.edu/soma2010/papers/soma2010_11.pdf (accessed 11 August 2016).

Merchant RM, Elmer S, Lurie N (2011) Integrating Social Media into Emergency-Preparedness Efforts. *The New England Journal of Medicine* 365: 289–291.

Mouffe C (2005) *On the Political.* London and New York: Routledge.

Morozov E (2014) The Rise of Data and the Death of Politics. *Observer*, 20 July: 1–14. Available at: www.theguardian.com/technology/2014/jul/20/rise-of-data-death-of-politics-evgeny-morozov-algorithmic-regulation (accessed 22 February 2016).

NOU (2012) Rapport fra 22. Juli-kommisjonen. 2012. 14. Departementenes servicesenter Informasjonsforvaltning. Norges offentlige utredniner, Oslo.

Nygren J (2015) The Resilience Protocol – On Incentives. Available at: https://resilience.press/the-resilience-protocol-on-incentives-5a4061d1f4b9#.e7oizsub9 (accessed 4 May 2016).

Paul G (2009) *Foundations of Digital Evidence.* Washington, DC: American Bar Association.

Purohit H, Castillo C, Diaz F, Sheth A, Meier P (2014) Emergency Relief Coordination on Social Media: Automatically Matching Resource Requests and Offers. *First Monday* 19(1). Available at: http://firstmonday.org/ojs/index.php/fm/article/view/4848/3809 (accessed 18 July 2016).

Rushe D (2013) Facebook Reveals Governments Asked for Data on 38,000 Users in 2013. *Guardian*, 28 August. Available at: www.theguardian.com/technology/2013/aug/27/facebook-government-user-requests (accessed 11 August 2016).

Sandvik KB (2013) *Drone Pilots, Humanitarians and the Videogame Analogy: Unpacking the Conversation, UAV – bare ny teknologi eller en ny strategisk virkelighet? Luftkrigsskolens skriftserie volum 29, 29.* Trondheim, Norway: Luftkrigsskolen.

Schmitt C (1921) *Die Diktatur.* Leipzig and Munich: Duncker & Humblot.

Stäheli U (2012a) Infrastruktiren des Kollektiven: Alte Medien – neue Kollektive? *Zeitschrift für Medien- und Kulturforschung* 2012/2: 99–116.

Stäheli U (2012b) Listing the Global: Dis/connectivity Beyond Representation? *Distinktion: Journal of Social Theory* 13(3): 233–246.

Stauffacher D, Hattotuwa S, Weekes B (2012) *The Potential and Challenges of Open Data for Crisis Information Management and Aid Efficiency: A Preliminary Assessment.* ICT4Peace Foundation, March.

Taylor M, Wells G, Howell G, Raphael B (2012) The Role of Social Media as Psychological First Aid as a Support to Community Resilience Building. *Australian Journal of Emergency Management* 27(1): 20–26.

Turner A (2006) Introduction to Neogeography. O'Reilly Media. Available at: http://highearthorbit.com/neogeography/book.pdf (accessed 11 August 2016).

UNGP (2013) *Mobile Phone Network Data for Development.* New York: United Nations Global Pulse.

Wexler MN (2011) Reconfiguring the Sociology of the Crowd: Exploring Crowdsourcing. *International Journal of Sociology and Social Policy* 31(1/2): 6–20.

Yates D, Paquette S (2011) Emergency Knowledge Management and Social Media Technologies: A Case Study of the 2010 Haitian Earthquake. *International Journal of Information Management* 31(1): 6–13.

8 Resilience and the network

Self-care and self-organization are central aspects of resilience. In the context of security governance they are technologies of the self (Foucault 1988a,b, 1993; cf. Chapters 3 and 4), which are now transformed by technologies off-the-shelf, that is, smart phones and computers, which feature access to the Internet as well as to social media specifically. Chapter 7 discussed the aspect of digital data for resilience programs and the way in which they can be used for resilience programming performed by governments. The computational turn has mainly led to the affirmative rhetoric about new sense-making opportunities during emergencies (as observed by Duffield 2016), while digital information redefines the practices, principles and rationalities of emergency management at the same time. As opposed to analyzing the digital and computational aspect of information circulating online and its relation to resilience programs, this chapter foregrounds the networked aspect of the Internet. This is not to say that the digital and the networked are oppositional. Quite the contrary, they are both fundamental charateristics of digital information (cf. Kaufmann and Jeandesboz 2016). However, while the digital aspect is associated with ones and zeros, with countability and computability, the networked aspect of digital information points to the social and relational dimension of information and not least to metadata that allows for information to travel. The digital and the networked also arguably establish different forms of reflexivity: while the digital instills reflexivity through numbers, the networked characteristics of information establish reflexivity through contacts, circulation and feedback loops. It is only the combination of the two – the digital and the networked – that allows for correlational forms of reasoning and the epistemology of the pattern that have risen as a rationality of governmental programming in the past years.

This chapter draws attention to the networked aspect of information by exploring the use of social media during the 2011 attacks in Norway. During that crisis, the use of social media for resilience emerged spontaneously from the population, or the digital *crowd*. It was only in the aftermath that governmental bodies identified the opportunities inherent in this trend and called for an expansion of policies that incorporate social media into emergency management (NOU 2012: 454–455). This is an important temporal dimension, since by today the integration of social media and digital information into resilience programs has indeed progressed. The use of social media for emergency management has become more institutionalized in research projects (Cordis 2016) and policy initiatives (UK Government 2012), dedicated apps such as "First Aid" by the Red Cross released in 2012 (American Red Cross 2012) and features, as for example, Facebook's Safety Check, introduced in 2014 (Gleit *et al.* 2014). The use of social media during emergencies has become so common that, today, news agencies and public television stations, for example, integrate a review of social media activities into their reporting on ongoing emergencies (e.g., BBC 2015; Tagesschau.de 2016a,b). Only few of such services and initiatives existed in 2011, which means that during the Norway attacks, social media users were fabricating solutions spontaneously – and without being directly instructed to do so. In interviews, users not only recounted stories about creative moments of bricolage, of "re-engineering or repurposing whatever technical skills or serviceable infrastructure is at hand" (Duffield 2016: 9) – a set of practices which we can also identify as technologies of the self. The interviewees reflected on the challenges that arise when social media use is appropriated and rendered efficient for resilience programming by both governments and the population. While Chapter 7 discussed the challenges that arise when online creativity is locked to binary code, the interview material featured in this chapter provides a critical appraisal of the way in which creativity is further enclosed by networked logics, but also by governmental codes of *making opinion* and media codes of sensationalism, misinformation and speculation.

Social media and (self-)care during emergencies

"Military police, ambulances etc. on the scene #osloexplosion" (hilango) was the very first tweet from a private person that was recorded in relation to the Norway attacks. What followed was an extensive mapping of tweets that were collected and translated by the Norwegian public broadcaster, *Norsk rikskringkasting* (NRK), into a timeline of the hours and days after the events (Nrk.no 2011). The title of this collection reads: "The terror-days on twitter. A visualization of 250.000 twitter-posts from the first days of terror."

At a more general level, different kinds of technology, for example, telecommunication technologies, geographic information systems (GIS), or traditional media technologies, have long been an integral part of emergency reporting and management. The incorporation of social media into resilience practices and reporting, however, is a relatively recent phenomenon. The collection of tweets during the 2011 terror attacks was the first time in Norway that social media technologies have got this much attention in the context of an ongoing emergency. Social media – often referred to as 2.0 technologies – allow users to interact, collaborate and become creators of user-generated content. These are important technical features in the rise of distributed information exchange as they reflect the idea of self-organized contents and practices. Communication and networking sites, such as Facebook, Twitter, and Instagram, are by now important media for producing and accessing information about emergencies.

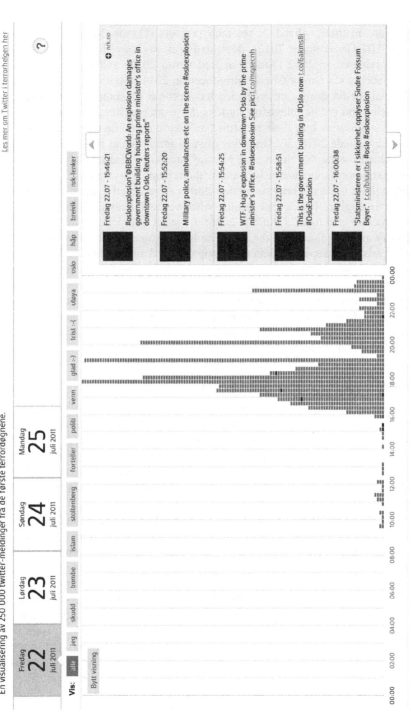

Figure 8.1 NRK Twitter-timeline of the 22 July Attacks in Norway.

Source: © nrk.no (http://snutt.nrk.no/multimedia/terrortwitter).

Resilience and the network 157

Studying the reactions to the 2011 Norway attacks as a case in point, this chapter asks: How are social media appropriated by average users for dealing with emergencies? And what does this shift toward social networks imply for resilience governance?

Resilience itself is not taken as a given capacity that is either enhanced or inhibited by social media use. Instead, the chapter explores how the multiple and diverse processes following emergencies are to an increasing extent incorporating social networking sites. It studies how average social media users in Oslo have appropriated Facebook and Twitter for dealing with the terrorist attack conducted by Anders Behring Breivik on 22 July 2011, when a car bomb in the Oslo government quarter killed eight people and a subsequent shooting at a worker's youth league summer camp on Utøya Island claimed 69 lives. The way in which social media have been utilized during and after these attacks, the chapter argues, is a specific expression of mediated and self-initiated governance of emergencies that resonates with resilience thinking, because it reflects and reinforces the principles and rationalities of self-organization, distribution and adaptation. How this form of resilience governance came about can in many ways be attributed to the interplay between 2.0 technologies and the (resilient) subject, which influence each other in the process.

The chapter's findings are based on 20 semi-structured, in-depth interviews, which were designed to explore what kind of functions social networking sites (Facebook), and microblogs (Twitter) fulfilled during the emergency situation and its aftermath, as well as the challenges connected to the use of social media. The interviews were organized in four thematic blocks: first, the interviewee's general use of social media; second, the specific online experience on 22 July; third, the different purposes of social media use in the aftermath of the attacks including topics, groups and pictures; and finally, the interviewee's own view on his or her social media experience, including expressions of emotions, values and opinions. The interviews were targeted at people between the age of 18 and 31 and included men and women, both with and without migration background. The interviewees were selected through a snowballing sample and included social media users who lived in Oslo at the time of the attacks and were either present in the city or traveling. More than half of the interviews were conducted in English; the others were translated from Norwegian for the purposes of the analysis. The transcriptions were coded using over 150 different theme clusters that were developed inductively from the material. The theme cluster on Facebook-related topics that were inferred from the interview material looked, for example, as in Figure 8.2.

The cluster included two higher-ranking thematic nodes, one of them covers anything about the use of Facebook during 22 July (Node: Use 22. Juli). Another node covers those statements that address why users have refrained from posting messages themselves and why (Node: Why people didn't post). The node "Use 22. Juli" is subdivided into further high-level nodes such as "Analysis," which collects any material that was relevant for a theoretical analysis of Facebook usage during emergencies; "Behavior," which covers how people described their

158 *Part III: Governing through the Internet*

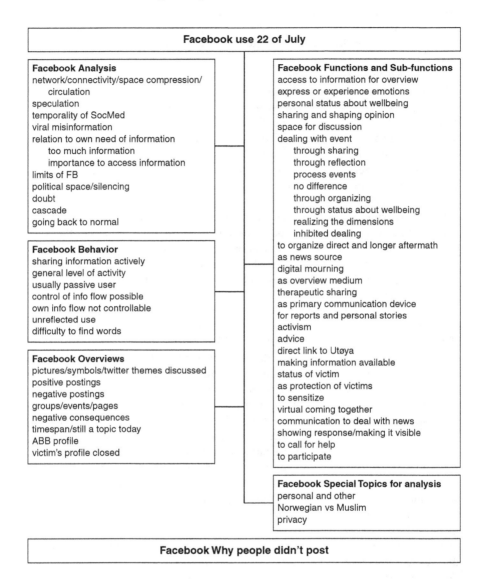

Figure 8.2 Coding nodes: theme cluster "Facebook".

own and others' behavior on Facebook in general; "Functions and Subfunctions" encodes any concrete functions that the interviewees mentioned Facebook fulfilled during the emergencies; "Overviews" covers a range of general and more overarching themes concerning Facebook usage during emergencies; and "Special topics for analysis" encodes topics that addressed issues of personal data, privacy and the relationship between Muslim and non-Muslim Norwegians.

The node-cluster for coding Facebook-related passages was one of approximately ten clusters that were used for the analysis. Other clusters included, for example, general information about the interviewees' online behavior, diverse Twitter-related topics, general statements about 22 July, the interviewee's views on or mentioning of values, media and emotions. While the compilation of the clusters was driven by and inferred from the interview material, meaning that many of these themes were in fact brought up by the interviewees themselves, the interviews were guided and structured by a set of questions, following the four thematic blocks described above. Most passages of the interviews were coded as relevant for several nodes.

Before going into the functions and challenges of social media use for resilience activities during 22 July, the following part introduces the theoretical approach of this chapter. It situates the use of social media for dealing with emergencies in the larger context of self-care and self-initiated governance. Drawing on the concept of mediality, it illustrates that the constitution of self-caring subjects is closely intertwined with the character of the infrastructure that is being used to express (self-)care. The third part will then explore the concrete examples of how social media have been actually appropriated to deal with the 2011 Norway attacks and points to the diverse manifestations of self-care that emerged from that use. This empirical material is discussed in the final section, which argues that the appropriation of social media for resilience practices not only generates mediated forms of resilience, but draws attention to an often under-analyzed aspect in this context, namely the way in which the networked character of social media influences the emergence of resilience practices and resilient subjects.

A new technology of the self?

Communicating about, managing and dealing with emergencies is, of course, never enabled through social media only. However, as online communication increases, the role social media play for such incidents increases, too (cf. IFRC 2013). Seven out of 20 interviewees state that social media were one of their initial points of contact with the Norway attacks – before they had checked traditional media. The trend to consult social media during emergencies has been explored academically in terms of social media's value for crowdsourcing information during disasters (Heinzelmann et al. 2011), to process visual information into maps (Sjöberg et al. 2013), to measure vulnerability (Birkmann 2006), to organize emergency relief, manage knowledge or utilize circulated information to engender resilience (Purohit et al. 2014; Yates and Paquette 2011; Keim and Noji 2011). Within this debate, scholars have discussed ethical frameworks for the use of big data to engender resilience (Crawford et al. 2013), challenges related to the veracity and validity of circulating information (Popoola et al. 2013; Meier 2014), and the rise of cyber-humanitarianism altogether (Duffield 2013, 2016; Sandvik et al. 2014). The majority of the academic literature on the use of social media for emergency management and resilience, however, explores such trends with considerable optimism and with the intent to identify opportunities for exploitation (for exceptions, cf. Duffield 2013, 2016; Sandvik *et al.* 2014). The issues of what kind of functions social media fulfill during emergencies and what this integration of networked technologies into emergency management processes implies for the sociology of resilience still need our critical attention. The aim of this chapter is, thus, not to assess whether the use of social media is constructive of or detrimental for resilience practices. Rather, it aims to understand what different roles social media fulfill during emergencies, explores how they reflect rationales and principles of resilience governance, and discusses what the turn from program to programming entails for the conceptualization of the resilient subject.

In order to investigate the connection between resilience and social media use during emergencies, it is instructive to trace how resilience has been theorized and how the use of 2.0 technologies for emergency management relates to that. Resilience thinking characteristically promotes self-organized crisis response (cf. Adger 2003). While socio-ecologists refer to the self-organizational capacities of systems, psychologists refer to the ability of subjects to deal with adversity through adaptation (Luthar *et al.* 2000; cf. Chapter 2). The notion of resilience has now been adopted into security policies as a form of re-organization after emergencies without obtaining "resources from the outside" (Longstaff *et al.* 2010: 7). All of these resilience conceptualizations refer to the necessity of self-care and the responsibilization of the individual that re-instantiates its own security after the event. Resilience is thus an act of self-care that draws upon peoples' self-governing capabilities, which becomes particularly apparent during the governance of emergencies. During emergencies, the resilient subject uses its calculating and rationalizing abilities to calibrate its own needs for security, and its entrepreneurship to overcome adversity.

In that sense, resilience can be considered a technology of the self, as it emphasizes the self-governing capabilities of the subject. Not only does the subject's behavior enable specific forms of governance, for example, by sharing information about itself, but it takes on an active role in caring for its own wellbeing (Foucault 1991; Rose 1996, 1999; Dean 1999). As discussed in Chapter 3, governmentality is here a useful lens to understand the broader development in which social media use for emergency management can be placed, especially when we explore how mediated and networked forms of self-care come about. As Berry (2012) notes, self-governance or self-care is manifested in different acts of individual consumption that follow a specific purpose, while this consumption is often facilitated through a specific infrastructure. As our lives are increasingly enmeshed with online networks, we can now witness how social media are appropriated as one of many infrastructures that are being used to share information about emergencies, in some cases with the deliberate intention to cope with and manage urgent situations.

In performing acts of self-governance, social media users rise as particular kinds of subjects (cf. Foucault 2010; Schecter 2010). They are not only self-caring, self-organizing, emergency-managing subjects, but their way of becoming particular subjects is enmeshed with 2.0 technologies. The specifics of becoming a self-caring subject are thus influenced by the character of the infrastructure that is used to perform self-caring practices (cf. Latour 2005). It means that the infrastructure, here off-the-shelf technologies and social media in particular, influences the way in which the subject, the care and the self-care comes about. That also becomes evident in the case study presented below: many of the emergency management functions that social media enabled during the Norway attacks could only emerge because the infrastructure was already deeply embedded in the users' everyday lives. Not only did users attribute additional functions to social media by using them for particular purposes, but the infrastructure's networked and distributed character also formed the emergence of these practices. The medium not only influenced the way in which knowledge about the emergency was accessed, produced and reproduced, but it also shaped the way in which users performed acts of self-care. It enabled distributed and networked forms of self-care.

The notion of mediality (Bolter and Grusin 1996; Grusin 2010) further conceptualizes this form of mediated (self-)governance. Most of Grusin's work explores the various forms through which media enable interactions between people with the aim of generating data that can be mined to effectively govern and discipline populations (Grusin and Cox 2010). Mediality is then a mode of governing and administrating that mobilizes the production and circulation of information through everyday media practices. Such modes of governing become all the more significant in societies where media and technologies of any kind play an increasingly central role. Mediality, however, not only refers to the way in which governments police and discipline populations through data, but the increasingly interactive character of media engenders modes of self-governing that can either be stimulated and instrumentalized by governments or by the populace itself, meaning these forms of governance can take place "within and outside the networks of state power" (Grusin 2010: 75). It is precisely in this notion of mediated self-governance where the idea of resilient self-organization and the use of 2.0 technologies for emergency management meet. It is within the use of social media where optimists see the opportunity to expedite self-governance during emergencies that is conducive to resilience. In addition to that, social media is not only a place where information is circulated, but where emotions are expressed and dealt with. We shall see in the case study below that mediated self-governance entails much potential for dealing with emotions. It is important not to dismiss, however, that all of these functions also involve related challenges that are discussed below, and that a moment of collective affect can be also exploited and manipulated to press for a specific political agenda or to present a specific account of the unfolding situation. The latter is also Grusin's main critique of the way in which media are used to affectively govern populations (2010). Such moments have also become more than visible in the debates that followed the role of social media during the Arab Spring and its fade, since social media also "help[s] dictators, not just protesters" (Gunitsky 2015). On a different and less dramatic level, the incorporation of social media into governmental emergency management efforts has already begun, and will continue to influence the way in which governments foresee the implementation of resilience agenda via digital technologies.

The concept of resilience in general and the use of technology to engender self-governance specifically have been subject to further criticism. While resilience policies promote a positive framing of self-organization, resilience has also been criticized for its proximity to neoliberal governance (cf. Zebrowski 2009; Joseph 2013). Resilience would be an expression of a subject that is responsibilized by the state and, following neoliberal market logics, requested to adapt to emergencies on its own account. Vis-à-vis the case discussed below, this criticism needs to be put into perspective. The way in which social media have been used to deal with the 2011 Norway attacks differs from prevalent examples of neoliberal governance in two ways. First, the fact that social media have been appropriated for emergency management was not directly or indirectly caused by governments that are "pushing for a certain agenda" (Joseph 2013: 44). If at all, the use during the 2011 attacks was an expression of the general governmental principles and liberal practices of our times. The form of self-governance described and discussed here was, in 2011, not yet the product of a social media initiative launched, for example, by the Norwegian government. It may only be the indirect result of a general move to outsource responsibility. As we shall see, the examples given below are rather instances of (self-)care that have grown out of a collective experience and that were enabled through networked infrastructure. To what extent this specific behavior could be an expression of a more deep-seated neoliberal culture or mentality is debatable. Second, the instance of (self-)care discussed here is also broader than its original meaning. It refers to individuals taking initiative, not only for their own, but also for each other's, wellbeing.

Finally, if social media are to an increasing extent integrated into resilience practices, another critical argument lies in the default translation of information about emergencies into digital data that can be traced, synthesized, measured and subjected to algorithmic analysis (Amoore 2009). In the context of an emergency, as explained in Chapter 7, digitized information about emergencies provides knowledge in the form of patterns: of behavior, of hubs of action, processes over time, movements of people and goods, of access to safe and dangerous areas. In the very sense of mediality and governmentality, such information has already begun to be incorporated into new practices of governance which seek to measure and engender resilience. As a result, resilience metrics will rise as one form of computed reasoning about resilience that influences the why and how of self-care. This development has been criticized as the facilitation of self-organization from a "control room" as new ways of knowing meet distance through cybernetic rationalities (Duffield 2013, 2016). This trend, however, has been discussed in more detail in Chapter 7.

While the above arguments about the digital need to be acknowledged as valid and important, we shall see that the empirical material of this chapter highlights a different aspect: the influence of the network. Social media are different from other digital media, as, for example, static websites, precisely because they depend more distinctly on an active network and contributors. In the same way, it is the subject that rises from these practices more than a subject that is defined through computable data: it also comes into existence through a network. It is this networked aspect of social media that the chapter brings back into the critical discussion on the technology-resilience nexus. That is why the case study not only illustrates a particular mediated experience of the Norway attacks and explores what forms mediated resilience can take, but it also draws attention to the granularity of digital networks, the discussion of which needs to include more facets than the computable. Showing that 2.0 technologies have more and less obvious affordances (Gibson 1977), the subsequent section will introduce the diverse functions and challenges that social media fulfilled in terms of resilience and reflect about the role that the networked character of social media played for the emergence of (self-)care.

Social media use during the Norway attacks – functions and challenges

> So it was this insane activity. There was a post every 30, 40 seconds on the same thing.
>
> (11)

After having heard of the attack, most interviewees refer to a moment of disbelief or confusion. They describe the situation as surreal, but are also filled with a worried kind of curiosity. This emotional status was counteracted with the attempt to access as much information, as soon as possible. In that moment, social media were not only consistently co-used with other media, but online newspapers and the Norwegian national broadcasting service were at times cited as the most important source of information. Most interviewees describe, however, that the selection of the medium was dependent on the purpose of its use. In general, the interviewees showed a tendency to access traditional online newspapers for facts, Twitter for analysis, and Facebook for personal statements, as well as the expression of emotions and interactive processes. The interactive aspects of dealing with the attacks were thus clearly ascribed to social media, the main focus of the chapter. In those cases, however, where social media constituted the direct link to the ongoing incidents, traditional media roles shifted, and social media were attributed with more factual credibility than traditional media. The trustworthiness of a source was thus assessed as dependent on the content and the situation.

The roles that social media fulfilled during the Norway attacks can be divided into two kinds – first-response and emotional functions. The first-response kind of functions, that mainly constitute the organizational and technical dimension of resilient self-organization, are collected in the first three function descriptions. These were different from the emotional functions that emerged in the longer aftermath of the attacks and can be associated with a sense of grief and coping, which are detailed in the last four function descriptions. While talking about the various functions that social media assumed in the process of dealing with the attacks, the interviewees also reflected on a range of challenges, which are presented in response to each function (function vs challenge). Since functions and challenges have been grouped and deduced from over 150 different codes, the different parts cannot always be clearly distinguished from one another. Despite their presentation as separate categories, they overlap and merge at various points, and some challenges apply to more than one function.

Gaining an overview vs misinformation and speculation

> In other settings I feel like it's too much information. Not at that day. That day you just dropped everything and said: this is what we do, we just try to find out what happened.
>
> (01)

> I heard about misinformation. It's easier to manufacture news. A small rumor gets quickly spread.
>
> (01)

The interviewees described their urge for information about the attacks as unusually intense. The first few days were characterized by the exchange of raw information and the effort to create a coherent picture of the situation: "Nothing of it made sense. Maybe I wanted to try to make sense, to get more and more information" (04). Like in a puzzle, different pieces of information were added together in a continuous update. Even though most of the interviewees considered themselves rather passive users, social media made a lot of information available to them. Many interviewees agree that this was important in order to gain an overview of the incident. Some interviewees also stated that at times there was too much information available, which meant that they either grew tired of the amount of information, or considered some information as too personal.

A core criticism was the room that social media left for speculation, which quickly went viral. Eighteen out of 20 interviewees mentioned that it didn't take much time before first speculations about the attacks being conducted by Muslims were posted: "I had a couple of [Facebook] friends writing some Islamic slurs on the newsfeed. And I remember deleting those friends the same day." (05). These speculations cascaded through the social network. It was not only considered difficult to distinguish trustworthy from deceptive information, but such speculative posts did also become a political act of digital discrimination and harassment, which was experienced by some interviewees at first hand. The cascade of information way beyond territorial borders also contributed to obscurity about the origin of the posts, which again posed problems for the validation of information.

At the same time, interviewees mentioned that social media, as opposed to online newspapers, offered the chance to identify the information they wanted to see more actively. They could filter what they wanted to read – a phenomenon that has changed since 2011 and which we will return to throughout the next paragraphs. Social media also allowed people to discuss the deceptive potential of information. In some cases, the cascade of deceptive information even led to forms of digital activism: people warned each other about deceptive information, they apologized for spreading wrongful information, or simply deleted those Facebook contacts who posted speculations, while the latter, however, may have also led to a suppression of the actual problem. Even though the verification of information was described as a challenge, social media at times gained more credibility than traditional media, precisely because the reporting was considered more authentic.

Using social media as a tool to gain an overview of the unfolding situation can be considered a first-response kind of resilience activity. The choice to utilize information circulating on social media for analysis and to access select sources in order to map ongoing situations is an expression of the self-initiative, actively rationalizing subject, who harnesses social media's affordances for handling emergencies. The availability and distributed character of social media, however, not only enables this interactive usage, but it also allows for different rationalizations and interpretations of the event. As such, social media presuppose reflexive usage, which cannot always be guaranteed – for several reasons.

An illustrative key challenge here is the problem about truth online, which was also brought up by the interviewees. Wrongful information has by now become a central concern in the debate about social media. The initiative to first filter information for its deceptive potential as described above is countervailed by an appetite for sensationalism. But the problem of truth online cannot be attributed to sensationalism alone. In her insightful analysis on how technology disrupts the truth, *Guardian* journalist Katharine Viner points to the trend that truth tends to be overridden by the novel media code of having to connect with people emotionally: "a fact begins to resemble whatever you *feel* is true" (Viner 2016: 3, emphasis added). The trend is much embodied by social media technology, where knowledge no longer comes in a fixed format – an outmoded model that also faced the problem of being difficult to challenge, but in networked environments, truth seems to follow the politics of clicks, of the popular and the self-validating. This social media trend to publish what is taken to be true is specifically visible "in emergency situations, when news is breaking in real time" (Viner 2016: 4). Meier suggests outsourcing verification tasks to users, such as online gamers, who judge whether the reported incidents correspond to ground truth (Meier 2013a). This, however, is difficult during emergencies, precisely because digital technology often works as a substitution for helpers on the ground or it is used to recapture remoteness that already exists (cf. Duffield 2016). Through the Internet, assumed truths can thus circulate at a considerable speed and with a wide reach, causing "information cascades" (Easley and Kleinberg 2010: 15) – as was the case for the 22 July attacks. This form of information circulation is not only powered by clicks and shares, but it is increasingly driven by algorithms that mean to detect those sets of information that match our interest best. This, again, relativizes the extent to which social media users can actually sort and identify deceptive information, since algorithms lead to what Internet activist Eli Pariser calls the "filter bubble" (Pariser and Helsper 2011). In that bubble, which is particularly vibrant in social media, steering information is no longer as easy as it seems to the user and, more importantly, we are also less likely to receive information that disproves our views (Viner 2016: 6). The algorithms that determine how information is found and forwarded are systematically opaque (Snake-Beings 2013) and cannot be challenged by the average social media user. This makes algorithmic control particularly powerful and reintroduces an element of centralization in otherwise distributed networks. The decisions taken about how to program algorithms are powerful, because the selection of information that reaches us influences our very debates on what is true and what it not.

This trend of cascading information and filter bubbles demonstrates the vigorous combination of the computability and the networked character of digital information. Together, both characteristics enable governmental rationalities of correlative and patterned reasoning. And this form of reasoning is spreading beyond social media. In fact, as Viner also points out, news organizations have already begun to tailor their own work to the demands of powerful "new media," where virality counts more than quality, as only a shared story is a news story (Viner 2016). A similar effect was also observable on 22 July, where social media and traditional news reporting had already begun to overlap and influence each other. Altogether, the trend to gain an overview of emergency situations via social media exhibits novel opportunities for situational awareness, but also challenges, such as the problem of misinformation, which can be particularly harmful in the context of an ongoing emergency. Above all, it is a trend that becomes again descriptive of a rationality that is deeply interwoven with and reflected in resilience governance. This rationality is reflected in the way in which social media enable populations to self-organize an overview about the emergency situation, through which they can even become part of determining the truth about themselves. Social media reflect the logic of distributed self-governing that is combined with a centralizing power, such as algorithms that reinforce the logic of effects and patterns. This specific combination of distributive and centralizing powers and practices can be ascribed to the fact that social media are a networked digital infrastructure.

Personal status of wellbeing vs sensationalism

> (T)here was this Facebook event that someone created saying: "I'm in Oslo, but I'm ok". So it was very easy for everyone to just join the event. And then everyone knew that this person was ok.
>
> (03)

Social media, especially Facebook's network, were used to spread updates about one's own wellbeing. Many interviewees describe how they and their contacts distributed status updates as a precautionary measure to avoid causing unnecessary worries. Since many users' networks included more distant friends, social media quickly enabled an overview of each other's wellbeing. Soon, this trend was identified and institutionalized in the form of a Facebook event, "Oslo er i god behold," which can be translated to "Oslo is doing well." The Facebook event was joined by more than 64,000 Osloers to signal that they were physically fine. The claim that one is alive and physically OK is, in the first instance, a manifestation of resilience, as it contributes to the idea of establishing normality and of spreading information about that. As a form of self-initiated control, self-care and care for each other, it also speaks to the idea of self-governing capabilities. The way this care came about was enabled by the interactive and networked character of the infrastructure.

A similar expression of resilience and mediated self-governance is that some interviewees utilized social media to actively identify who was in danger. They followed the status updates of acquaintances and friends on Utøya Island, where the situation was still evolving, given the time delay between the bomb explosion in the city and the shootings on the island. Such updates would, for the majority of users, cause relief through almost real-time responses about people's physical conditions or whereabouts. Some interviewees describe that the absence of status updates also created worry or confirmed sad news. In the context of checking each other's wellbeing, the specific format of the Facebook posting was also used in order not to impose on other people's private sphere. Some interviewees deliberately used social networking technologies to grant potential victims the freedom to answer or not, which is yet another notion of self-initiated care that is tied to the specifics of the medium.

Using social networks to identify and potentially act upon dangerous situations can instantiate resilient reaction – at least it can initiate it in a very condensed form. However, it also nurtures the attraction to sensational and extreme information, as some interviewees described. Amongst other things, this resulted in the fact that also the attacker's Facebook profile and his manifest were frequently visited. Some interviewees criticized this behavior, since it answered the attacker's aim to get attention, which is why protest was expressed by "not clicking" on particular kinds of information: "I never watched the video that he posted. The manifest. I didn't wanna give it a click" (02). Other users wanted to form a resistance to the attack by spreading positive posts and through "claiming the Norwegian flag back" from the attacker by adding it to their own profile; both of which are forms of social media use for emergency management that presuppose a rationalizing subject.

Today, social media use has become more deeply embedded into everyday activities, and the functions that they fulfill have become more fine-grained. Facebook has identified the kind of usage during emergencies described above as a programming opportunity. Inspired by the use of Facebook in the wake of the 2011 Tohoku earthquake and tsunami (Chowdhry 2014), Facebook introduced their Safety Check, which was released in 2014 (Gleit *et al.* 2014). The feature has been used during the 2015 Nepal earthquakes, the 2015 Paris attacks, and the 2016 Nice attacks, but also during bombing events, floods and shootings. Before it can be used, however, Safety Check first needs to be activated by Facebook. This implies that Facebook takes a decision about which kind of emergency actually warrants the feature – and they need to take that decision early during ongoing emergencies in order for it to work. To avoid misuse, Facebook then sends a notification to users who can choose to answer. Within that notification, however, there is currently no function to indicate that you are not safe. The answer is condensed to "safe," which may indeed "reduce our biggest fears" (Walker 2015), at the same time as it may also reduce further communication about a complex situation, where safety has many facets. Unanswered notifications, whether they are a result of choice, reduced Internet access or oblivion, are, on the other hand, a source of worry. Glitches in the system, such as notifications accidentally sent to the wrong geographic region – as has been reported after a 2016 explosion in Lahore, Pakistan – have led to insecurity and false alarms (Chaykowski 2016). Whether Safety Check is an effective tool for emergency management is thus open for discussion. Apart from that, the design of the feature and the way in which it is engineered and steered by Facebook signifies the turn from programs of resilience to programming resilience. Vis-à-vis the spontaneous use of Facebook in 2011, the now-institutionalised Safety Check indicates that a centralized actor has begun to influence the way in which distributed activities of self-governance during emergencies are being enacted. The instigation of resilience is now written into applications, programs and digital features.

Direct link to the event, organization and advice vs the omnipresence of terror

> [B]eing on Twitter I could read the closest information to the incident.
>
> (04)

> [E]very time I went online, on Facebook or Twitter or visiting an online newspaper it popped up in my head. I couldn't escape it. My boyfriend and I had to arrange breaks from the Internet.
>
> (16)

Facebook and Twitter were used as an entry point to identify relevant information. Particularly for those who traveled outside of Oslo, social media served as a direct link to the event, since Norwegian public television did not broadcast outside of national borders and online newspapers did not at first have much information available. Social media enabled the users to inform themselves in a more direct and personal way than traditional media would cover. The high number of postings made it possible for readers to follow the situation promptly, not only because smart phones could "report from anywhere," including the sites of the attacks, but also since those posts would not be edited into a news story at first. For some interviewees, social media became a primary communication device during the emergency. They deployed Facebook as the primary medium of contacting friends and family – mostly because it was more efficient than calling via phone. A few victims even used social media to call for help, because they would put themselves into danger by speaking out loud or by being called. In general, people were instructed not to use phones to avoid blocking the lines for those who would need them. Some victims had lost their phones: "Because I heard – afterwards – that they had dropped their phones in the water and Facebook was the only channel they were able to let people know that they were ok" (06).

Social media were not only a source of information about the attacks. They were also used to spread advice about how to deal with the ongoing situation and to organize response in the city and on Utøya: "Someone wrote: avoid crowded areas, don't use cell phones in Oslo, don't occupy the net, go home, don't use public transportation, don't panic – in a matter-of-factly way" (17). Information about the victims' whereabouts, including details about hospitalization and private contact information was distributed via social media. While the sharing of private information on semi-public media created considerable challenges vis-à-vis personal data protection on the one hand, it also contributed to the governance of the attack's aftermath on the other, since it could be translated into concrete advice. The latter was, for example, reflected in the different Facebook groups and Twitter posts that were used to organize the chaos caused by the attacks.

Facebook events were created to suggest where people could meet up and talk about the event physically or online. One of the founders of the Norwegian event "Standing Together Against Terrorism" got more than 100,000 members in just a few hours. After realizing its potential, he changed the name of the group in order to help organize the "rose march" event that took place three days after the attacks. Interviewees have described that such Facebook events brought people together, on social media, but also physically, which can be considered an instance of resilience and of governing the aftermath of the terror attacks in a self-initiated manner. As such, social media networks not only enabled the efficient distribution of information, but also incited concrete action.

These examples can be understood as resilient forms of emergency communication and management, which was enabled through the particulars of social media infrastructure. In the sense of self-governance, the population performed a very first approach of dealing with the attacks in creating a direct link to the event, in finding alternative means of communication, in giving advice and in organizing concrete response activities – a behavior that is not only expressive of self-care, but also of care about each other. While most interviewees agreed that social media played an important role for communication and advice, the high amount of postings also entailed substantial efforts to filter out the relevant information and make sense of it. Some interviewees stated that all of these processes could also have taken place without social media. Others went a step further and mentioned that social media also inhibited coping to a certain extent. The fact that every member of one's social media network posted about the attacks brought the events from public into personal space that was difficult to escape. As a result, users were unable to avoid the topic even when they followed their habit of browsing social media for everyday purposes. The social network constantly reminded its members of the attacks.

The wide-ranging use of social media has by today been identified as an effective tool for emergency communication and management. The reaction on social media after the 2015 terror attacks in Paris added yet another dimension to emergency communication as the Twitter hashtag #PorteOuverte, meaning "open door" was used to signal that those seeking safety from the attacks or in need of a place to sleep could find somewhere in proximity to the site (Ross 2015). The same hashtag was used in the wake of the Munich attacks on 22 July 2016 (Twitter 2016a). Social media, however, not only give rise to emergency communication and management, where they enable concrete functions. At the same time, it has become even more evident that social media also play a role in the promotion of extreme views and the advertisement of terrorist acts. In 2011, the person responsible for the Norway attacks – Anders Breivik – used Facebook as a platform to spread his message and advertise his views. The attacker of the 2016 Orlando shootings – Omar Mateen – equally used social media as a stage to create an attention buzz, checking while he was performing his acts (Nicks 2016). Other attackers have used Facebook to broadcast their acts (McAuley 2016). The publicity coverage of emergencies via social media thus contains both information that may contribute to and that may inhibit coping.

As mentioned by some of the interviewees, the presence of uncomfortable information via social media is something that they were not able to escape. This is the case because both sets of information follow the same distributive mechanisms of clicking, sharing and circulation.[1] The disentanglement of both is eventually a combination of algorithms that filter information for the user on the one hand, and the user's own responsibility to evaluate the information her- or himself on the other. The latter is yet another instance of self-initiated governance during emergencies, especially when users are given concrete advice about the emergency situation that requires their decision as to whether they should follow or ignore this advice.

Express and experience emotions vs un-reflected use

> In terms of information there wouldn't be much of a difference. But maybe in terms of expressing feelings. Expressing support, there's definitely a way to do that.
>
> (15)

> Young people that were involved got interviewed and started blogging shortly after the attack. These things will be there forever. Online.
>
> (03)

Dealing with the attacks was not only a matter of technical and practical self-organization, but also an act of handling emotions. A trajectory of emotions that was experienced by the interviewees included shock, confusion, disbelief, worry and fear at first. This was followed by the urge to access information, which was accompanied by a sense of sensationalism. After this first phase, most interviewees entered moments of grief, sympathy, compassion, and sadness, which endured for a longer period. Some of these moments translated into love, care, unity, solidarity, support and mutual respect on the one hand, but also into hate, anger and disagreement with the terrorist views on the other. As part of this second phase, interviewees also described how a moment of pride about the Norwegian's official reactions to the attacks was coupled with a moment of self-inquiry, asking what would have happened if the attacker had not been a Norwegian national. Indicators for returning to normality after the attacks were everyday-style postings and the return of humor on social media.

While social media were not judged instrumental in bringing about these emotions, they were still described as a platform, which allowed its users to affect and to be affected: emotions were described, distributed, consumed, experienced and conserved in a networked manner. Where emotions could not be expressed in words, pictures and symbols were used as a visual way of communicating, for example, through roses and hearts, Norwegian flag badges, candles, but also pictures of the bombed government quarter or the victims. These became powerful symbols because they cascaded, like all the other expressions of emotions, through the network. To what extent they contributed to emotional resilience cannot be generalized. Some interviewees, however, mentioned that social media were approached to calibrate one's own emotions toward a community of grief, but also to reassure oneself of one's own emotions through sharing. It is thus likely that social media enabled and reinforced a form of dealing with the attacks on an emotional level, as well as instances of care and self-care that were enabled through the specific networked infrastructure of social media.

The high level of shared information about one's private emotions was, however, to a certain extent regarded as un-reflected. Posts containing personal thoughts, ideas and opinions cascaded through the social network by being reposted, which made this information available to an almost unknown amount of other users, online, for an indeterminate length of time. In addition, information was posted that could have played into the hands of the attacker himself. One interviewee, for example, referred to a post by a person on Utøya who updated his followers about the place where he was hiding. This information, even if it was meant to calm down worried followers, could also have been harvested by other parties. The accessibility of social media here presents a challenge that has also become more prominent during the past years. At the attacks of 22 July 2016 in a Munich shopping mall – a date which the German-Iranian teenage gunman appears not to have chosen coincidentally (BBC 2016) – the attacker not only used Facebook to invite targeted victims to a specific spot (Alexander *et al*. 2016), but the police repeatedly appealed to the public not to post videos via social media in case they revealed police strategy to the attacking party (Twitter 2016b).

At the same time that social media enabled the access to a discourse of coping, it also led this discourse in semi-public on privately owned media that will not only have access, but also opportunity to share this information – with all parties involved in the emergency and beyond. This raises questions about privacy and the status of personal information, which we will turn to now.

Therapeutic sharing and digital mourning vs infringements upon privacy

> [Name] has his own memory page. I think his cousin made it. It's a page you can like. Yes, I like it. I haven't written – that doesn't feel right. I didn't know him. But it's a very active page in general.
>
> (16)

> People might have been offended that their personal information was shared and distributed so freely as it was then. As well as their whereabouts, etc., names, pictures being distributed by people they do not know.
>
> (11)

Both victims and their friends used social media amongst other things to talk about and share experiences, for example, by posting pictures of Utøya from before 2011 to symbolize that good memories of Utøya would not be destroyed by the attack. Some victims also used the virtual proximity, but physical distance of social media to share their experiences, and yet avoid direct physical reactions of pity toward them. Others used social media as a platform to signal whether they would want attention or not. While many interviewees would not post much about their personal feelings, some still appreciated the opportunity to send condolences virtually. It was a way of "letting the victims know" and also of saying goodbye to the deceased, but in a manner that does not require face-to-face contact or a phone call with the affected, which, in some cases, was considered as too direct a medium.

Other mediated instances of grief were online minutes of silence, pictures of candles, personal letters and entries for victims, so-called human chains of virtually holding hands, and memory pages that were established for the deceased victims. To some, these served as an important instance of not forgetting, since memories and stories about victims were shared here. This networked aspect of sharing and caring about each other was described as impressive and even those who would not post anything personal said that it helped to see how people remembered victims. The network instantiated new, mediated forms of mourning that were characterized by a non-physical contact with victims on the one hand, but engendered on the other hand a collective, cascading form of care for each other that clearly exceeds the notion of self-care that is so often foregrounded in resilience studies. How this behavior was experienced by victims, and how it changes the sociology of grief and resilience, still needs to be assessed and discussed.

While many positive aspects about this form of grieving were mentioned, some interviewees considered it problematic that a deceased person was somehow kept alive virtually and in a semi-public space where questions of post-mortem privacy would also play an important role. In that respect, the process of balancing personal, private and public information was one of the main challenges. Many interviewees made a distinction between personal and private information. Postings were personal if they included information about someone being physically affected by the events, if feelings or personal thoughts were shared. Privacy, however, was defined as something factual: names, contact details and photos in which you could identify a victim. Others thought that private information was that the kind of personal information which was simply too unpleasant to know. Speculating whether the attacker was of a Muslim faith for example, was also considered a thought you may have in private, but should not share. Most interviewees, however, mentioned that expressions can be personal without being private. In the context of the attacks, for example, people seemed to have been willing to share personal thoughts publicly for different reasons, but mostly because "we were all in it together" (01). Thus, showing otherwise private emotions publicly was considered as something positive, as a credible statement.

In fact, the problem of emergency information being harvested by other parties has become a major debate (cf. Boyd and Crawford 2012; Crawford *et al.* 2013; Meier 2013b). The problem of sharing private information on semi-public and privately owned platforms becomes even more pressing when considered on a global scale. Duffield points here to the unequal global distribution of data protection laws and regulatory regimes: where information technologies may be "subject to public oversight, legal safeguards and increasing privacy concerns in the global North […] regulation, safeguards and protection are absent or weak" in the global South (Duffield 2016: 12; Hosein and Nyst 2013). When mentioned in the emergency management context, such concerns, Duffield continues, are generally countered and overridden by "the need for speed demanded by the humanitarian imperative" (Duffield 2016: 12; cf. Taylor 2013).

What has become most obvious from the use of social media during the 2011 attacks is that what is considered public, and what is private knowledge, first needs to be negotiated. The different views on privacy presented above indicate that this debate is still to be had and that it is once again up to the user to define which kind of information to share and which information to withhold. After all, the network inspired a form of emotional coping and self-governance through the sharing of personal information. The considerations as to which kind of information should and should not be shared, presuppose a user who rationalizes and reviews these different options carefully, one who understands the importance of information to private companies and who considers the way in which this information may circulate and the effects that may create. In general, this is a level of reflexivity and self-governance that is not only under the circumstance of an emergency a challenge to social media users.

Shaping vs making opinion

> [A]nd it was a general attempt in trying to process everything that was going on. I mean, people also talked about it face-to-face. I know they did, but I guess on Facebook you could put thoughts out there and you could get different reactions from different people potentially.
>
> (10)

Vis-à-vis the traditional media, social media offered a forum where people accessed different personal views, where opinions were shaped and moral standpoints were calibrated: What is extreme? What is a just reaction? What are shared Norwegian values? While defining one's own position was an important part of creating resilience by processing and dealing with the events, some have described the information exchange on social media rather as a process of making opinion – as opposed to really discussing perspectives. This was appointed to the limited format of the postings. Other interviewees mentioned that they were not comfortable with posting opinions themselves, which is why they refrained from taking part in these processes as an active user. Some interviewees, however, agree that the debate, especially without Twitter, would have been different. Twitter played a unique role in dealing with the event with respect to political questions and different perspectives.

This goes to show that the networked character of social media had a concrete impact on how opinions, views and certain rationales came about. Even though it was mentioned that the format left little space for discussion itself, it allowed for accessing different perspectives and comments. Disentangling, organizing and assessing these different views from each other was an important instance of the rationalizing subject, who seeks to (re-)construct a sense of normality by getting hold of different views. It presupposes, though, a reflected media use and the access to different perspectives must by now, however, be considered vis-à-vis the phenomenon of the "filter bubble" described above (Pariser and Helsper 2011).

Virtual unity vs unanswered ambiguities

> So the parade was the physical coming-together and then the pictures and the status-updates of support [...] that's the virtual coming-together [...] which is probably just as important, if not more.
>
> (17)

By collecting and producing expressions of how people felt, social media created a virtual sense of unity that was often compared to the solidarity expressed during the rose marches. The interviewees felt that they were part of something bigger. While the networked aspect of social media created a sense of a digital coming together, which – according to some interviewees – may have had an impact on the way that solidarity, support, care, pride, and empathy were expressed, other interviewees mentioned that social media could also have inspired a form of slacktivism (17): the sheer mass of mourning users would force each other into creating unity online, which didn't even take much energy to express.

While most interviewees emphasized the positive sides of digital unity, the use of social media for purposes of collective coping has now raised a debate about the substantiveness and the sincerity of online mourning and activism. This was particularly visible in the aftermath of the attacks by two Islamist gunmen on the satirical newspaper *Charlie Hebdo* in January 2015. With the use of the phrase and hashtag "Je suis Charlie" ("I am Charlie"), meant to express one's association with the victims and the ideals they would stand for as writers, social media were discussed as an "empathy engine" (Garber 2015). At the same time, this gave rise to the question as to whether empathy itself became a meme (ibid.), or part of a social media etiquette – for better or worse. Others argued that such complex issues can and should not be reduced to a simple slogan, the lifespan of which is not only short, but abridges a more profound dispute about "how we resolve the struggle between two competing political and religious ideologies," and how one insures that "tolerance works both ways" (Kelner 2015), instead of providing a simplistic answer to a complicated issue. During the 2011 Norway attacks, not only were the simplistic digital forms of expression considered to be problematic, but – so the interviewees' critical remarks highlighted – social media enabled the silencing of voices and the expression of hate and anger. These were phenomena that were not countered or discussed properly, especially in the context of the attacker's extreme views on Norwegian culture, politics, and society. This left some interviewees with a feeling of hypocrisy: Norway's way of dealing with the attacks was not only about care and unity; it also included aspects that were too complex or too unpopular to be discussed online.

Thus, in a positive sense social media enabled a form of dealing with the attacks that was not just a matter of the individual self, but it gave rise to a collective, social self. This digital social self was enabled through the networked character of social media. At the same time, social media did not give space to the uncomfortable debates that were needed according to the interviewees, but instead to a collective that could easily be subjected to diverse political currents.

Resilience 2.0 and the (self-)caring subject

> [P]eople tried to make social media [help] to go back to their lives by organizing: oh this has happened, but we're going to bring some flowers, bring some hearts and then we're going to continue with our lives. And restoring that sense of normality.
>
> (11)

The networked character of social media implicates many affordances that social media users translated into concrete resilience practices during the 2011 Norway attacks, that have, today, become more institutionalized. Departing from the understanding that resilience is a technique and mentality of self-governance during emergencies, this chapter has shown how the networked character of the medium influenced the way in which practices of self-governance came about, and how these practices presupposed a rationalizing user that engages with the networked logics and effects of social media. As such, it built on Grusin's notion of mediality and illustrated how the everyday technology of social media contributed to the production and circulation of information during emergencies. Together, social media infrastructures and its users created new forms of self-initiated and mediated resilience governance, each of which entailed its own set of challenges. Even though most of these practices emerged spontaneously, this trend has already been integrated into programs to enhance social media use for emergency management. The chapter's case study, however, invites conclusions about more overarching questions that concern both the spontaneous and the politicized forms of social media use for crisis management, namely: How do the ontology of resilience practices and the resilient subject itself change under the influence of 2.0 technologies?

Space – the network mediated the experience of space, since both the event itself and physically distant friends and family members were virtually as close as on the screen as they were in the living room: "It somehow brings people closer in time and space, because you can have everyone gathered in Facebook" (10). This created a perception of proximity to other users in general, but to the scene of the attacks in particular. This change in spatial perception not only contributed to a collective mediated experience of the incident, but also influenced how social media users became part of the various instances of dealing with the attacks. It was through the connectivity between users across space that social media users were drawn into the event – irrespective of their physical whereabouts. As a result, most social media users who became interested in the incident would also contribute to the production and circulation of information about it, whether that happened through the recirculation of advice or the experience of mediated unity. At the same time, the use of social media also contributed to a new form of governing at distance, through programming efforts and digital methods that partly replace on-the-ground commitment (cf. Duffield 2016).

Time – the networked character of 2.0 technologies also mediated the experience of the emergent present by effectively influencing information flows. Information moved faster though social networks and seemed more instant than information distributed by other media. This influenced both the experience of urgency and emergency, but also the process of dealing with worries about the physical wellbeing of one's closest contacts. While the time-efficient information exchange may have accelerated response, it also entailed negative consequences for coping with the event, such as the fast travel of deceptive information, abbreviations of otherwise complicated and much-needed discussions and the making of opinion, as well as the difficulty to organize the overwhelming amount of information, views and expressions.

Vision – social networking sites also engendered new ways of seeing, watching and viewing the emergency, since all of the circulated information could be collected on one platform. This contributed to the identification of dangerous areas and of people in danger, which could be translated into concrete emergency response. Beyond that, social media also enabled the *watching* of the attacks in the sense of sensationalism on the one hand, and as a practice of censoring difficult themes on the other. As one interviewee mentioned, "you could have the whole nation against you if you said something wrong that day" (15). At the same time, did social media enable a form of *watching out* for each other, in the positive sense of sharing and caring? As such, it engendered mediated forms of sharing, of community and unity. Even though this unity was a mediated experience and did not happen face-to-face, people felt that they were part of "something bigger" that spread all over the country, which may have contributed to societal resilience, on the one hand, or may have taken momentum away from more direct forms of social contact and in-depth attempts to deal with the emergency, on the other.

On an overarching level, this chapter has illustrated how subjects form technologies and technologies form subjects: the networked character of social media had a direct effect on how (self-)caring subjects came into existence, at the same time as these subjects translated the various affordances of the network into concrete resilience practices. From this interaction between subjects and technologies new ways of governing emergencies arose, including technical and emotional forms of self-organization, with potential for both positive or negative effects. Such technologies of governing emergencies are by today increasingly standardized, they have become subject to programming efforts and have been written into applications. Within this world of 2.0 technologies, the resilient subject is situated in a network and thus also in a potentially unlimited collective. It is a subject whose experiences of urgency are not only mediated, but shared and individuated at the same time, and whose actions are enabled and constrained by the networked infrastructure. As such, resilience is no longer only about the *self* in self-organization, but the subject's governance of emergencies necessarily needs to incorporate the idea of collectivity. The subject's resilient (re-)actions are mediated, which may not only affect itself and its reality of the emergency experience, but they also affect a potentially unknown collectivity of users. This may produce positive as well as negative effects for its own and collective resilience – a fact that in an ideal world should not only inform the subject's processes of rationalization and mediated interactions, but also the future governance efforts that include 2.0 technologies for emergency management.

Note

1 For an analysis of how the digital enhances commercial forms of circulation that percolate both extremist and classic Western digital video material, read Leander (2016).

References

Adger WN (2003) Building Resilience to Promote Sustainability: An Agenda for Coping with Globalisation and Promoting Justice. *IHDP Update* 2: 1–3.

Alexander H, Henderson B, Palazzo C, Heighton L, Rothwell J, Weise Z, Tuner C, Huggler J (2016) *Munich Shooting: Teenage Killer Ali Sonboly "Inspired By Far-right Terrorist Anders Breivik" and "Used Facebook Offer of Free Mcdonald's Food to Lure Victims."* Available at: www.telegraph.co.uk/news/2016/07/23/munich-shooting-german-iranian-gunman-targeted-children-outside (accessed 25 July 2016).

American Red Cross (2012) *First Aid by American Red Cross.* Available at: https://itunes.apple.com/US/app/first-aid-by-american-red-cross/id529160691 (accessed 21 July 2016).

Amoore L (2009) Algorithmic War: Everyday Geographies of the War on Terror. *Antipode* 41(1): 49–69.

BBC (2015) How the Paris Attacks Unfolded on Social Media. Available at: www.bbc.com/news/blogs-trending-34836214 (accessed 25 July 2016).

BBC (2016) Munich Gunman "Obsessed with Mass Shootings." Available at: www.bbc.com/news/world-europe-36874497 (accessed 25 July 2016).

Berry DM (2012) Code, Foucault and Neoliberal Governmentality. Available at: http://stunlaw.blogspot.no/2012/03/code-foucault-and-neoliberal.html (accessed 11 August 2016).

Birkmann J (2006) *Measuring Vulnerability to Natural Hazards: Toward Disaster Resilient Societies.* Tokyo: United Nations University Press.

Bolter JD, Grusin RA (1996) Remediation. *Configurations* 4(3): 311–358.

Boyd D, Crawford K (2012) Critical Questions for Big Data. Provocations for a Cultural, Technological, and Scholarly Phenomenon. *Information, Communication and Society* 15 (5): 662–679.

Chaykowski K (2016) Facebook "Safety Check" Glitch Asks Users Far from Lahore, Pakistan if They Are Safe After Explosion. *Forbes*, 27 March. Available at: www.forbes.com/sites/kathleenchaykowski/2016/03/27/facebook-safety-check-glitch-asks-users-far-from-lahore-pakistan-if-they-are-safe-after-explosion/#48849ae01585 (accessed 22 July 2016).

Chowdhry A (2014) Facebook "Safety Check" Tells Your Friends That You Are Safe During a Disaster in the Area. *Forbes*, 16 October. Available at: www.forbes.com/sites/amitchowdhry/2014/10/16/facebook-launches-disaster-notification-feature-safety-check/#2bc245e84127 (accessed 22 July 2016).

Cordis (2016) How Social Media Can Improve Emergency Service Responses. Community Research and Development Information Service. Available at http://cordis.europa.eu/news/rcn/122383_en.html (accessed 8 July 2016).

Crawford K, Faleiros G, Luers A, Meier P, Perlich C, Thorp J (2013) Big Data, Communities and Ethical Resilience: A Framework for Action. *White Paper for PopTech and Rockefeller Foundation.* Available at: www.rockefellerfoundation.org/app/uploads/71b4c457-cdb7-47ec-81a9-a617c956e6af.pdf (accessed 11 August 2016).

Dean M (1999) *Governmentality: Power and Rule in Modern Society.* London: Sage.

Duffield M (2013) *The Human Trace: The Rise of Cyber-Humanitarianism.* Seminar presentation, Danish Institute for International Studies. Copenhagen, 16 May. Available at: www.bristol.ac.uk/global-insecurities/commentary/humantrace.html (accessed 11 August 2016).

Duffield M (2016) The Resilience of the Ruins: Toward a Critique of Digital Humanitarianism. *Resilience: International Policies, Practices and Discourses.* 15 March: 1–19.

Easley D, Kleinberg J (2010) *Networks, Crowds, and Markets: Reasoning about a Highly Connected World.* Cambridge: Cambridge University Press.

Foucault M (1988a) *The History of Sexuality. Volume 3: The Care of the Self.* New York: Vintage Books.

Foucault M (1988b) Technologies of the Self. A Seminar with Michel Foucault at the University of Vermont, October 1982. In: Martin LH, Gutman H, Hutton PH (eds) *Technologies of the Self: A Seminar with Michel Foucault.* Amherst, MA: University of Massachusetts Press. 16–49.

Foucault M (1991) Governmentality. In: Burchell G, Gordon C, Miller P (eds) *The Foucault Effect: Studies in Governmentality.* Chicago, IL: University of Chicago Press. 87–104.

Foucault M (1993) About the Beginning of the Hermeneutics of the Self. *Political Theory* 21(2): 198–227.

Foucault M (2010) *The Birth of Biopolitics: Lectures at the Collège De France, 1978–1979.* New York: Palgrave Macmillan.

Garber M (2015) #PrayForParis: When Empathy Becomes a Meme. Available at: www.theatlantic.com/entertainment/archive/2015/11/pray-for-paris-empathy-facebook/416196 (accessed 22 July 2016).

Gibson JJ (1977) The Theory of Affordances. In: Shaw R, Bransford J (eds) *Perceiving, Acting, and Knowing.* Hillsdale, NJ: Erlbaum. 67–83.

Gleit N, Zeng S, Cottle P (2014) Introducing Safety Check. Facebook Newsroom, 15 October. Available at: http://newsroom.fb.com/news/2014/10/introducing-safety-check (accessed 29 April 2016).

Grusin R (2010) *Premediation: Affect and Mediality after 9/11.* New York: Palgrave.

Grusin R, Cox G (2010) On Premediation. Interview with Richard Grusin Led by Geoff Cox. Available at: www.academia.edu/4754419/Grusin-Interview_With_Geoff_Cox_2010_ (accessed 11 August 2016).

Gunitsky S (2015) Social Media Helps Dictators, Not Just Protesters. Available at: www.washingtonpost.com/blogs/monkey-cage/wp/2015/03/30/social-media-helps-dictators-not-just-protesters (accessed 21 July 2016).

Heinzelman J, Gordon R, Meier P (2011) Mobile Technology, Crowdsourcing and Peace Mapping: New Theory and Applications for Conflict Management. In: Poblet M (ed.) *Mobile Technologies for Conflict Management: New Avenues for Online Dispute Resolution.* London: Springer.

Hosein G, Nyst C (2013) *Aiding Surveillance: An Exploration of How Development and Humanitarian Aid Initiatives Are Enabling Surveillance in Developing Countries.* London: Privacy International.

IFRC (2013) *World Disasters Report. Focus on Technology and the Future of Humanitarian Action.* International Federation of Red Cross and Red Crescent Societies, Geneva. Available at: http://worlddisastersreport.org/en (accessed 11 August 2016).

Joseph J (2013) Resilience as Embedded in Neoliberalism: A Governmentality Approach. *Resilience: International Policies, Practices and Discourses* 1(1): 38–52.

Kaufmann M, Jeandesboz J (2016) Politics and the Digital. *European Journal of Social Theory.* DOI: 10.1177/1368431016677976: 1–20 (accessed 25 March 2017).

Keim ME, Noji E (2011) Emergent Use of Social Media: A New Age of Opportunity for Disaster Resilience. *American Journal of Disaster Medicine* 6(1): 47–54.

Kelner S (2015) I Am No More Charlie than George Clooney or Helen Mirren Is. Available at: www.independent.co.uk/voices/comment/i-am-no-more-charlie-than-george-clooney-or-helen-mirren-is-9974998.html (accessed 22 July 2016).

Latour B (2005) *Reassembling the Social: An Introduction to Actor-Network-Theory.* Oxford: Oxford University Press.

Leander A (2016) Digital/Commercial Visibility: The Politics of DAESH Recruitment Videos. *European Journal of Social Theory.* DOI: 10.1177/1368431016668365 (accessed 25 March 2017).

Longstaff PH, Armstrong NJ, Perrin K, Parker WM, Hidek MA (2010) Building Resilient Communities: A Preliminary Framework for Assessment. *Homeland Security Affairs* VI(3): 1–23.

Luthar SS, Cicchetti, D, Becker B (2000) The Construct of Resilience: A Critical Evaluation and Guidelines for Future Work. *Child Development* 71(3): 543–562.

McAuley J (2016) ISIS-inspired Attacker Kills French Police Officer and Streams it on Facebook. Available at: www.washingtonpost.com/world/french-president-killing-of-police-officials-undeniably-a-terrorist-attack/2016/06/14/db71760f-68be-48d3-96e9-df35dc5d7e5b_story.html (accessed 22 July 2016).

Meier P (2013a) *Disaster Response Plugin for Online Games.* Available at: https://irevolutions.org/2013/07/17/disaster-response-for-online-games (accessed 25 July 2016).

Meier P (2013b) #NoShare: A Personal Twist on Data Privacy. Available at: https://irevolutions.org/2013/09/15/noshare-hashtag (accessed 22 July 2016).

Meier P (2014) Adding the Computer Crowd to the Human Crowd. In: Silverman C, Tsubaki R (eds) *The Verification Handbook.* Available at: http://verificationhandbook.com/book.

Nicks D (2016) Orlando Shooter Checked Facebook to See if His Attack Went Viral. Available at: http://time.com/4371910/orlando-shooting-omar-mateen-facebook/ (22 July 2016).

NOU (2012) Rapport fra 22. Juli-kommisjonen. 2012. 14. Departementenes servicesenter Informasjonsforvaltning. Norges offentlige utredninger, Oslo.

Nrk.no (2011) Terrordøgnene på twitter [The Days of Terror on Twitter]. Available at: http://snutt.nrk.no/multimedia/terrortwitter (accessed 20 July 2016).

Pariser E, Helsper E (2011) *The Filter Bubble: What the Internet Is Hiding from You.* LSE public lecture. Available at: www.lse.ac.uk/assets/richmedia/channels/publicLecturesAndEvents/slides/20110620_1830_theFilterBubble_sl.pdf (accessed 21 July 2016).

Popoola A, Krasnoshtan D, Toth A, Naroditskiy V, Castillo C, Meier P, Rahwan I (2013) *Information Verification During Natural Disasters. Paper Presented at the Social Web for Disaster Management Workshop, WWW 2013 Rio, Brazil.* Available at: http://irevolution.files.wordpress.com/2011/07/verily-swdmwww13.pdf (accessed 11 August 2016).

Purohit H, Castillo C, Diaz F, Sheth A, Meier P (2014) Emergency Relief Coordination on Social Media: Automatically Matching Resource Requests and Offers. *First Monday* 19(1). Available at: http://firstmonday.org/ojs/index.php/fm/article/view/4848/3809 (accessed 11 August 2016).

Rose N (1996) *Inventing Our Selves.* Cambridge: Cambridge University Press.

Rose N (1999) *Powers of Freedom: Reframing Political Thought.* Cambridge: Cambridge University Press.

Ross A (2015) Parisians Use #PorteOuverte Hashtag for Those Seeking Safety from Attacks. Available at: http://time.com/4112428/paris-shootings-porte-ouverte (accessed 25 July 2016).

Sandvik KB, Jumbert MG, Karlsrud J, Kaufmann M (2014) Humanitarian Technology: A Critical Research Agenda. *International Review of the Red Cross* 96(893): 219–242.

Schecter D (2010) *The Critique of Instrumental Reason from Weber to Habermas.* New York: Continuum.

Sjöberg E, Barker GC, Landgren J, Grierg I, Skiby JE, Tubbin A, von Stapelmohr A, Härenstam M, Jannson M, Knutsson R (2013) Social Media and Its Dual Use in Biopreparedness: Communication and Visualization Tools in an Animal Bioterrorism Incident. *Biosecurity and Bioterrorism: Biodefense Strategy, Practice and Science* 11(S1): 264–275.

Tagesschau.de (2016a) Vielsprachige Polizei, offene Türen [Multilingual Police, Open Doors]. Available at: www.tagesschau.de/inland/muenchen-schiesserei-socialmedia-101.html (accessed 25 July 2016).

Tagesschau.de (2016b) Wie die Polizei die sozialen Medien nutzt: B. Rasem, NDR, mit Informationen [How the Police Uses Social Media: B. Rasem, NDR, with Information]. Available at: www.tagesschau.de/multimedia/video/video-201999.html (accessed 25 July 2016).

Taylor L (2013) Surveil the Rich. Observe the Poor: Big Data at the Internet Governance Forum 2013. Available at: http://linnettaylor.wordpress.com/2013/10/25/surveil-the-rich-observe-the-poor-big-data-at-the-internet-governance-forum-2013 (accessed 25 July 2016).

Twitter (2016a) #offenetuer #muenchen. 22 July 2016. Available at: https://twitter.com/search?q=%23offenetuer%20%23muenchen (accessed 25 July 2016).

Twitter (2016b) @Polizei München: NOCHMAL: KEINE Videos oder Bilder von Polizeikräften im Einsatz online stellen, helft nicht den Tätern!!! #muechen#oez# schießerei. 11:20AM, 22 Jul 2016. Available at: https://twitter.com/polizeimuenchen/status/756554483845459969 (accessed 25 July 2016).

Snake-Beings E (2013) From Ideology to Algorithm: The Opaque Politics of the Internet. *Transformations* 23 (The Internet as Politicizing Instrument). Available at: www.transformationsjournal.org/wp-content/uploads/2016/12/Snake-Beings_Trans23.pdf (accessed 22 July 2016).

UK Government (2012) *Using Social Media in Emergencies: Smart Practices.* Available at: www.gov.uk/government/uploads/system/uploads/attachment_data/file/85946/Using-social-media-in-emergencies-smart-tips.pdf (accessed 8 July 2016).

Viner K (2016) How Technology Disrupted the Truth. *Guardian*, 12 July. Available at: www.theguardian.com/media/2016/jul/12/how-technology-disrupted-the-truth (accessed 21 July 2016).

Walker J (2015) Facebook Has a Safety Check to Reduce Our Biggest Fears. Whitridge Associates, 2 December. Available at: www.whitridge.com/news/facebook-has-safety-check-reduce-our-biggest-fears (accessed 22 July 2016).

Yates D, Paquette S (2011) Emergency Knowledge Management and Social Media Technologies: A Case Study of the 2010 Haitian Earthquake. *International Journal of Information Management* 31(1): 6–13.

Zebrowski C (2009) Governing the Network Society: A Biopolitical Critique of Resilience. *Political Perspectives* 3(1): 1–41.

Part IV
Conclusions

9 A theory of resilience and the relational

Resilience speaks to an understanding of the world as relational, as interconnected and in-formation. This book has explored several empirical and theoretical avenues to better conceptualize resilience as a way of governing in interconnected societies. In particular, it focused on the relationship between the Internet and security governance. By studying resilience as a way of *governing the Internet* and of *governing through the Internet*, a range of recurring themes were addressed. Such cross-cutting threads include the ontological arguments that the different resilience discourses imply, how these arguments are reflected in conceptualizations of resilient space, and which temporalities resilience as a way of governing incorporates and operates. As we shall see, these arguments about being, space and time, furthermore, feed into the epistemology of resilience, which entails a specific understanding of the role that in/security plays for resilience governance. These ontological, spatial, temporal and epistemological motifs are reflected in the practices and subjectifications that resilience generates, which recur to self-organization and distributed rule – legacies of the scientific ethos of complexity thinking. All of these cross-cutting themes are discussed below with the intent not to merely reiterate what the different chapters have to say about them, but to extrapolate and condense these findings into a theory about resilience as a way of governing in interconnected societies.

This account of resilience as a way of governing, however, is not exhaustive. Since security policies and studies largely invoke the ecological and systemic roots of resilience (Holling 1973), this book does not elaborate, for example, on the conceptual history of resilience in psychology, even though the self-governed individual plays an equally strong role here. Since the specific focus of this book is resilience within societies that embrace the Internet into societal interactions, the following sections reflect upon the relatively novel dimension of digital connectivity within the resilience discourse and what it adds to a concept that already embraces complexity. While I am well aware that there is always more to be said about complexity or the role of technology within society, the discussion of these themes is limited here to the recurring and novel aspects. The discussion also picks up on some of the paradoxes that have been carved out in the different chapters. In doing so, this book does not make an ontological statement about the world as complex or networked. Interconnectedness, as made clear in various chapters, does not include or concern everyone in the same way. It is selective, and there are different forms of interconnectedness. In particular, digital connectivity is not global, since various digital divides persist. What has become clear throughout the book is, however, the way that interconnectedness and the relational are tied to governmental narratives and translated into practices of in/security. Rather than referring to them as a fact, the book took narratives about interconnectedness and the relational, which equally include discourses of science, politics and art, as an analytical vantage point. It studied how these narratives are at times even used strategically to produce a perception, a *sense* of interconnectedness, the relational and complexity. In that context, the relational refers to both: the way in which interconnectedness induces emergencies as well as the way in which digital data and networks are now used to respond to emergencies. Vis-à-vis such governmental discourses, the book asks whether the resilient subject always has the freedom to react as it wishes, whether any kind of creativity through the subject is politically desired, and how both governmentalities of risk and resilience are employed at the same time. Thus, this book does not forward a critique of resilience that can be misread as a fear of change, as a critique of the ability to deal with challenges, or to let life become something better. What is subject to criticism is a politics that produces concrete narratives, practices and expectations toward resilience, the resilient subject and the interconnected, insecure world. Each of the sections below will briefly reflect on the particular contributions to the critical study of resilience, summarizing how they either advance existing critical arguments about resilience or discuss a new aspect. Most importantly, the presentation of these cross-cutting themes is meant as an introduction to a dialogue on a combination of topics that are likely to stay prominent within security-oriented practices of governing in the next few years: the complex world, the struggle with epistemological limits, the response to unforeseen disruption, the self-organized subject as an instance of distributed rule, and the embrace of digital technologies into security practices.

Ontology

The idea of existing in and through interconnectedness and relations is central to the concept of resilience and has been discussed at many points throughout this book. Systems of interconnection have become a main frame of reference for societal interaction, the fabric of societal existence or the medium through which society operates. While such theorizations sound profane at first, discourses and theories about interconnected states of existence seem to have become ubiquitous: whether they refer to neuronal interaction in the brain, electrical pulses in power grids, microbiological processes in bodies, feedback mechanisms in ecosystems or electronic information exchange within the Internet. And, most importantly, the interconnected state of existence as such seems to justify the existence of resilience: in case of disruption, so complexity theories argue, systems would disintegrate. They would cease to exist. Resilience, however, is presented as the answer to complex and unpredictable environments that are prone to disruption. In a world of rapid change, it gains prominence as a mechanism to deal with uncertainty and contingency.

The discourses of resilience and interconnectedness are entwined to such a high degree that they seem to be constitutive of each other: resilience is both result and promoter of the relational, of interconnectedness and complexity. Resilience is the consequence of networks because it needs connections to arise and to handle disruptions, at the same time as it contributes to their preservation and continuation, which, in turn, conceptualizes insecurity as an integral part of systems. Interconnectedness and complexity are thus not just models to theorize societal interaction, but being interconnected becomes the basis for a specific theorization of existence. Resilience is here the vital mechanism insuring that random interruptions do not persist and life in its interconnected form continues to exist. Within this logic, however, disruption also has its function. The interplay between disruptions and resilience is not only accepted as a natural dynamic of complex systems, but the systems need this interplay to trigger adaptation and to evolve. With that, resilience becomes a form of living through emergencies, of being in-formation.

In developing this argument, the book builds upon and advances Walker and Cooper's argument about resilience as a "generalization of complex systems theory" (2011: 143). Resilience has become a political program based on the acceptance of relational ontologies and epistemologies of the emergency. Complexity thinking, here, also resonates with network theories – a connection that has not been made in the discussion about the genealogies of resilience before. The understanding of society as a continuous form of exchange processes has influenced security narratives since the conceptualization of the feedback loop in the 1940s (Wiener 1948; cf. Chapters 1 and 3). However, the way in which telecommunication, the digital, and the Internet reinforce narratives of interconnectedness has only recently moved to the center of attention (cf. Chapter 4). This latter discussion adds a new dimension to feedback loops or information exchange and how they relate to the world as being in-formation. The increased integration of digital technologies into modes of societal interrelation perpetuates ontological narratives of complexity and interconnectedness that are paired with narratives about the necessary existence of resilience. Not only have these narratives become widely accepted within political discourses, but the digital and networked characteristics of information now allow for the translation of resilience programs that are based on rationalities of complexity and being in-formation into forms of programming resilience.

Discourses on cyber-security, in particular, embrace these rationalities and practices. In fact, they promote these rationalities to such an extent that the Internet has been recast as a specific form of space, namely as the "interconnection ecosystem" (ENISA 2011b) and that resilience and self x become the programs through which such spaces need to be governed. This reconceptualization of space fundamentally acknowledges the ontology of complexity, while it legitimizes and promotes resilience as the answer that can be written into the interconnection ecosystem. Chapter 6 deepens this empirical investigation on cyber-security and finds that the scenario of the cyber-attack functions as an epitome of the complex emergency, invoking powerful images of cascade and the intense impact they can have on societal functioning altogether. The language of the scenario employs metaphors of interconnectedness and unidentified vulnerabilities, which constitute the main justification for enhancing response through exercising. Resilience here becomes a necessary means to secure also digital interconnectedness and circulation, which endues the concept of resilience with a totalizing force.

Chapters 7 and 8 provide a different take on the relationship between resilience, the ontology of interconnectedness and the Internet. Both chapters discuss resilience as a way of responding to the emergency that arises from a complex whole, but they focus on the way in which digital and networked technologies of interconnectedness bring about new resilience practices. Social media and digital information serve here as a fabric that gives rise to resilience as a form of self-organized response to emergencies. Internet-enabled resilience practices foreground the use of digital information for processes of being in-formation that utilize association and algorithmic analyses to instill change, whereas they also foreground the crowd as an important local actor and provider of information. Once again, both chapters illustrate that at a conceptual level resilience and the ontology of interconnectedness seem to constitute each other.

Spatiality

Interconnectedness is also the vantage point for understanding how resilience has become a way of governing complex spaces. Critical discussions about the Internet, spatiality, or their specific combination for the resilience discourse have been extremely rare, with two exceptions. While Zebrowski argued that resilience as mode of governing can be understood through the logic of protocol – a specific form of regulating the Internet (2009), Duffield wrote about digital humanitarianism and resilience, where he focuses on the use of distant-sensing and remote government in the context of humanitarian missions (Duffield 2016). The discussions of this book, however, concentrate on the spatiality of the Internet with its heterogeneous infrastructures, as well as networked and digital forms of information flow, which partly draw upon and extend Zebrowski's and Duffield's important observations.

The Internet has a history of being understood as space. However, ideas about its internal organization and the power-knowledge at work vary with the respective spatial concept, whether that is the elusive *cyberspace* or an understanding of the internet as *just-a-network* (cf. Cohen 2007). The most recent spatial conception of the Internet as *ecosystem* embraces narratives of heterogeneity and the complex workings of the Internet. The term reflects the variety of soft- and hardware, physical and logical infrastructures, designers, engineers and end users that constitute this highly fluid, ever-changing space. Most importantly, its heterogeneous character legitimizes resilience as a strategy to organize the Internet: the more complex and dynamic its topology, the more there is a space in need of a mechanism that secures its interconnectedness, its mode of existence. Resilience is presented here as the evident and superordinate concept that combines the various mechanisms of flexibility and adaptation to assure information circulation. These mechanisms are so central to the governance and administration of the Internet ecosystem that they, in fact, become part of the materiality of this space: headroom and redundancies are engineering strategies which function on the assumption that disruption will occur. The result is a space that embraces insecurity and, with that, the limits of the preventative logic of a firewall.

Beyond this material dimension, ecosystemic space also speaks to a political dimension. Like any other space, it is a site for the production and extension of power. As a space of heterogeneity, the ecosystem combines different governmental rationalities and practices of negotiating the control over connectivity. Within this heteroscape of power one recognizes familiar dynamics: the local is a new locale for response and responsibility, which is reflected in subsidiarity and sub-national approaches to Internet security. This distributive approach is combined with the need for a central actor that defines universal standards and undertakes harmonizing efforts, such as the conducting of exercises, the establishment of global codes of conduct, a standardization of gaps and mutual aid agreements. Power correspondingly lies with those who define global standards. Yet, the exercise of this power is more intricate than traditional dominating modes of power, because the owners of this position only act as facilitators, which ultimately ask local actors to follow the logic of self x: self-organization, self-repair, self-reflection and the like (cf. ENISA 2011a: 31).

This combination of local power and overarching standards, as well as the interplay between the maintenance of a status quo and disturbance is also reflected in the logic of protocol (cf. Galloway and Thacker 2007). As a mechanism of regulation that supports robustness, contingency, interoperability, flexibility and heterogeneity, protocol works through negotiation, with the aim to organize and control information circulation. With protocol, topologies are enabled to cooperate with each other, meaning that concrete tasks are spread to concrete layers. Protocol manages the information flow between networks of any kind, not as a sovereign top-down modus of discipline, neither as an emancipatory, self-determined bottom-up modus that wins over centralized power, but as a modus of orchestration, of immanent, decentralized guidance of information flow with an eye on organizational evolution (cf. Zebrowski 2009). This is also what makes protocol different from autopoiesis. Instead of each layer conducting autonomous work only, higher layers are encapsulating lower layers, which make all the layers dependent on each other. Through that, protocol not only admits heterogeneity, but insures that each layer becomes part of rendering emergencies and disruptions productive. Protocol combines moments of standardization with the creation of possibilities for further development through self-organization.

The Internet ecosystem, protocol and self x are not just words, but they turn the spatial reconceptualization of the Internet into a strategic move. They translate the resilience program into resilience programming by instantiating the local as a new security actor that holds the responsibility for adequate response. At the same time, the ecosystem, protocol and self x suggest that a centralized facilitator defines insecurities and standards which serve as a basis for any governmental action. This power, however, cannot simply be declared, which also creates a contested space, where different actors struggle over the power to define the standards of what it means to be secure. As expressed through the spatial concepts of the ecosystem, protocol and self x, resilience is a mode of governing that works with heterogeneity, it seeks to regulate relations between different parts of a system, shape self-responsible, active calculating subjects while delimiting disciplinary control. The notions of local and global are no longer limited to geographic topologies, but they are redefined constantly. Resilience gives guidance on how emergencies are used as opportunities by training creativity and spontaneity; it indicates the way in which systems evolve, but this indication is emergent.

The book has documented how resilience strategies do not just speak to the spatial notions of the Internet ecosystem, protocol or self x, but it has also documented the way in which information becomes the substance of controlling evolution. This concerns an additional dimension of interconnected, heterogeneous space. Chapters 7 and 8 investigated the way in which the digital connectivity of the Internet provides for the transformation of information exchange into digital bits. The digitality of the Internet not only allows for a specific mode of knowledge production and related resilience practices, but it also stretches, compresses and expands the experience of spatiality, which plays an important role in the instantiation of resilience. For example, digital connectivity redefines proximity by granting mediated access to emergency sites. It draws Internet users into the emergent event as it broadens capacities for information access and brings those who analyze emergencies closer to the situation, thus creating a different space for participating in emergencies and instantiating resilience. At the same time, it realizes a physical distance between, for example, analyzers or emergency managers and the emergency, which again entails structural invisibilities. Duffield's argument about remote management and the way in which everyday activities move away from face-to-face interaction is here a prominent one (Duffield 2016). However, it needs to be emphasized that the entanglement of mediated proximity and physical remoteness creates both opportunities and challenges for resilience management. It instantiates new visibilities and invisibilities of emergencies, as well as collective and individual experiences of emergency that can be beneficial and detrimental for dealing with disruption. The trend that circulating digital information during emergencies is used for the mapping of hot spots is only one indication here. This mapping serves as a basis for instigating emergency response and learning. Such forms of digital analytics create new visibilities and novel entry points for resilience-oriented practices. At the same time, they render disconnected hot spots invisible. In a different way, the use of social media in the aftermath of the 2011 terror attacks in Norway provided users with a virtual access to the emergency site that they otherwise wouldn't have had. This virtual access provided the information needed to understand what happened, but, at the same time, it brought the emergency into a private space, constantly reminding social media users of the emergency situation and disconnecting them from discussions they would otherwise have had face-to-face.

Temporality

What defines the temporality of resilience is the emergency. The emergent event is intimately linked to ontological and spatial narratives of interconnectedness and the relational. Interconnectedness entails that both disruption and resilience are system-inherent, or, as framed in resilience policies, they are inherent to the complex society. From the perspective of concrete political programs that focus on the optimal recovery from adverse events, an emergency can take place in the past, the present or the future. That being said, critical assessments of resilience temporalities commonly focus on the future (Lentzos and Rose 2009; Walker and Cooper 2011; Aradau 2014, to name a few) – a trend this book seeks to realign to a certain extent.

Intuitively, resilience actually seems to be tied to the past. Due to the prefix "Re-" the term itself suggests a backwards-orientation. Resilience then appears to be a way of governing and of dealing with emergencies that materializes post-disruption. The momentousness of the disruptive event, however, may vary throughout society and even individually as it may extend into the present. What the different experiences of disruption have in common is a reference to an event that has already begun, one that commenced in the past. The instantiation of resilience after the 22 July attacks in Norway illustrates this case in point. This form of governing and dealing with past events can, for example, take shape as discourses of memorialization and visualization that serve as a vantage point for re-establishing a new sense of normality. Instances of resilience can then be understood a reworking and a reorganization of the past. Resilience, so policy discourses would describe it, is instantiated if all of these backwards-oriented activities feed into a process of adaptation and create a new normal (cf. Chapter 2). Digital connectivity can influence the temporality of relating to past events as it changes information flows and the access to knowledge. It compresses and expands the temporal relation to the past event, allowing for speedy access to information, but also for the continuous presence of the event. Chapter 8, for example, illustrates this more closely. It shows how digital technologies influence the experience of the 22 July attacks in Norway and, paradoxically, engender both the acceleration and the deceleration of dealing with these attacks. While it was considered helpful by Internet users to gather as much information about the event as possible at a considerable speed, in order to make sense of what had happened, online activity was also marked by constant reminders of the attacks, which slowed processes of establishing normality down.

Furthermore, political perspectives often frame resilience as a learning process. In order to learn from emergency situations, experiences of the past are utilized to draw conclusions for the preparation of pending disruptions. Here, resilience practices establish a link from the past to the future. This link is further enhanced through the availability of digital information about past events for analysis, which is used, for example, for the development of resilience patterns and metrics to prepare for future disruption.

Due to the fact that theories of interconnectedness frame disruption as constantly pending or imminent, resilience also feeds into the expansive project of governing the future (as, for example, used by Aradau and van Munster 2008). However, it does so only by accepting or building upon the insight that a disruptive future may not be prevented. In particular, this book discusses preparatory governmental practices of resilience that are supposed to snap into action when future disruption occurs: exercising is one of them (cf. Chapter 6), and the preparation of technical and material solutions to enhance infrastructural resilience is another (cf. Chapter 5). While it has been well illustrated how anticipatory practices of governing and narratives of the catastrophic future re-determine the present (e.g., Aradau and van Munster 2008, 2011; de Goede 2008, 2012), the question remains as to whether such governmental attempts to establish resilience *ex ante* – before the occurrence of disruption – gains actual momentum during the emergent event. Chapter 6 not only discusses the exercise as one practice of installing future resilience, but it also illustrates how the response to emergency is characterized by both trained and emergent practices of resilience. Emergent practices of resilience, however, are arguably not instantiated by exercising, but occur spontaneously. In that respect, Chapter 8 illustrates how the use of social media to respond to and deal with the Norway attacks in 2011 was exclusively emergent and spontaneous. Despite this structural potentiality for resilience programs to fail or to be overridden by spontaneous, unintended response during the actualization of emergencies, the future remains prominent in resilience discourses – not only as the imagined disruptive event that needs preparation, but also for conceptual reasons. Resilience as a way of governing may seek to answer events at any point in time, but it always does so with a more global orientation toward the future, because it is safeguarding circulation, adaptation and evolution, that is the future of human (or systemic) existence.

In order to safeguard the future of existence, however, insecurity must be addressed continuously. This argument is implied in the conceptual foundations of resilience. At this point, it is helpful to distinguish between the conceptual and the practical dimension of resilience. Political practices aimed to instigate resilience may address disruptions of the past (such as the Norway terror attacks discussed in Chapter 8), or even chronic emergencies of the present (such as the Internet's exposure to potential infrastructural failure at any point in time, cf. Chapter 5) and imagined events of the future (such as large-scale cyber-attacks that are explored in Chapter 6). As a result, resilience as a practice of governing speaks to any temporal dimension. However, in contradistinction to concrete instances that these practices seek to address at any point in time, the resilience concept presupposes a temporality of continuity. Past, future and present may be relevant for governmental programs that seek to address and deal with specific events. The distinction of these three temporal dimensions, however, is irrelevant for the resilience concept as such. Conceptually, resilience as a way of governing seeks to safeguard life by sustaining the continuity of interconnectedness, circulation and information exchange. In doing so, it thrives on emergence. Emergence is an all-encompassing precondition for resilience and it requires the continuous dealing with insecurity to make life live. While the political category of the emergency may interweave different temporal strands, the concept of emergence extends the event ad infinitum, which perpetuates and stabilizes a resilience temporality of continuity. Living through emergencies, being information, or life made live through resilience is thus subjected to insecurity that is temporally nonfinite.

Epistemology

What can be known in an interconnected, complex world is that knowledge about the future is radically limited or not knowable. Ontologies and epistemologies of complexity condition each other. The concept of emergence epitomizes this ultimate limit to knowledge: the internal workings of the complex system world eventually give rise to emergence, phenomena which exhibit characteristics that did not exist beforehand. As such, they cannot be known in advance. In security discourses, emergence describes the dimension of the "unknown unknowns" (Rumsfeld 2002) and is framed as that which confronts life with the unexpected. The relational or connectivity merely intensify this trend with images of cascading disruptions, snowball and domino effects. In an interconnected, complex world the episteme of risk and probability is thus pushed to its limits and possibility and plausibility are introduced into discourses and practices as new modes of dealing with the unknown. Eventually, knowing the causes of insecurity is replaced by knowing that insecurity will appear. This specific epistemology becomes apparent when thinking about resilience on a conceptual level. Resilience epistemology does not just incorporate the unknowability of the future, but what becomes prominent from resilience discourses is the expectation that future emergence eventually brings about some form of disruption. The latter could be captured in the term *negative epistemology*: what is known is that emergence will take place, but which form it takes, at what point in time it appears and its consequences cannot be known. This combination of the paradox (the unknowable future) and the negative (the disruptive, emergent future) characterizes the epistemology of resilience and fundamentally justifies its existence. An emergent event that cannot be known may ultimately not be prevented from happening, which necessitates resilience as a means to deal with disruption. These are the narratives invoked to justify resilience practices.

Indeed, this epistemology no longer concerns the conceptual level alone, but it informs political discourses and practices. In fact, accepting the ontology of complexity as well as the unknowable, yet disruptive future event as a given includes power: uncertainty is here invoked to implement specific forms of government, namely resilience. In tracing these discourses, this book ties existing conceptual discussions on resilience epistemology (cf. Aradau 2014; Chandler 2014) more distinctly to the empirical level, providing examples of specific governmental discourses in relation to Internet security, cyber-emergency exercises and concrete epistemological practices of, for example mapping of emergencies (cf. Chapters 5, 6 and 7). It finds that in the domain of security policy, this epistemology is reflected in various narratives of the inability to foresee and prevent emergencies in full (cf. Chapters 1 and 2). Most strikingly, these narratives not only exist as stand-alones – without further context – but they are explicitly tied to narratives of complexity, as is the case in ENISA's approach to Internet security (cf. Chapter 5). The expanding integration of complexity thinking into political discourses thus leads to an acceptance of the future as – at least partly – unknowable.

Under this condition, practices of resilience have no knowledge about future disruption to offer, but know-how: the appearance of emergence cannot be known and stopped, but resilience as a way of governing offers knowledge for how to respond. Practices of knowing the future are thus not completely abandoned within a paradigm of complexity and interconnectedness. Quite the contrary, it seems that such practices are constantly re-invented and becoming more ubiquitous, especially with the rise of digital technologies (cf. Chapter 7 on digital methods). However, the acknowledgment of contingency, unpredictability and unknowability of disruption is endorsed and reinforced by the rise of resilience as a way of governing. The changing role of the complex emergency within security discourses and practices, as is the case in certain discourses around cyber-emergencies, substantiates this trend. The cyber-security discourse altogether embraces narratives of complexity, contingency and nonlinear cascade within interconnected societies (cf. Chapters 5 and 6). It subscribes to the apparent ubiquity of interconnectedness, which is framed as that which perpetuates the unknowability of disruption. Dealing with or governing emergencies thus becomes a necessity and resilience exercises represent one mode of answering them. The acting-out of scenarios is a politically promoted practice of producing knowledge about future response, for example, by training participants to develop routines of meeting the emergent.

An additional approach of dealing with future emergence and disruption is the resurgence of calculative knowledge production (Ewald 2002; Amoore 2009, 2013; de Goede 2012; to name a few). However, the relevance of this trend for resilience-oriented practices of governing has been surprisingly under-discussed in the critical literature. This is a gap that this book addresses. Even though probability calculation may have reached its limits, and discourses about the unknowability of the future are at their peak, calculation and computation still find their place in resilience governance. Digital technologies provide here a novel access point to knowledge production. They enable the development and use of new analytical tools to overcome future disruption with the help of, for example, responsiveness metrics. Information about past events can be analyzed, learned from and translated into models for knowing and strategizing future response. Equally, this knowledge can be utilized for dealing with the aftermath of an event in the present (cf. Chapters 7 and 8). As Chapter 7 illustrates, big data is already embraced by those actors that seek to engender resilience. Here, digital technologies are used for situational analysis and the identification of self-organizational patterns for lessons learned activities.

While much attention is currently paid to the way in which such analytical practices need to address critical questions about privacy, reliability and research ethics (cf. Buchanan and Ess 2008; Boyd and Crawford 2012; Crawford *et al.* 2013), little reflection exists on how digital information influences the epistemology of resilience and resilience-oriented practices. Chapter 7 argues that the usage of digital data and associated analytical tools gives rise to the crowd as a new epistemic community and the pattern as a new epistemological authority for practices of resilience programming: resilience can now be analyzed through the logic of mass in the form of frequency and behavioral patterns. This is possible because digital technologies codify information. Codification allows for the circulation of information over long distances and at considerable speed, which seems especially relevant in the context of the emergency. Digital metadata can, furthermore, offer information about geographic locations, making contents traceable and searchable. Its codified existence also makes digital information storable, reproducible, countable and computable, leaving many opportunities for associating pieces of information with each other. This availability of information in codified format allows for new ways of gathering, assembling and reassembling information, giving rise to form and pattern as analytic authorities in emergency management. Algorithms play an important role in this context, because they are utilized to make visible and knowable those complex processes that resilience management practices seek to target.

Chapter 7 further discusses these practices of *connecting the dots* as vehicles to make knowledge actionable: dynamic maps, visual reports, and the identification of activity hubs allow for situational overview and provide a knowledge base for resilience measures. A practical challenge here is the circulation of deceptive and wrongful information, which by no means leads to an abandonment of the digital. Quite the contrary, it reinforces epistemological practices of establishing truth by numbers: the more users confirm a piece of information, the more trustworthy it is. This form of establishing truths about resilience based on mass, however, re-injects a sense of speculation into the gained knowledge and engenders a strategic reproduction of visibilities and invisibilities (as discussed in previous sections).

In sum, the digital changes the way in which knowledge is produced to engender resilience as a response to the unknown. In emphasizing the analytics of effects over causes, the digital promotes a way of governing emergencies that is based on patterns, drawing the focus away from underlying explanations. This reinforces the already existing trend in governmental resilience practices to provide response to emergencies, as opposed to stopping them from happening in the first place. Furthermore, the digital foregrounds an epistemological practices of the countable and numerical to form the resilient subject. In doing so, it ties the accountable, the self-organized responsible subject, to the countable.

In/security

The limited possibilities of knowing the emergent future and the various efforts to create knowledge in order to meet future disruption are directly linked to the concepts of in/security that resilience as a way of governing is operating with. From the information above, it not only becomes apparent that the narrative of the interconnected, emergence-driven world stabilizes a temporality of the infinite and engenders various practices of grappling with the limits of the knowable, but it also presupposes a specific relationship to insecurity. This relationship has been discussed by many resilience critics, especially by Evans and Reid (2013, 2014) but also by Chandler (2014), Walker and Cooper (2011) and Aradau (2014), to name some prominent examples. Even though Walker and Cooper (2011) do mention the conceptual embeddedness of resilience in complexity thinking, they could have expanded on a theorization of what happens to the concept of security when understood through complexity. Chandler (2014) establishes a conceptual link between security, resilience and emergency, but does not discuss what that means for the temporality of security. Aradau (2014) conceptualizes resilience as a promise of security that is never redeemed, while Evans and Reid (2013) forward a powerful criticism on the insecure subject, claiming that with resilience security in fact dies. This book expands on these insightful discussions about security by further developing the different traits of resilience as a way of governing in/security in interconnected societies.

The unending expectation of future disruption is the dominant form of insecurity in interconnected societies. The central reason for that is the feedback loop, which enables openness and multiplicity. The feedback loop is the reason for emergence to appear. As discussed above, the trajectory of these multiple feedback processes cannot be known, but they are expected to eventually cause emergence, which are framed within the policy discourse as complications, vulnerability, susceptibility to harm and emergencies. The ever-changing *Internet interconnection ecosystem* is but one example that illustrates how this narrative of complexity-induced disruption and cascading failure is incorporated into the policy discourse. However, in the theories that inform such views, the information-rich feedback of disruptions and emergencies is also what causes change and drives the system forwards. As argued in the previous section, insecurity is therewith internal to the system, a permanent condition and a necessary driver for systems to evolve. As a result, security in interconnected societies is no longer a state of being protected and intact, but through the logic of resilience security is recast as the process of overcoming and dealing with disruption in order to create change. This response needs to be enacted constantly in order to maintain circulation and insure the continuity of existence and evolution.

Conceptually, resilience thus denotes a continuous struggle of redefining security. When put into practice, resilience is a way of governing that constantly invokes insecurity, which explains its popularity as an object of study in International Relations and security studies. The annulment of security-as-protection, which is also increasingly reflected in the discourses and practices of security-oriented governance, is here the most prominent criticism of resilience (cf. Evans and Reid 2014). However, a critical appraisal of the entanglement of resilience with insecurity cannot stop here; not least, because the definition of security as the absence of insecurity is overhauled since relational and constructivist security studies developed in opposition to (neo-)realist security conceptions (Buzan 1991; Buzan *et al.* 1993; Krause and Williams 1996). Viewed from the poststructuralist perspective used in this book, a state marked by the absence of insecurity is an impossibility, since the existence of the radically different and the non-signifiable (Dillon 2000: 4f.) – here the radically insecure – would always be drawn into security. Security is thus neither the absence nor the opposite of insecurity (cf. CASE Collective 2006). This book argues that it is better grasped by a logic of in/security, which refers to a process of negotiation between security and insecurity and an activity of constant differentiation. Besides, from a critical security studies standpoint, a security politics of protection through a sovereign state presupposes conditions that can also be identified as depoliticizing, patronizing and even insecuritizing, thus being productive of a subject that either does not seem to have anything to do with the condition of its own security or of one that is rendered insecure and suspect (cf. Bigo 1995 on the inseparability of securitization and insecuritization). From this, however, no inference can be made that resilience as a way of governing represents a less problematic alternative to sovereign modes of security-as-protection.

The critical argument developed throughout this book is not only that the protection from harm is framed as an impossibility in a complex world, but that insecurity is being strategically engaged as a tool to instigate the self-organization of populations. Further, it argues that resilience as a way of governing is based on the idea that insecurity is a precondition for life to exist. Insecurity is understood as an opportunity to evolve – or as Dillon would say: resilience epitomizes the idea being in-formation (Dillon 2000). It is, thus, the way in which insecurity is reconceptualized as the driving force for the capacity of becoming (Dillon and Reid 2009: 55ff.) that needs critical attention. Reflecting that, Chapters 5, 6 and 8 discuss the way in which security is recast as a process and as a pathway to becoming. As opposed to a passive state of being protected from harm, security in interconnected societies is an activity; through resilience, it is always in the making. Put differently, security is the constant unmaking of insecurity and thus strictly emergent. It is *in-formation* (ibid.). This ontology of in/security is heavily based on the complexity narratives, where it is the feedback of information flows that creates emergence and processes of being in-formation.

Security as being *in-formation* has thus multiple meanings. At a simple level, it refers to the fact that current resilience policies are still *in the making* (cf. Chapters 1, 2 and 5). It also conveys that digital *information* plays an increasingly important role in processes of resilience (cf. Chapters 7 and 8). Most importantly, it means that *information circulation* is the theoretical baseline of complexity and resilience thinking; circulation is the main rationale that informs the contemporary notion of in/security as being in constant formation. In accordance with the continuous temporality of insecurity that is present within the resilience concept, security is only existent as long as it is being acted out in response to insecurity. This strategic engagement of insecurity that is present in resilience also points to its main difference from a poststructuralist understanding of in/security. If insecurity is not recognized, strategized and engaged as an engine for evolution, life ceases to exist. As a result, the responsibility to thrive on insecurity and to act out security lies within the resilient subject. Security is *self-made*, because the subject needs to reinvent itself and its security actively, vis-à-vis the constant presence of insecurity. Each of the four case studies presented and discussed in this book illustrates the notion of the subject that engages with insecurity and reinstates its own security, whether it is a system that is programmed to self-learn and -heal, whether it is the subject who acts out security within an emergency exercise, or the subject that re-appropriates digital technologies in response to an attack. The way in which resilience as a way of governing requires self-organization thus needs to be addressed as an important cross-cutting theme of this book.

The resilient subject and self-organization

Resilience as a way of governing emphasizes the importance of the active individual or the self-organized system. Governing, then, is primarily a concern of the *self*, and political leadership becomes a matter of enabling and facilitating options for self-organization. Due to the strong emphasis on the self in resilience as a way of governing, it is instructive to explore whom and what that designates. The self does not necessarily denote singularity. It may be a reference to an individual, but also to a community, the more abstract crowd (cf. Chapters 7 and 8), the local (cf. Chapter 5), or even a non-human self-learning system (cf. Chapter 5). The common denominator of these different subjects is that they distinguish themselves from the others: the organization of security is not a matter left to be dealt with by others, but oneself takes action. It is assumed that the best knowledge and equipment for dealing with disruption is placed within the self or the local, which is why the responsibility to act and the possibilities of blame are located here as well.

While the actual practices of self-organization do vary, the more fundamental question remains as to what self-organization represents conceptually. Drawing on Carpenter *et al.*, self-organization is the opposite of a lack of organization (2001; cf. Chapter 2), which once more stresses the indebtedness of resilience to the scientific ethos of orchestration. Resilient individuals or systems are organized, they do not act randomly. They learn from past failure and strategically employ this knowledge for survival. In addition to that, self-organization means the opposite of organization forced by external factors (ibid.), which again presupposes autonomy. This autonomy, however, is contentious, given that the self-organized individual or system can be considered a formation of political resilience programming.

The resilient subject, formed by a political program, may act out security, but does it have agency? This question introduces one of the most significant debates about resilient subjects and self-organization that takes place most notably between socio-ecological research (cf. Walker *et al*. 2002; Adger 2003), psychological research (cf. Luthar and Zigler 1991; Masten and Powell 2003) or policy-oriented publications (cf. UNISDR 2005; European Commission 2013a,b; Longstaff *et al*. 2010; IFRC 2012) on the one side and critical security research on the other (cf. Zebrowski 2009; Evans and Reid 2014; Joseph 2013; Grove 2014; Howell 2014; Oels and Methmann 2015). The tension sits between two antithetically poled conceptualizations of self-organization. One position argues that engendering resilience in fact empowers individuals, allowing them to assume agency, act autonomously or shape the course of emergence according to their will (cf. Luthar and Zigler 1991; Masten and Powell 2003; UNISDR 2005; European Commission 2013a,b; Longstaff *et al*. 2010; IFRC 2012). The other forwards the argument that the subject is merely the product of a political program, whose conduct is being conducted and whose actions may be no more than automatism (cf. Zebrowski 2009; Joseph 2013; Evans and Reid 2014; Howell 2014; Oels and Methmann 2015). The performance of given political principles would then be inherently depoliticizing: the subject would resign from its political responsibility to engage with governmental programs by willingly enacting what is politically desired. Whereas the position arguing for agency considers the individual's self-organization an expression of autonomy and self-determined engagement with insecurity that can only be positive, the position arguing for the political construction of self-organization describes the resilient subject as a mere playball of political or systemic power, assuming that techniques of conducting the conduct of populations do not fail. Surely, both positions here are described in their extremes. A variety of positions can be found between those two extreme poles. What they do signify, however, is that the issue of self-organization and agency is contentious. It recurs regularly within the larger resilience discourse, as also reflected throughout this book. At times, this creates the impression that resilience as a way of governing is characterized by contradictions. Instead of rejecting or actively ignoring such tensions, contradictions and paradoxes within the resilience discourse, this book seeks to embrace and disentangle them.

In general, the book refers to self-organization as a specific form of governing. This way of governing neither follows a top-down, nor a bottom-up logic, but constitutes an immanent expression of power. In most instances, the book analyzes the increase of the resilience discourse in the field of security policy in terms of its programmatic function, which is much in line with the critical arguments described above. Such resilience programs are discussed as the guidance of self-organization, a distributed form of rule that incites self-organizational practices, which adhere to common guiding principles. These guiding principles are the assurance of interconnectedness, circulation and evolution. Much in line with governmentality, resilience programs are understood as a form of conducting the conduct of disaster populations as they seek to engage societal members as active and self-managing citizens.

However, the extent to which such programs work or actively influence disaster populations, and at what point self-organization may also escape programming through the generation of unforeseen, creative practices of self-governing are recurring issues that this book pursues without necessarily refraining from an overall understanding of self-organization as a way of governing. Governing implies both political resilience programs that seek to forge specific forms of self-organization, on the one hand, as well as the more complex forms of spontaneous or creative self-organization, on the other. Both forms of self-organization, however, subscribe to the overarching governmental logic that resilient individuals or systems have no choice but to act out security or react to insecurity.

The focus on self-organization does not necessarily result in the forming of one kind of subject, but leaves room for a multiplicity of resilient subjects. Chapters 5 and 7, for example, focus on political programs of resilience that seek to actively forge resilient subjects and specific forms of self-organization, such as ENISA's Internet resilience program or the trend to utilize digital tools and information for programming a specific form of resilience. Chapters 6 and 8, however, explore instances of self-governing that escape such programs, for example, the way in which exercise participants challenge the exercise scripts or social media users creatively re-appropriate social networking sites for emergency management. Taken together, the book discusses apparent contradictions, paradoxes and ambiguities as variations and multiplicities of resilience as a way of governing. The following paragraphs portray a few instances of how self-organization comes about. Particular attention is given to the role that digital technologies play in the generation of self-organization, as well as the theorization of variations in self-organization through affect, and the ambiguities concerning the purpose of self-organization and resilience.

Digital technologies, so Chapters 7 and 8 suggest, bring about distinct modes of self-organization that could be both an instance of targeted resilience programming or spontaneous response to disaster. The fact that online communication technologies have become a part of everyday practices in many societies influences the way in which information is created, retrieved, analyzed and engaged for self-organization during emergencies. Vis-à-vis this trend, it is helpful to distinguish between the digital and the networked character of such technologies and the way in which they engender new and different forms of self-organization and resilient subjects.

Chapter 7 discusses digital bits in terms of their traceable, storable and computable character. With the increased use of digital technologies for emergency management, the conceptual orientation of resilience, namely to learn from incidents, is translated into new analytic practices. The digital provides for the introduction of calculative and associative reasoning into resilience as a way of governing, which further redefines the relationship between authorities and the self-organized subject. Through computational analytics, new programs for emergency response can be designed on the basis of association and patterns. Programs that foresee the forming of the resilient subject are, then, no longer based on insights from individual responses, but developed on the basis of measurable mass response. Through digital practices, the resilient subject is no longer understood as individual, neither as abstract mass, but as dividual (cf. Deleuze 1992). The rise of digital resilience programming would not only imply the training and responsibilization of self-organized disaster populations that are productive of politically desired forms of adaptation, but this programming would be based on computed patterns. Digitized resilience practices of governing thus combine the accountable with the countable.

Internet-based communication tools are, however, not only digital, but also networked in character. Chapter 8 therefore investigates how 2.0 technologies, specifically Twitter and Facebook, were enmeshed in the way self-organization came about in the aftermath of the 2011 Norway attacks. Here, social media engendered both organizational as well as emotional aspects of self-organization. Yet, all these instances of self-organization were marked by internal tensions. Social media were, for example, utilized to access novel and individualized information about emergencies, which aided the organization of advice and fast response at the same time as they promoted the omnipresence of terror. Social media served as a means to communicate statuses of wellbeing, but equally nurtured sensationalism. They constituted a medium to express emotions or to communicate mourning, while they also inspired un-reflected use and infringements upon privacy. They contributed to the shaping of opinions and to the creation of virtual unity, while at the same time, they granted room for propaganda and left users in many instances with unanswered ambiguities. In light of all these different forms of self-organization, one point remains striking, namely that the way in which the networked character of social media emphasizes interaction, the social. The network introduces a novel nuance to the resilient individual that acts as an engaged, responsible, self-organized citizen: care is not instantiated for the dissociated *self* only, but it incorporates a sense of mediated sociality, as opposed to self-organization merely based on mass (cf. Chapter 7). It allows for a networked, social self, that is, however, social only in the mediated and limited ways described above. Most importantly, the different instances of self-organization, discussed in Chapter 8, were not explicitly planned or trained by political programs. Self-organization was the result of spontaneous media usage, which implies the inventive and original exploitation of social media's affordances by the acting users. This mode of self-organization is different from programmed self-organization, which is, as discussed in Chapter 7, the result of a response strategy, an orchestration of self-organization powered by data analytics and metrics that seek to foster specific modes of resilient behavior.

In the context of online practices, however, both kinds of self-organization – the one performed by the networked and the digital self – converge. Galloway and Thacker describe how Foucault's (2005) closer look at the concept of care is here particularly insightful. According to classical Greek culture, the concept of caring-for-others was not only intimately related to the care and responsibility for one's self (*epimeleia heautou*), but also to the way in which one conducted self-observation and self-examination that include the change of oneself (Galloway and Thacker 2007: 108). The very notion of care, then, brings together a triad of care for the self, care-for-others and change-of-self that is also reflected in the notion of being in-formation, especially when looked at in the context of resilience as a way of governing (through) the Internet. We will return to further variations of self-organization in the concluding section of this chapter, since this book suggests such variations as the starting point for more differentiated critical resilience research.

Concluding findings and suggestions for future research

Resilience is a way of governing interconnected societies. On a conceptual level, resilience subscribes to complexity, which means that interconnectedness is accepted as the condition in and through which everything exists. This interconnectedness gives rise to the emergency paradigm, for which resilience presents itself as the answer. Resilience fulfills here a double role: like emergence, it rises from interconnected structures at the same time as it is a means to sustain interconnectedness if it comes to emergencies. Emergencies exist for a reason: the constant interplay between emergencies and resilience – so the rationalities of complexity theories purport – leads interconnected societies to progress and unfold. This is an important asset for security policy, because through that, resilience becomes not only a means to govern interconnectedness and its inherent emergencies, but it is a way of living and striving through emergencies. It signifies a life in which security is constantly in-formation. Resilience is a way of governing that doesn't stop emergencies from materializing, but it utilizes them to steer interconnected societies by addressing and forming effects. Accordingly, resilience prioritizes the governance of effects over the governance of causes.

This relationship between interconnectedness, emergencies and resilience is not only an abstract, theoretical one. This book has documented how it has been translated into concrete policy narratives and practices. It is, for example, prominent in the domain of Internet security, where each step in the handling of emergencies and the steering of effects is organized in a distributed fashion through the logics of *self x* and protocol (cf. Chapter 5). In a similar manner, the exercise of cyber-emergencies is a strategy to govern interconnectedness and form resilient subjects that self-organize in emergency situations (cf. Chapter 6). The growing use of digital technologies engenders new governmental strategies to foster self-organization and resilience in emergencies through data analytics (cf. Chapter 7), while digital technologies have also been used by citizens to self-organize in unanticipated ways after they have been affected by terror attacks (cf. Chapter 8).

Within all these processes, the connection between information and being in-formation is of particular interest. In societies that are interconnected via the Internet, information circulation is not only the object of security governance – where resilience is a way of governing the Internet, of governing information circulation and effects. But digital information also actively feeds into processes of being in-formation – where resilience becomes a way of governing through the Internet, of governing through information circulation and through effects. As such, it is no surprise that resilience rises as a form of governing at this specific point in time. However, it is likely to be more than just a temporary fashion or a buzzword in security policy. The rise of resilience signifies a bigger shift. The increasing importance of the Internet and digital technologies for societal processes of circulation, related governmental practices of big data and algorithmic analysis, and the way in which both are accompanied by the call for self-organized, creative subjects that deal responsibly with the challenges of a more complex world are aspects of resilience that characterize the governance of our time. It is a time when smart technologies track subjects for data in order to perform analyses, provide feedback and guide them; for example, to optimize their self-organization and effectualness. As such, most of this book's conclusions are relevant for a critical evaluation of security governance in interconnected societies at large.

As a way of governing, resilience not only embraces narratives of interconnectedness that concern our understanding of being and space, but it also exhibits a specific temporality, epistemology, a particular understanding of in/security and of dealing with insecurity. Interconnectedness and complexity lead, so the narrative goes, to the emergence of the disruptive event. The emergency determines the temporality of resilience. In the domain of security policy, it is either the emergency of the past, the present or the future that requires resilience. By interweaving these different temporal strands, political practices of resilience tend to perpetuate and extend the regime of insecurity. On a conceptual level, however, the differentiation between past, present and future is obliterated. Resilience here presupposes a temporality of the nonfinite, extending the interplay between disruption and response indefinitely: emergence becomes a permanent condition and, in order to secure the continuation of life, resilience needs to be instantiated continuously.

Epistemologically, resilience combines the paradoxical with the negative: its particular approach to knowing is concerned with that which cannot be known. On a political level, this translates into narratives of expectable disruption. Digital interconnectedness feeds into the larger project of governing the expectable emergency in a particular way, because it emphasizes in-formation and effects. It helps to generate patterns of past disruption that can be consulted when dealing with emergencies to come. As such, resilience never provides knowledge about future disruption itself, but rather a know-how-to-respond, which can be derived from patterns of earlier response.

These ontological, temporal and epistemological characteristics of resilience imply a notion of security that is a process, not a state. In an interconnected world where emergence is ubiquitous security is constantly in the making, it is in-formation (Dillon and Reid 2009). It emerges as a response to insecurity, which leads to the most central conclusion of this book, namely that resilience as a way of governing is based on the strategic engagement of insecurity to foster life's continuation in its interconnected form.

With that, governing in the interconnected, complex world is primarily a concern of the *self* and political leadership becomes a matter of enabling, forging or facilitating options for self-organization. While at first sight, this relationship between in/security and self-governing seems to be a continuation of the risk discourse (as suggested by Lentzos and Rose 2009; Walker and Cooper 2011), there are important conceptual differences between the subjects that risk and resilience as different ways of governing seek to install. Both presuppose an active, planning, rational, calculating subject. However, while risk-oriented ways of governing presuppose a subject that manages to invest sensibly into measures that stop insecurity from materializing, resilience as a way of governing requires a subject that reacts flexibly to the inherent insecurities of the interconnected world and learns from them. Even though both ways of governing are based on a subject that plays a major role in practices of dealing with insecurity, prevention and resilience strategies are not to be confused, as the latter is based on a notion of insecurity that is internal to the system.

The conceptualization of self-organization, however, does not stop here. What this book suggests is for future resilience research to further a critique that accounts for the different forms of power that are inherent in self-organization and thus also in the practices of resilience. Chapter 6 theorizes variations of self-organization through different types of power that arise from affect. A cyber-resilience exercise serves here as site of study, where moments of the encounter between the participants and an emergency situation are observed. These moments are filled with the pressure to react to disruption and to act out security. Following affect theory, the participants' bodies are at a receiving state at these moments of the encounter and their ability of being affected translates into action. The chapter investigates exactly this argument as an entry point for the further conceptualization of self-organization. Both the empirical study of how participants reacted to pressures at the site, and the theorization of affect as the onset for action are useful to understand variations in self-organization. Most critical investigations of the role of affect in the context of security governance focus on the affective forging of relationships between the governing and the governed (cf. Massumi 1995, 2005; Grusin 2004; Grusin and Cox 2010; Anderson and Adey 2011). Following that, exercises could easily be identified as a distinct instance of programming disaster populations, not necessarily because they actively train specific responses, but because exercises affectively forge a specific relationship between the emergent event and the self-evidence of the responsible, active subject. However, studying the theoretical foundation of affect and observing instances of affect and acting at work during the cyber-exercise inspired an investigation as to whether self-organization is only ever programmed or affectively forged. By drawing on Spinoza (Spinoza 2002; Seyfert 2012), the chapter argues that affect constitutes the power of acting, which can be an instance of dominating (potestas) or constitutive (potentia) forms of power.

Even though, in practice, both instances may be intertwined to the point of irrecognizability, potestas and potentia offer important conceptual insights that can be applied to better understand different facets of self-organization. While potentia refers to the spontaneous moments of self-organization that set energy free, potestas refers to political practices that canonize the energies of the subject and lock self-organization to specific intentionalities and programs. Such programmatic resilience practices often approach self-organization as something that needs to be conducted in a particular fashion. Resilience programs more explicitly conduct the conduct of resilient subjects. They are designed to create subjects that voluntarily exercise specific resilience practices. In doing so, resilience programs extend control all the way toward the *self*. Instances of potestas refer to the orchestration of self-organization, which in its extreme form may lead to automatism. As that, so this book argues, resilience becomes a form of intervention. This intervention takes place on a distributed level, as it inculcates norms and standards of organization into entrepreneurial *selves*. The political intentions of emergency exercises represent this distributed form of power by training the subject to self-organize in a specific manner. There are many ways of how such instances of potestas come about. This book has discussed, for example, how resilience programs tend to form subjects through the formulation of standards (cf. Chapter 5) or through measuring and indexing resilient behavior (cf. Chapters 7 and 8). It is thus rather obvious that the more resilience programs foresee a specific form of forging subjects, the less room they leave for political agency. Resilience programs are likely to create a subject that simply performs – like an automat – according to performance indicators. Here, the resilient subject does not have ownership of the resilience process.

This is different when one looks at resilience as an instance of potentia. Potentia refers to the power of individuals to organize themselves in a self-determined manner, without any constraints or standards. A similar position has been formulated by Grove, who asks whether resilience is "something to be technocratically managed" or whether it can "be allowed to flourish in whatever direction it may take?" (Grove 2014: 253). This means that, in principle, resilience leaves room for spontaneity and creativity. Even though creativity can only ever manifest itself *ex post facto* and is thus restricted to re-action, these creative instances of response are the variations in self-governance, which leave room for agency. There are many ways in which potentia may play out. During the cyber-exercise discussed in Chapter 6, for example, participants invented responses that changed the overall situation of the exercising scenario. Similarly, in the aftermath of the Norway attacks social media users employed the Internet for creative forms of self-organization that included a social form of self-care (cf. Chapter 8). Resilient individuals do not have the political choice as to whether to transform the cause of their problem, but, in principle, they can still choose a mode of organizing themselves.

When it comes to resilience as a constitutive form of self-organization, Schmidt points to the importance of experience (2014). She invokes Dewey's pragmatist concept of agency (2012 [1927]), which speaks to a non-foundational, relational, thus complex world. It is a form of agency that arises in exchange with the environment and is characterized through meaningful learning processes by the subject. As such, it is less targeted at a specific aim, but at the meaningful dealing with a consequence of an experience – which is also the aim of resilience. While habits or behavioral patterns provide the disposition for acting, new know-how can be formed in exchange with the environment. Dewey then sees agency no longer as causal and targeted acting, but as a pragmatic and know-how-oriented agency (Schmidt 2014). This notion of agency also favors adaptation over goal-oriented or purposeful decisions; it favors effects over causes. Through this focus on learning, emergence is equally not devalued as an emergency, but it is recognized as a part of life itself. One can thus see how Dewey's agency much reflects the rationalities and ethos of resilience, precisely because it favors the empowered and constantly creative subject. Dewey's ideas of enrichment through learning are very close to the vocabulary of evolution and fine-tuning. There is, however, no room in his understanding of agency to identify the depoliticizing effects of resilience.

Vis-à-vis Dewey's notion of agency, the distinction between potentia and potestas may thus provide for a more fine-grained conceptualization of power in resilience governance, even though this distinction may also not question the role of adaptation as such. Potestas and potentia, however, theorize more facets of self-goverance. Indeed, potestas and potentia are both ways of governing emergencies. The difference between them is that the actual mode of self-organization may be determined by the individual itself. While potentia opens up for the integration of spontaneity and resignification, such as Dewey's notion of agency would suggest, potestas points more clearly to those instances of resilience that seek to program or order meaningful learning experiences. If conceptualized through potestas and potentia, self-organization can be both trained as well as self-determined. Or to put it on the level of the crowd in the context of digital practices: crowds can be tasked to behave in a specific way as captured in the notion of crowd-tasking or crowd-sourcing (cf. Chapter 7), or crowds can arise as an instance of passion and association (Mouffe 2005; Borch 2009; cf. Chapters 7 and 8). Both of these become manifest during emergencies and even emergency exercises, which neither instantiate fully empowered, nor completely automated subjects. Through this, the book provides a further theorization of self-organization in the critical discourse, which invites researchers to take a closer look at the power dynamics that are at play in a given instantiation of resilience. It shows that resilience does not necessarily engender one particular kind of power relationship between the governing and the subjects. Variations in self-organization and crowds do exist and they are expressive of different kinds of power. The subject can perform according to programs or it can influence the norms of given programs. Acknowledging this distinction is one of this book's suggestions for future research.

What should be clear, however, is that despite their more fine-grained conceptualization of power, the notions of potestas or potentia fail to question the ethos of adaptation that is embedded within resilience, because both of them are only ever realized as a response to given uncertainty. Potestas and potentia equally push for constant adaptation in the face of ontological insecurity. Neither of them ever eradicates the necessity for self-governing, because without self-organized responses to insecurities the *system life* is believed to disintegrate. This necessity for self-governing is a fundamental constituent of the resilience program and part of its ethos. Complexity theory's supposed dead end of governing, namely that a "right" answer to emergency cannot exist except for adaptation itself, translates into a culture of learning, preparedness and self-organization at large. The way in which strategic discourses of uncertainty, resilience-programs and -programming efforts seek to engender patterns of preparedness and adaptive capabilities, as well as the way in which such programs inscribe insecurity and emergence into the concept of life cannot be questioned through either of the concepts described above. Rather, all of them embrace the program of adaptation as the only way to deal with insecurity. As such, they also accept the premise that resilient individuals and systems need insecurity to thrive; that the resilient subject dwells on danger. As a way of governing, resilience thus forges new linkages between threats and threatened, as well as between effects and affected, through which the state of vulnerability is reproduced. This permanent state of insecurity requires a continuous struggle for survival without an option for finitude. Eventually, this leads to the preservation of qualified life only: resilient systems or individuals are not allowed to forget about their vulnerabilities, but they are expected to constantly engage and reflect about them for the sake of their own evolution. The program and programming of self-organization and adaptation through creativity is in that respect particularly depoliticizing, because it seeks to regulate and governmentalize a per se constitutive moment of the subject. With that, creativity becomes a technology of the self (cf. Bröckling 2004), where the subject is governed through liberties. This liberty needs to be used to organize oneself productively. The aim of resilience is to make creativity productive for evolution, to orchestrate it via incentives, animation, facilitation, and instigation. Even if resilience is an instance of agency and potentia, liberty becomes the programmatic power over the subject's acts, because it operates with possibilities.

Another aspect that neither Dewey's pragmatist agency, nor the distinction between potestas and potentia can grasp is that in practice subjects also encounter failure, powerlessness or mis-enunciation. Resilience programs, however, expect a subject that never halts, resists or overhauls itself completely. In fact, Chapter 6 highlights this important point about resilience as a way of governing that neither scholarship nor policy discourses have addressed so far. The moments where self-organization fails altogether are instances of powerlessness in which affect does not translate into action. This absence of powerlessness from resilience and the emphasis on self-organization once again emphasize the strategic element of resilience and its indebtedness to orchestration. By focusing exclusively on the necessity to act and self-organize after disruption, resilience ignores one of the most blatant reactions to the overwhelming affect of emergency: the inability to act or organize. This discontinuation or failure to act out security thus represents the intractable, that which cannot be drawn into the logics of resilience as a way of governing, but which is nonetheless a reality.

Due to the strategic ethos of resilience – that is to retain the connectedness, continuity and adaptivity of any system – powerlessness is a reality that cannot be addressed by it.

Most importantly, this need for adaptation also precludes transformation. Resilience may be productive of change, but it is a change that is temporally bound to the ex post facto. Change is only ever required after disruption has appeared. Complex systems deal with disruption with the aim of systemic or conceptual closure: complete systemic breakdown cannot take place, because systems need to function (cf. Stäheli 2000: 310ff.). Building on Dillon's argument (2000), this book highlights that resilience is embedded in a strategic ethos of orchestration, of organizing adaptability, and of seeing life as a flexible form of continuous survival. This is a form of change that is based on responsive modulation. As that, it excludes a transformation of the conditions that actually cause the problem. As a strategy of governing, resilience does not address causes, but it requests a change within the subject instead. The continuous effort of dealing with insecurity through adaptation, whether through creative or programmed forms of self-organization, is inscribed into the resilient subject. Resilience thus embodies a logic that is different from différance, because it only ever adapts and modulates life. It never overhauls, transforms or substantially confounds the conditions for life in a political sense, because adaptation cannot account for the non-relational, that which is radically different from interconnectedness.

Poststructuralist theories break with this totalizing idea of resilience and complexity thinking. They consider life as marked by alterity, difference and finitude (Dillon 2000). Poststructuralism continuously draws in the non-relational to deconstruct the modulatory, adaptation-based workings resilience. Through that poststructuralism defies the attempted conceptual closure of complexity thinking. While resilience is eventually a request for infinite survival though modulation and being "in-formation" (Dillon and Reid 2009), the non-relational is that which contributes to the option for thinking *the other* and thus for instantiating the political transformation of the cause. Generally speaking, agency finds little place in poststructuralist theory, but in this context, one could say that agency appears where critique of given conditions takes place, where the radically different is invoked and where power relations are deconstructed.

By tying the assessment of resilience back to a broader theoretical discourse, namely the difference between poststructuralist and complexity accounts of interconnectedness, vertices (1) and (2) of this book, the attention of future research endeavors is drawn to that which is truly different and which cannot be drawn into the totalizing logics of complexity and resilience thinking. If, in the context of resilience, instances of potestas and potentia are essentially about self-organization and adaptive capacities, the non-relational or that which constitutes counter-conduct is accordingly powerlessness, mis-enunciation or failure. The fact that powerlessness is absent from resilience in theory and practice reiterates that resilience always expresses a need to govern. In particular, critical resilience literature from the field of Political Sciences and International Relations tend to overlook this aspect, since governance and power are here, too, such ubiquitous concepts. The reality of these moments of powerlessness, however, introduces a need to further investigate exactly those fissures and ruptures, the moments of inability, failure and finitude that cannot be drawn into the all-encompassing logics of complexity and interconnectedness – or, as Galloway and Thacker suggest, to investigate the moments of counter-protocol, where notions of life resist the power over life through species-being: "Resistance-to-life is thus a challenge posed to any situation in which a normative definition of "life itself" dovetails with an instrumental use of that definition" (2007: 79). Investigating these moments of rupture and resistance is pivotal, because their presence radically challenges complexity thinking and related ways of governing that already permeate so many aspects of societal life. It is time to make a *différance*.

References

Adger WN (2003) Building Resilience to Promote Sustainability: An Agenda for Coping with Globalisation and Promoting Justice. *IHDP Update* 2: 1–3.

Amoore L (2009) Algorithmic War: Everyday Geographies of the War on Terror. *Antipode* 41(1): 49–69.

Amoore L (2013) *The Politics of Possibility. Risk and Security Beyond Probability.* Durham, NC: Duke University Press.

Anderson B, Adey P (2011) Affect and Security: Exercising Emergency in "UK Civil Contingencies." *Environment and Planning D: Society and Space* (29): 1092–1109.

Aradau C (2014) The Promise of Security: Resilience, Surprise and Epistemic Politics. *Resilience: International Policies, Practices and Discourses* 2(2): 73–87.

Aradau C, van Munster R (2008) Taming the Future: The Dispositif of Risk in the War on Terror. In: Amoore L, de Goede M (eds) *Risk and the War on Terror.* London: Routledge. 23–40

Aradau C, van Munster R (2011) *Politics of Catastrophe. Genealogies of the Unknown.* Abingdon, Oxon: Routledge.

Bigo D (1995) Grands débats dans un petit monde. Les débats en relations internationales et leur lien avec le monde de la sécurité [Great Debates in a Little World: Debates in International Relations and Their Link with the World of Security]. *Cultures & Conflits* 19–20: 9–48.

Borch C (2012) *The Politics of Crowds. An Alternative History of Sociology.* Cambridge: Cambridge University Press.

Boyd D, Crawford K (2012) Critical Questions for Big Data. Provocations for a Cultural, Technological, and Scholarly Phenomenon. *Information, Communication and Society* 15(5): 662–679.

Bröckling U (2004) Über Kreativität: ein Brainstorming. In: Bröckling B, Paul AT, Kaufmann S, Eßbach W (eds) *Vernunft – Entwicklung – Leben.* Munich: Fink. 225–243.

Buchanan EA, Ess C (2008) Internet Research Ethics: The Field and Its Critical Issues. In: Himma E, Tavani HT (eds): *The Handbook of Information and Computer Ethics.* Chichester, Sussex: Wiley.

Buzan B (1991) *People, States and Fear.* 2nd edn. Hemel Hempstead, Herts: Harvester Wheatsheaf.

Buzan B, Jones C, Little R (1993) *The Logic of Anarchy*. New York: Columbia University Press.

Carpenter S, Walker B, Anderies JM, Abel N (2001) From Metaphor to Measurement: Resilience of What to What? *Ecosystems* 4: 765–781.

CASE Collective (2006) Critical Approaches to Security in Europe: A Networked Manifesto. *Security Dialogue* 37(4): 443–487.

Chandler D (2014) *Resilience. The Governance of Complexity*. London and New York: Routledge.

Cohen JE (2007) Cyberspace as/and Space. *Columbia Law Review* 107(201): 210–256.

Crawford K, Faleiros G, Luers A, Meier P, Perlich C, Thorp J (2013) Big Data, Communities and Ethical Resilience: A Framework for Action. *White Paper for PopTech and Rockefeller Foundation*. Available at: www.rockefellerfoundation.org/app/uploads/71b4c457-cdb7-47ec-81a9-a617c956e6af.pdf (accessed 11 August 2016).

de Goede M (2008) Beyond Risk: Premediation and the Post-9/11 Security Imagination. *Security Dialogue* 39(2/3): 155–176.

de Goede M (2012) *Speculative Security: The Politics of Pursuing Terrorist Monies*. Minneapolis, MN: University of Minnesota Press.

Deleuze G (1992) Postscript on the Societies of Control. *October* 59 (Winter): 3–7.

Dewey J (2012 [1927]) *The Public and its Problems: An Essay in Political Inquiry*. University Park, PA: Pennsylvania State University Press.

Dillon M (2000) Poststructuralism, Complexity and Poetics. *Theory, Culture & Society* 17(5): 1–26.

Dillon M, Reid J (2009) *The Liberal Way of War. Killing to Make Life Live*. London: Routledge.

Duffield M (2016) The Resilience of the Ruins: Toward a Critique of Digital Humanitarianism. *Resilience: International Policies, Practices and Discourses*. 15 March: 1–19.

ENISA (2011a) *Analysis of Cyber Security Aspects in the Maritime Sector. Heraklios*. Available at: www.enisa.europa.eu/activities/Resilience-and-CIIP/critical-infrastructure-and-services/dependencies-of-maritime-transport-to-icts/cyber-security-aspects-in-the-maritime-sector-1 (accessed 15 July 2016).

ENISA (2011b) *Inter-X: Resilience of the Internet Interconnection Ecosystem*. Full report. Available at: www.enisa.europa.eu/publications/interx-report/at_download/fullReport (accessed 11 August 2016).

European Commission (2013a) *Action Plan for Resilience in Crisis Prone Countries 2013–2020*. Available at: http://ec.europa.eu/echo/files/policies/resilience/com_2013_227_ap_crisis_prone_countries_en.pdf (accessed 11 August 2016).

European Commission (2013b) *Disaster Risk Reduction. Increasing Resilience by Reducing Disaster Risk in Humanitarian Action*. Available at: http://ec.europa.eu/echo/files/policies/prevention_preparedness/DRR_thematic_policy_doc.pdf (accessed 11 August 2016).

Evans B, Reid J (2013) Dangerously Exposed: The Life and Death of the Resilient Subject. *Resilience: International Policies, Practices and Discourses* 1(2): 83–98.

Evans B, Reid J (2014) *Resilient Life. The Art of Living Dangerously*. Cambridge: Polity Press.

Ewald F (2002) The Return of Descartes' Malicious Demon: An Outline of a Philosophy of Precaution. In: Baker T, Simon J (eds) *Embracing Risk. The Changing Culture of Insurance and Responsibility*. Chicago: University of Chicago Press. 273–302.

Foucault M (2005) *The Hermeneutics of the Subject: Lectures at the Collège de France, 1981–82*. New York: Palgrave Macmillan.

Galloway AR, Thacker E (2007) *Exploit: A Theory of Networks*. Minneapolis, MN: University of Minnesota Press.
Grove K (2014) Agency, Affect, and the Immunological Politics of Disaster Resilience. *Environment and Planning D: Society and Space* 32(2): 240–256.
Grusin R (2004) Premediation. *Criticism* 46(1): 17–39.
Grusin R, Cox G (2010) *On Premediation. Interview with Richard Grusin led by Geoff Cox*. Available at: www.academia.edu/4754419/Grusin-Interview_With_Geoff_Cox_2010_ (accessed 11 August 2016).
Holling CS (1973) Resilience and Stability of Ecological Systems. *Annual Review of Ecology and Systematics* 4: 1–23.
Howell A (2014) Resilience, War, and Austerity: The Ethics of Military Human Enhancement and the Politics of Data. *Security Dialogue* 46(1): 15–31.
IFRC (2012) *The Road to Resilience: Bridging Relief and Development for a More Sustainable Future*. International Federation of the Red Cross and Red Crescent Societies. Available at: www.ifrc.org/PageFiles/96178/1224500-Road%20to%20resilience-EN-LowRes%20%282%29.pdf (accessed 11 August 2016).
Joseph J (2013) Resilience as Embedded in Neoliberalism: A Governmentality Approach. *Resilience: International Policies, Practices and Discourses* 1(1): 38–52.
Krause K, Williams MC (1996) Broadening the Agenda of Security Studies: Politics and Methods. *Mershon International Studies Review* 40(2): 229–254.
Lentzos F, Rose N (2009) Governing Insecurity: Contingency Planning, Protection, Resilience. *Economy and Society* 38(2): 230–254.
Longstaff PH, Armstrong NJ, Perrin K, Parker WM, Hidek MA (2010) Building Resilient Communities: A Preliminary Framework for Assessment. *Homeland Security Affairs* 6(3): 1–23.
Luthar SS, Zigler E (1991) Vulnerability and Competence: A Review of Research on Resilience in Childhood. *American Journal of Orthopsychiatry* 61(1): 6–22.
Massumi B (1995) The Autonomy of Affect. *Cultural Critique* 31(2): 83–109.
Massumi B (2005) Fear (The Spectrum Said). *Positions* 13: 31–48.
Masten AS, Powell JL (2003) A Resilience Framework for Research, Policy and Practice. In: Luthar SS (ed.) *Resilience and Vulnerability. Adaptation in the Context of Childhood Adversities*. Cambridge: Cambridge University Press. 1–28.
Mouffe C (2005) *On the Political*. London, New York: Routledge.
Oels A, Methmann C (2015) From "Fearing" to "Empowering" Climate Refugees: Governing Climate-Induced Migration in the Name of Resilience. *Security Dialogue* 46(1): 51–68.
Rumsfeld D (2002) *DoD News Briefing – Secretary Rumsfeld and Gen. Myers. Presenter: Secretary of Defense Donald H. Rumsfeld. February 12, 2002 11:30 AM EDT*. Available at: http://archive.defense.gov/Transcripts/Transcript.aspx?TranscriptID=2636 (accessed 1 August 2016).
Schmidt J (2014) Intuitively Neoliberal? Towards a Critical Understanding of Resilience Governance. *European Journal of International Relations* 21(2): 402–426.
Seyfert R (2012) Beyond Personal Feelings and Collective Emotions: Toward a Theory of Social Affect. *Theory, Culture & Society* 29(6) 27–46.
Spinoza B (2002) *Spinoza – Complete Works*. Trans: Shirley S. Indianapolis, IN: Hackett Publishing Co.
Stäheli U (2000) *Sinnzusammenbrüche. Eine dekonstruktive Lektüre von Niklas Luhmanns Systemtheorie*. Weilerswist, Germany: Velbrück Wissenschaft.
UNISDR (2005) *Hyogo Framework for Action (2005–2015) Building the Resilience of*

Nations and Communities to Disasters. Available at: www.unisdr.org/2005/wcdr/intergover/official-doc/L-docs/Hyogo-framework-for-action-english.pdf (accessed 11 August 2016).

Walker B, Carpenter S, Anderies J, Abel N, Cumming G, Janssen MA, Lebel L, Norberg J, Peterson GD, Pritchard R (2002) Resilience Management in Social-Ecological Systems: A Working Hypothesis for a Participatory Approach. *Conservation Ecology* 6(1): Article 14. Available at: www.ecologyandsociety.org/vol6/iss1/art14/print.pdf (accessed 15 July 2016).

Walker J, Cooper M (2011) Genealogies of Resilience: From Systems Ecology to the Political Economy of Crisis Adaptation. *Security Dialogue* 42(2): 143–160.

Wiener N (1948) *Cybernetics: Or Control and Communication in the Animal and the Machine*. Paris and Cambridge, MA: MIT Press.

Zebrowski C (2009) Governing the Network Society: A Biopolitical Critique of Resilience. *Political Perspectives* 3(1): 1–44.

Index

action, and affect 102, 107–12, 114–17, 118–19
active subject 102, 104–5, 129
adaptation 21–2, 26, 34, 47, 48, 49, 51, 54, 56, 64, 65, 69, 160, 191, 206, 207, 208
Adey, P. 101, 102, 105–6, 111, 119
Adger, WN 20
adversity 21
affect 6, 52, 54, 58–9, 204; and action 102, 107–12, 114–17, 118–19; as a capacity of the body 107; as constitutive of the body 108; definition of 107; emergent character 108, 111; and emotion distinguished 108, 111; encounter between people as source of 114; media as source of 113–14; and narration 111–12; technical failure as source of 114
affordances, of digital information 131–3, 135, 136, 145–6
Agamben, G 53, 58, 101, 148
agency 12, 13, 28, 31, 32, 33, 57, 58, 82, 102, 199, 205–6, 207, 208
aid 19, 56
algorithms 17, 73, 129, 132, 139, 144, 147–8, 165–6, 188, 195, 203
ambiguity 48, 54
Amoore, L 17, 132
Anderson, B 104, 105–6, 108, 111
Andrejevic, M 132, 133, 148
anticipation 17, 18, 192
apparatuses 53, 54
apps 130, 135, 137
Arab Spring 161
Aradau, C 26, 27, 106, 145, 147, 192, 196
assemblage 48, 52, 53–4
association 132, 138, 143, 147, 188, 200
Atnanasiou, A 112
autonomy 198, 199

autopoiesis 8, 47, 49, 189

Barabási, AL 47, 51
Beck, U 16
becoming 54, 108, 197
Behr, I von 12
Bender, I 54
Bendiek, A 93
Berger, G 31
Berry, DM 160
big data 129, 130, 159, 195, 203
biopolitics 27, 28
Blanke, T 145, 147
Blum, A 83
Blumer, H 145, 146
Boin, A 12
Borch, C 146
Bourbeau, P 23, 105
Boyd, D 134
Brassett, J 19, 29, 34
Breivik, AB 157, 170; *see also* Norway terror attacks (2010)
Bröckling, U et al. 55, 56, 57, 59, 65–6
Brown, KA 11
Burch, H 86
Butler, J 44, 47, 52, 59, 80, 82

calculation 56, 73, 74, 194
Canetti, E 145
care 201–2; *see also* self-care
Carpenter, S 22, 198
cascade effects 11, 67, 79, 86, 113, 165, 166, 193
Castells, M 7, 9, 47, 92, 94
Chandler, D 18–19, 23, 31, 32–3, 46, 196
change 208
Charlie Hebdo attacks (2015) 175
Cheswick, W 85–6
Cilliers, P 47, 52

circulation 55, 56, 70, 72, 154; of information 197–8, 202–3
citizen-detective 104
climate change 12, 19, 24, 27–8, 29
Clough, PT 107, 108, 112, 119
Coaffee, J 29
codification of information 8, 72, 195
collective resilience 177
community 56–7
complex emergency 103, 112, 194
complexity xi, xiii, 4, 21, 67, 185, 186, 187, 202
complexity thinking 4, 7–9, 10, 11, 33–4, 46, 47–8, 55, 187, 196; and digital technology 67–70, 72; ethos of 49–50; and poststructuralism, similarities and differences 45, 48–51
constitutive power (potentia) 118, 119, 120, 204–5, 206–7
constructivism 82, 197
contingency 23, 30, 48, 55, 69, 105, 187, 189, 194
Cooper, M 30, 33, 187, 196
Council of the European Union 89
Cox, G 70, 72
Crawford, K 134, 136
critical security studies 197, 199
critique, resilience as 32–5
crowd-sourcing 130, 135, 137–8, 141, 159, 206
crowd-tasking 135, 137, 144, 206
crowds 144–9, 188, 195, 206
Cyber Europe exercises 89
cyber-attacks 67, 101, 103, 112, 188
cyber-security exercises 5, 6, 89, 101, 103, 188, 194, 200; German Federal Office of Civil Protection and Disaster Assistance (BBK) 109–11, 112–17, 118–19
cybernetics 8
cyberspace 82–3, 94, 188

data protection issues 133, 136, 173
de Goede, M 103, 113, 119
Dean, M 56, 57, 59
deconstruction 46–50
Deleuze, G 44, 48, 52, 53, 54, 68, 69, 74, 83, 107, 108, 111
Demchak, CC 88
depoliticization 27–8, 31, 199
Derrida, J 46–7
Deutscher, P 47
Dewey, J 51, 205–6
différance 46, 47, 50, 54, 208
Digital Agenda for Europe 81, 85

digital code 5
digital contagions 12
digital crowds 144–9
digital divide 66, 84, 147, 186
digital enclosure 133, 136
digital information 6, 17, 65, 71, 188, 197, 202–3; affordances 131–3, 135, 136, 145–6; analysis 132, 133–4, 138, 148, 192; as capital 133; and the crowd 130, 135, 137–8, 141, 144–9; and decision-making 133; and directing emergencies 140–2; exchange 8, 9–10; hardware 131, 133; interpretation of 134; and learning for future emergencies 142–3; and mapping of emergencies 73, 130, 136–40; networked aspect of *see* social media; privacy and data protection issues 133, 136; processing infrastructure 133–4; properties of 131–5; as real-time information 137; and remote management 141–2, 190; and resilience 129–53; as traceable, storable and computable 130, 132, 145–6; truthfulness of 139, 165
digital labor 133
digital recapture 141, 142
digital technology 4, 5, 9, 71–2, 187, 194–5, 200; access to 66, 67; and complexity thinking 67–70, 72; and digitization of information exchange 71; and temporality 70, 137, 147, 154, 176; ubiquity of 67, 68, 72; vitality in 69
Dillon, M xii, xiii, 10, 44, 46, 48, 49, 50, 69, 73, 197, 208
disciplinary power 118
discourse 18, 52, 55, 80–1, 82, 84, 111
dispositif 53
disruption 20, 21, 49–50, 186, 187, 192, 193
disturbance 21
dividuals 44, 74, 201
Doherty, GW 25
dominating power (potestas) 118–19, 120, 204–5, 206–7
domino effects 11, 96, 113, 193
Dover, SR 22
drones 141
Duffield, M 8, 12, 17, 25, 27, 66, 67, 71, 72, 73, 130, 142, 144, 148, 173, 188, 190
Dunn Cavelty, M 11, 18

Ebola virus 12

ecology 19, 20
economic crises 24
Effective Altruism movement 130
effects 144–9, 166, 195, 202, 203, 206
emergence 5, 8, 10, 11, 46, 47, 48, 51, 55, 56, 68, 70, 192, 193, 194, 196, 203, 207
emergency 4, 17, 101–2, 202; complex 103, 112, 194; mapping of 73, 130, 136–40, 190, 194; as paradigmatic form of insecurity 10–12; as site of power 102
emergency services 140–1
emotions 140, 161; and affect distinguished 108, 111; social media and expression of 161, 163, 170–2, 173
empowerment 105; resilience as 23–5, 31, 199
engineering science 20, 21
entrepreneurship 56, 57, 72
epistemology of resilience 185, 193–5, 203
ethos 48–9; of complexity thinking 49–50; poststructuralist 50, 51
European Commission 82, 130; Digital Agenda for Europe 81, 85
European Committee for Standardization (CEN) 90
European Parliament 81
European Union Agency for Network and Information Security (ENISA) 5, 6, 19, 81; Internet security policies 79–80, 85–96, 194, 200
European Union (EU) 4, 24, 81, 104–5; Internal Security Strategy 25; Internet security policies 25; *see also* European Union Agency for Network and Information Security (ENISA)
Evans, B 25, 27, 28, 31, 196

Facebook 155, 201; and Norway terror attacks (201) 157–9, 163, 166–8, 169; Safety Check 135, 147, 167–8
Farías, I 54
feedback loops 8–9, 10, 11, 16, 47, 154, 187, 196
Feenberg, A 68
filter bubbles 166, 174
Folke, C 19, 26
food crises 24
Foucault, M 4, 27, 29, 30, 44, 47, 49, 52, 53, 55–6, 57, 58, 59, 64, 65, 80, 82, 83, 84, 91, 106, 201
freedom 55, 56, 58, 66, 70, 72

Galloway, AR 9, 47, 67–8, 69, 201–2, 209

gamification 141
Gaouette, N 12
Garmezy, N 20
Gates, K 132, 148
German Federal Office of Civil Protection and Disaster Assistance (BBK), cyber-security exercise 109–11, 112–17, 118–19
Gerrie, J 66
Gibson, JJ 131
Giroux, J 18
Gitelman, L 134
Global Network Society 9
Global Network Theory 47
global warming 16
Goldsmith, JL 83
Google 133; Person Finder 135
Google Crisis Response 140
governance xi, 80; laissez-faire 30; security 4, 5; self- 4, 28–32, 160, 161, 162, 167, 169, 170, 176, 205, 206
governmental programs 64–5; role of language in 80; *see also* resilience as political program
governmentality 29, 44, 52, 55–8, 59, 64–5, 160, 162, 199
Graham, M 84
Granovetter, MS 47
grieving 172–3
Grove, K 26, 27, 28, 105, 205
Grusin, R 70, 72, 73, 111, 161, 176
Guardian newspaper 3
Guattari, F 52
Gustavsson, R 22

Habermas, J 16
Haiti earthquake (2010) 129–30
Handmer, JW 22
Hansen, M 111
Hardt, M 7, 8, 118
Hayek, F 29
Hayles, K 10
Heath-Kelly, C 18, 104, 120–1
Heidegger, M 68
Hildebrandt, M 134
Holling, CS 19–20
Howell, A 29, 104
humanitarianism 159, 188
hybridity 48, 54
Hyvönen, AE 27

idisasters 138
imagination 17
individuation 48

216 Index

information 16; circulation of 197–8, 202–3; codification of 8, 72, 195; invisible 140; misinformation 164–6; *see also* digital information
in-formation xiii, 5–10, 48, 59, 74, 102, 107, 129, 137, 185–8, 197, 202–3, 208
Information Age 7, 9
information cascades 165, 166
information and communication technology (ICT) 68, 69
information exchange 9–10, 11, 47, 70, 74, 187; *see also* digital information, exchange
Innis, HA 70
insecurity 4, 7–10, 16, 19, 21, 22, 187, 192, 196–8, 203, 207; emergency as paradigmatic form of 10–12; governing through 17, 18; and interconnectedness 11, 12, 21, 68–9, 79; resilience as 26–8
in/security xiii, 7, 81, 185–6, 196–8, 203–4
Instagram 135, 137, 155
interconnectedness xi, 4, 5, 7, 9, 16, 34, 44, 45, 46, 113, 185–6, 187, 191, 202; and insecurity 11, 12, 21, 68–9, 79
International Federation of the Red Cross (IFRC) xii, 25
International Network of Crisis Mappers 137
International Organization for Standardization (ISO) 90
Internet 4, 5, 6, 20, 25, 34, 44, 45, 58, 65, 67, 69, 129; access to 66, 67, 154; cyberspace conceptualization of 82–3, 188; and the digital crowd 146; just-a-network conceptualization of 83, 188; networked aspect of *see* social media; spatiality of 80, 81, 82–96, 188–90
Internet Corporation for Assigned Names and Numbers 90
Internet as ecosystem 80, 81, 84, 85–96, 187, 188–90, 196; material/infrastructural dimension of 85–8; power-related aspects 85, 88–94
Internet Mapping Project 85–6
Internet Response League 137
Internet security 79–80; exercises 89, 200; harmonization/standardization of approaches to 89–90, 91, 92–3, 189; local level responsibilities 89, 90, 91–2, 189; and private sector 93; protocols 72, 81, 90–1, 92, 188, 190, 202; *see also* Internet as ecosystem
intervention 30–1, 32, 33, 51, 57, 58, 205

iRevolutions 71
iteration 48

Jackson, V 134
Jontunen, T 27
Joseph, J 30, 31, 162
Juniper, T 3

Kelner, S 175
Kempis, GK 49
Kitchin, R 83
knowledge 84; *see also* epistemology; power-knowledge

language 80, 82; and affect 111–12; of resilience programs 65
Lash, S 103
Latour, B 47, 83, 131
Le Bon, G 145
learning 31, 32, 73, 142–3, 191–2, 194–5, 205–6
Lentzos, F 26
Lévi-Strauss, C 46
liberal interventionism 30–1, 33
liberalism 55–6
Liddle, H 26
local responsibility 89, 90, 91–2, 189–90, 198
Longstaff, PH 21, 22
Luhmann, N 16
Luthar, SS 19, 20

McCormack, D 103
MacCormack, P 108
Malcolm, JA 28, 105
Manovich, L 134, 148
mapping: digital 73, 130, 136–40, 190, 194; Internet infrastructure 86
markets, neoliberal 29, 32
Massey, D. 52, 83
Massumi, B 52, 107, 108, 111, 119, 120
Mateen, O 170
media: as source of affect 113–14; *see also* social media
mediality 159, 161, 162, 176
Meier, P 71, 139, 140, 165
memorialization 191
Mendoza, M 139
Merchant, RM 139, 142, 143
metadata 132, 154
Methmann, C 18, 27–8
MicroMappers 138
Miller, P 65
misinformation 155, 164–6

Morozov, E 138–9
Moskovitz, D 130
Mouffe, C 145
mourning 172–3, 175
multiplicity 48, 53, 54
Munich terror attacks (2016) 170, 171
Munster, R van 106, 192
Mutual Aid Agreements 90

narration, and affect 111–12
Negri, A 7, 8, 52, 118
Neocleous, M xii, xiii, 54
neogeography 137
neoliberalism 29–30, 31–2, 46, 64, 102, 104, 162
network theories 47
networked power 94
networks 6–7, 8–9, 47, 59, 88–9, 96, 187; *see also* social media; *see also* Internet
new prudentialism 56
Newsweek magazine 3
non-relationality 50, 51, 54, 208
Norsk rikskringkasting (NRK) 155
Norway terror attacks (2011), role of social media during 6–7, 142–3, 145, 146, 147, 154, 155–9, 162, 163–77, 190–1, 192, 201; advice, source of 169, 170; as constant reminder of attacks 169–70, 191; direct link to the event 168–9; emotional function 163, 170–2, 173; first-response function 163, 165; gaining an overview vs misinformation and speculation 164–6; opinion shaping/making 174, 201; privacy concerns 173, 201; self-organization 205; sensationalism 165, 167, 171, 177, 201; spatial aspects 176; temporal aspects 176; therapeutic sharing and mourning 172–3, 175, 177; unifying aspect 174–5, 177, 201; visual aspects 177; wellbeing updates 166–8, 201

Oels, A 18, 27–8
O'Malley, P 30
Ong, A 109
ontology and relationality 46–7, 54, 70; of networks and of complexity 8, 10, 18–19, 27–8, 30–4; of the Internet 86, 94–5; of resilience 144, 176, 186–8
Open Street Maps 137
opinion, social media and shaping/making of 174, 201
Orlando shootings (2016) 170
Other 50, 208

Paquette, S 129
Parikka, J 12
Paris terror attacks (2015) 170, 175
Pariser, E 166
patterns 17, 130, 132, 138–9, 143, 147, 148, 162, 166, 195, 200, 201
Paul, G 131
Peace Research Institute Oslo xii
Pelosky, RJ 11
performativity 44, 47, 52, 54, 80, 81, 82, 84, 94
political science 19
popular resilience literature 25
population, role of 65
poststructuralism xii–xiii, 33–4, 44, 45, 46–7, 80–1, 83–4, 197, 198, 208; and complexity thinking, similarities and differences 45, 48–51; ethos 50, 51
potentia 118, 119, 120, 204–5, 206–7
potestas 118–19, 120, 204–5, 206–7
power 12, 66, 81, 84, 106, 193; constitutive form of (potentia) 118, 119, 120, 204–5, 206–7; disciplinary 118; dominating form of (potestas) 118–19, 120, 204–5, 206–7; and ecosystemic space 85, 88–94, 189, 190; emergency as site of 102; networked 94
power-knowledge 50, 72, 188
powerlessness 120, 121, 207–8, 208–9; *see also* resilience, limits to/"Ohnmacht"
pragmatism 51, 205
premediation 17
prevention 17, 18, 73
Prigogine, I 11, 16
privacy 133, 158, 173, 195, 201
private sector 93
probability 17, 19, 193, 194
processuality 54
programming 71–4, 130, 144
protocols 6, 58, 81, 90–1, 92, 96, 188, 189, 190, 202
psychological support, social media as source of 140
psychology 19, 20, 21–2, 23, 185, 199
public—private partnerships 93

radicalization 12
Random Hacks of Kindness 137
real-time information 137
reflexivity 47, 48, 54–5, 154
Reid, J xii, 10, 25, 27, 28, 31, 69, 73, 196, 197
relatedness xi
relational society 4

relational space 52, 81, 83, 84, 94
relationality xii, 33, 44, 45, 45–6, 50, 52–9, 84, 185, 186, 187; mere 44; radical 44, 46, 51, 54
remote management 141–2, 190
resilience xi–xii, 3–4, 5, 8, 10, 18–19, 49–50; and affect 101–25; ambiguity of concept 19; circulation of concept across disciplines 19–21; as critique 32–5; definition of 19, 20, 21; as depoliticizing 27–8; and the digital 129–53; as empowerment 23–5, 31, 199; epistemology of 185, 193–5, 203; etymology of 19; as insecurity 26–8; limits to/*Ohnmacht* 21, 27, 120–1, 207–9,; and the network 154–81; as political program xi, 4–7, 18, 28, 32, 64–7, 70–5, 79–82, 84, 89, 95–6, 101–2, 105–7, 118–20, 129, 140, 144, 154, 187, 191, 199–207; as self-governance 28–32; and spatiality 79–100, 188–91; temporality of 191–3, 203
resilient subject 198–200
responsibility to protect 29
responsibilization 29, 56, 57, 73, 102, 105, 160, 162, 201
Reynolds, N 49
Rhinard, M 11
risk 16–17, 18, 21, 22, 26, 73, 193, 204
Rogers, P 28–9, 105
Rose, N 26, 64, 65, 66, 67
Rosenow, D 31, 33
Ruddick, S 108

Schalhorn, A xi
Schmidt, J 31–2, 33, 105, 205
Schneier, B 11
Schoon, M 19
security-as-protection 196–7
security xi, xiii, 16, 28, 196–8; as an activity 101–6; as in-formation 5, 102, 197–8, 202, 203; Internet *see* Internet security; as social fiction 16
security exercises 6, 89, 101, 105–6, 192; *see also* cyber-security exercises
security failure 104, 207–8
security governance 4, 5
security policy 3, 4, 194, 199, 202, 203
self x 6, 58, 81, 91, 187, 189, 190, 202
self-care 155–9, 160–1, 162, 175–7, 202, 205
self-governance 4, 28–32, 160, 161, 162, 167, 169, 170, 176, 205, 206
self-help literature 25

self-organization 6, 22–3, 29, 47, 50–1, 64, 65, 68, 72, 73, 96, 101, 102, 103, 105, 106, 129, 138, 140, 160, 162, 177, 185, 198–202, 203; and adaptation 28, 51, 56, 208; and agency 199; digital 144, 146, 200–1; failure of 207–8; and intervention 57, 58; political construction of 199; and power 204–5, 206–7; and protocol 90, 91; and social media usage 201
self-reflection 28, 29, 33
self-reflexivity 47, 48
self-transformation 31, 32
sensationalism 155, 165, 167, 171, 177, 201
September 11 terrorist attacks 3
Seriously Rapid Source Review 139
Serres, M 113
Seyfert, R 108, 111
Siapno, JA 25
Simon, S 103, 113, 119
Singer, P 130
smartphones 130, 154; apps 130, 135, 137; ownership 66–7
snowballing of disasters 11
social media 5, 22, 34, 59, 65, 67, 71, 135, 136, 137, 145, 154–5, 159–63, 188, 200; emotional expressional and 161, 163, 170–2, 173; and Haiti earthquake (2010) 129–30; and promotion of extreme views 170; and psychological support 140; and (self-)care during emergencies 155–9, 160–1, 162; and self-organization 201; *see also* Facebook; Norway terror attacks (2011); Twitter
social movements 130
social self 175
socio-ecology 23, 199
sovereignty 57
space/spatiality 5, 34, 49, 70, 71, 72, 79–100, 141, 142, 147, 185, 187, 188–91; of Internet 80, 81, 82–96, 188–90; and Norway terror attacks (2010) 176; relational space 52, 81, 83, 84, 94
speculation 17, 155, 164, 165, 195
Spinoza, B 107, 118, 204
Stäheli, U 111, 132
Ståhl, B 22
standardization, and Internet security 89–90, 91, 92–3, 189
Standing Together Against Terrorism event 169
Stern, M 104

stress 21
subjectification 44, 52, 58, 59, 70, 74, 185
Sundelius, B 12
system world xi

Tampio, N 53–4
Taylor, M 140
technical failure, as source of affect 114
technologies 65–6; role in society 68; technologies of the self 66–7, 67, 70, 91, 154, 160; technologies-off-the-shelf 66–7, 154; *see also* digital technology
telos 49
temporality 5, 10, 18, 34, 46, 49, 185, 191, 203; of affect 108; and digital technology 70, 137, 147, 154, 176
terror attacks 3, 12, 16, 18, 112, 170; *see also* Munich terror Attacks (2016); Norway terror attacks (2011); Paris terror attacks (2015)
Thacker, E 9, 47, 67–8, 69, 201–2, 209
Thrift, N 7, 8
Time magazine 3
tragedy of the commons 11, 87–8
tragedy of the Internet commons 95
transboundary threats 11, 12
transformation 48, 50, 51, 54, 208; self-31, 32
trolling 139
truth 195; of digital information 139, 165
Tumblr 135
Twitter 135, 137, 155, 157, 163, 168, 170, 174, 201

uncertainty 3, 4, 26, 46, 64, 86, 187, 193, 207; governing 16–19

United Nations 4, 24
United Nations Development Program (UNDP) 19, 24
United Nations Office for Disaster Risk Reduction (UNISDR), Hyogo Framework for Action (HFA) 24
United States (US), Federal Emergency Management Agency 138
unity, social media and creation of 174–5, 177, 201
unknowns 16, 18, 29, 193, 194
urgency 102, 108–9, 113, 114, 116, 119, 176, 177
Urry, J 7, 8, 10, 11
Ushahidi 71

Vaughan-Williams, N 102
Viner, K 165
visualization 177, 191
Voight, J, "Staat/Random IV and V" x, xi
vulnerability 29, 113, 159, 196, 207

Walker, B 20
Walker, J 30, 33, 187, 196
war 29
wellbeing 166–8, 201
Wiener, N 8, 47, 187
Wired magazine 87
Wood, DM 29

Yates, D 130
Yeatman, A 56

Zebrowski, C 30, 188

Taylor & Francis eBooks

Helping you to choose the right eBooks for your Library

Add Routledge titles to your library's digital collection today. Taylor and Francis ebooks contains over 50,000 titles in the Humanities, Social Sciences, Behavioural Sciences, Built Environment and Law.

Choose from a range of subject packages or create your own!

Benefits for you
- Free MARC records
- COUNTER-compliant usage statistics
- Flexible purchase and pricing options
- All titles DRM-free.

Benefits for your user
- Off-site, anytime access via Athens or referring URL
- Print or copy pages or chapters
- Full content search
- Bookmark, highlight and annotate text
- Access to thousands of pages of quality research at the click of a button.

REQUEST YOUR FREE INSTITUTIONAL TRIAL TODAY — **Free Trials Available** We offer free trials to qualifying academic, corporate and government customers.

eCollections – Choose from over 30 subject eCollections, including:

Archaeology	Language Learning
Architecture	Law
Asian Studies	Literature
Business & Management	Media & Communication
Classical Studies	Middle East Studies
Construction	Music
Creative & Media Arts	Philosophy
Criminology & Criminal Justice	Planning
Economics	Politics
Education	Psychology & Mental Health
Energy	Religion
Engineering	Security
English Language & Linguistics	Social Work
Environment & Sustainability	Sociology
Geography	Sport
Health Studies	Theatre & Performance
History	Tourism, Hospitality & Events

For more information, pricing enquiries or to order a free trial, please contact your local sales team:
www.tandfebooks.com/page/sales

 Routledge Taylor & Francis Group | The home of Routledge books

www.tandfebooks.com